By Gilberto Freyre

THE MASTERS AND THE SLAVES
[*Casa-Grande & Senzala*] (*1956, 1946*)

NEW WORLD IN THE TROPICS:
The Culture of Modern Brazil (*1959*)

THESE ARE BORZOI BOOKS
published in New York by Alfred A. Knopf

NEW WORLD
IN THE TROPICS

NEW WORLD
IN THE TROPICS

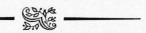

The Culture of Modern Brazil

BY

Gilberto Freyre

Alfred A. Knopf   New York

1959

L. C. Catalog card number: 59-5488

© Gilberto Freyre, 1959

THIS IS A BORZOI BOOK,

PUBLISHED BY ALFRED A. KNOPF, INC.

FIRST EDITION

This is a very much expanded and completely rewritten version of Brazil: An Interpretation, *originally published in 1945, which consisted of the Patten Foundation Lectures given at the University of Indiana, 1944-5.*

TO

Heitor Villa-Lobos,

MY FRIEND

AUTHOR'S ACKNOWLEDGMENTS

I SHOULD LIKE TO EXPRESS MY THANKS *to Mr. Herbert Wein-stock for help and advice in the planning of this book, and to Miss Violet Serwin for her assistance in preparing the type-script for these pages—an extremely difficult task because my handwriting is so obscure as to be a sort of neo-Chinese.*

G . F .

Apipucos, Recife, Brazil
1958

Contents

INTRODUCTION   3

I   THE EUROPEAN BACKGROUND OF BRAZILIAN HISTORY   39

II   FRONTIER AND PLANTATION IN BRAZIL   67

III BRAZILIAN UNITY AND BRAZILIAN REGIONAL
     DIVERSITY   93

IV   ETHNIC AND SOCIAL CONDITIONS IN MODERN BRAZIL   114

V   BRAZIL AS A EUROPEAN CIVILIZATION IN THE TROPICS   141

VI   BRAZILIAN FOREIGN POLICY AS CONDITIONED BY BRA-
     ZIL'S ETHNIC, CULTURAL, AND GEOGRAPHICAL SIT-
     UATION   166

VII SLAVERY, MONARCHY, AND MODERN BRAZIL   193

VIII THE MODERN LITERATURE OF BRAZIL: ITS RELATION
     TO BRAZILIAN SOCIAL PROBLEMS   209

IX   BRAZILIAN ARCHITECTURE: "MOORISH" AND
     "ROMAN"   230

X   WHY A TROPICAL CHINA?   257

     INDEX   follows page 286

NEW WORLD
IN THE TROPICS

Introduction

This is the revised edition of a book on Brazil written and published in English in 1945 as *Brazil: An Interpretation*. It is not only a revised edition: it is so enlarged as to be a new book, having four new chapters and this introduction. Some of the new material has appeared in the United States in *The Atlantic Monthly*, *Foreign Affairs*, and *The Encyclopedia Americana;* in *Civilizations* (Brussels); in *Progress* and *The Listener* (both London), in the *Year Book of Education* of the University of London; and in *Kontinent* (Vienna). But it appears now, expanded and revised. However, for the use of this material I want to thank the editors of these publications.

No Latin American country seems at present to attract the amount of Anglo-American attention which some countries of Europe, Asia, and Africa are attracting. But Latin America is not a geographical space that Anglo-Americans or West Europeans can afford to disdain entirely for the sake of new loves or enthusiasms. It is too European and too Western to be considered entirely exotic from a European or Western point of view; and too exotic to be treated as a mere European extension in America—mainly in the tropics—or a mere "Latin" annex to Anglo-America. It is different. And Brazil is so different even from Spanish America as to ask for special treatment as an anthropological or sociological subject. So specifically Brazilian is its way of being both "Latin" and "American" that some have gone so far as to suggest that its mystery reminds one of China or Russia: it could even be described as a tropical China. Rapid and easy travel today has made countries appear less mysterious and much less different from each other than they were half a century ago. But in a world that is passing through a process of intense standardization of dress, architecture, food, and even drink, these differences still exist.

There was a time when the foreigner arriving in even the capital of Brazil found himself in entirely unfamiliar surroundings. At the same time he himself excited the curiosity of the less sophisticated Brazilians as much as if he had come from another planet.

How human was the intruder? How Christian? At that time Brazilians believed that the English, heretics from the orthodox Roman Catholic point of view, were perhaps devils in the guise of humans, even had webbed feet like devils. And, ironically, the foreigner often imagined he was coming to a heathen country, while some orthodox Protestant and evangelical missionaries expected to find people not only heathen but also almost subhuman.

The fact, however, was that Brazilians were human and had been a Christianized people since the early days of the Portuguese colonization of their country in the sixteenth century. Pagan survivals can, of course, be found in their civilization, as they can in the purest form of European Christianity practiced by common people (as opposed to minority groups of theologically strict Christians).

Sociologically, Brazilian development viewed as a whole may be considered predominantly Christian. As a "human"— in the sense of humane—expression of American culture, it is characterized more by the desire of the typical Brazilian to enjoy life—through the appreciation of a well-cooked fish, a good cigar, fine guitar music, and kindness and tolerance to others—than by the pursuit of material gain or highly intellectual conquests that might prove detrimental to a slow and pleasant rhythm of existence.

4

Europeans familiar with Brazil during the colonial era (from the sixteenth century to the beginning of the nineteenth) were surprised at the lack of interest shown by Brazilians in books, natural history, natural science, and even art. Only music was an exception, for the notes of a guitar were always to be heard coming from some window opened for the fresh breeze, a guitar usually played by a woman with fine dark eyes, with her husband or father as an appreciative audience.

The Inquisition's limitation of reading matter to Roman Catholic religious books is a possible explanation of the fact that the study of books was mainly restricted to a few colonists. In spite of this, however, literature began to appear as early as the sixteenth century. In those days, to be a military man was a great distinction, but it was equally distinguished to be a scholar, to wear glasses and be able to read Latin or write Portuguese; and one of the early leaders of Pernambuco, a man of aristocratic Portuguese birth, was both a soldier and a literary man. Trade, industry, and any form of manual labor were not so highly considered, and from the earliest colonial days the Brazilians left the conduct of business affairs to Portuguese of humble origin or to other Europeans, and all manual work to Negro slaves or free mulattoes. They themselves adopted the attitude of landed gentry, giving orders to their slaves from the height of their horses or the depth of their luxurious hammocks, where they passed the day in comparative idleness. Those who were not landowners were satisfied to possess a few slaves to work for them.

This widespread lack of ambition for material gain or intellectual improvement was characteristic of the Brazil of that period. It had, however, its compensation in an equally general Brazilian disposition to enjoy life and leisure—a disposition lacking in more energetic and progressive countries in which industrial slaves had replaced agrarian slaves, and industrial barons feudal land barons, losing in the process the capacity to appreciate music and art, to eat a good dinner (except Christmas dinner!) slowly, to linger over a cup of coffee, a glass of port, and a Bahia cigar, or to enjoy aromatic snuff.

Colonial Brazilians also had a particular love of finery, appearing in public in clothes "bedaubed with embroidery," according to an early nineteenth-century writer. But at home they dressed simply, the men in shirts and trousers, the women in thin muslin petticoats over an embroidered chemise, anticipating present-day Europeans in the hygienic reduction of dress in the tropics to a minimum. They can indeed claim credit for having "humanized" dress for the tropics, despite the fact that they continued passively to copy European dress for public functions, suffering even in the present century the torments of top hats, frock coats, and furs.

Such tropical habits—habits of natives of the tropics—already followed by the indigenous population and by the Africans imported to Brazil since the early sixteenth century, as sleeping in hammocks, using clay vases for fresh drinking water, and cooking fish in coconut milk, were adopted and improved by the Portuguese and their descendants in Brazil, who at the same time gradually assimilated the native customs, styles, and values. By a cultural compromise and by their genius in combining civilized and indigenous values, they have been able, perhaps better than any other people of predominantly European origin, to adapt a European civilization to the tropics. They have made a considerable tropical area a place in which European values now flourish and where men of European culture can live, enjoy life, and prosper. In such cities as Rio de Janeiro and Santos, they have defeated the tropical enemies of Europeans: yellow fever and bubonic plague. The Oswaldo Cruz Institute in Rio is one of the foremost centers for the study of tropical diseases. In the country areas the dangers of malaria and ancylostomiasis are being overcome, and in the Butantan Institute in São Paulo, Brazilian scientists, following the example of Dr. Vital Brasil, are fighting the perils of snake bite with carefully prepared serum. These great Brazilian victories in the humanization of the tropics have contributed much to destroying the European idea that these evils are inseparable from tropical conditions.

The secret of Brazil's success in building a humane, Christian, and modern civilization in tropical America has been her genius for compromise. While the British, as no other people, have had this genius for compromise in the political sphere— their political system is a masterly combination of apparently antagonistic values—the Brazilians have been successful in using this same power of compromise in the cultural and social spheres. Hence their ethnic democracy, the almost perfect equality of opportunity for all men regardless of race or color. The successful and almost free mingling of different cultures can also be seen in the assimilation of values as diverse as British football and the French taste for pastry, the East Indian love of rice and the North American sewing machine, the Amerindian hammock and the Portuguese toothpick, the African dish *couscous* and the Chinese style of roof. But it is not mere passive imitation, for Brazilian footballers dance with the ball as if they were doing the samba; *couscous* is made with the local products (manioc and corn), instead of the African; and sewing machines have been used to produce clothes in traditional Brazilian styles. The old art of hand embroidery is not forgotten in such a region as Alagoas, and girls in convents are still taught the lacemaking and handwork of colonial days. For though, in the last half century, parts of Brazil have gone through an intense process of North- or Anglo-Americanization, the typical Brazilian has a deep aversion to standardization, including ethnic standardization.

The mixture of races produces regions in which the population is a constant surprise to a European because of its variation of color and anthropology. A large family in northeastern or central Brazil may represent three or four anthropological types and various skin colors through the father's marriage first to an Amerindian and then to a Negress. And though each one may have a family nickname according to the color of his eyes, the type of his hair, or the shape of his nose, they love each other as brothers. This "family" situation—though many Brazilian families pride themselves on being exclusively white—is to a large extent typical of the Brazilian population. Men regard each other as fellow citizens and fellow Christians without regard to color or ethnic differences. Not that there is no race or color prejudice mixed with class prejudice in Brazil. There is. But no one would think of having churches only for whites. No one in Brazil would think of laws against interracial marriage. No one would think of barring colored people from theaters or residential sections of a town. A general spirit of human brotherhood is much stronger among Brazilians than race, color, class, or religious prejudice.

It is true that racial equality did not become absolute with the abolition of slavery in Brazil in 1888. But it is true also that even before the 1888 law the relations between whites and colored, between masters and slaves, in Brazil attracted the attention of foreign observers as being particularly cordial and humane. Even before that law, miscegenation had occurred, freely practiced among the people in general, and on rare occasions a member of a distinguished white or white-Amerindian family married outside his color caste.

As a Brazilian historian who was also a philosopher has said, the Brazilian solution of the racial question is certainly wiser, more promising, and, above all, more humane than any solution that operates through separation or segregation. He suggests that because of the fraternal relations between individuals of different races there exists a certain Brazilian "happiness," though, as a good philosopher, he refuses to admit that Amerigo Vespucci was right when he located the Earthly Paradise in Brazil. There is in all likelihood no earthly paradise, but in respect of race relations the Brazilian situation is probably the nearest approach to a paradise to be found anywhere in the world.

Brazilian happiness is, however, relative, for there are still, for a large part of the population, a poverty, a misery, and a series of diseases which probably account for the sadness expressed in Brazilian folk music and guitar songs. To some extent, this sadness is to be explained also by a trauma in the social past of a large part of the population: slavery. The slave, even when well treated, felt vaguely nostalgic, which made his song one of sadness, though his dance was often one of joy. From the Portuguese the Brazilians inherited the well-known nostalgia of the sailor, who is frequently far from his home; a feeling expressed in the Portuguese language by the word *saudade*.

In a country where women have been oppressed by men, some hypercritical foreigners think it pure fiction to speak of social democracy, but the truth is that for years Brazilian women have been as nearly the equal of men as colored are the equal of white and native the equal of European. The first woman governor in the history of the Americas was Dona Brites, of Pernambuco, in the sixteenth century, and both in the early colonial days and during the Empire numerous widows took charge of large plantations and were accepted as real substitutes for their dead husbands.

In modern Brazil women enjoy more freedom of expression

than in any other Latin American country, and today any talented woman can take up a career as doctor, writer, civil servant, nurse, musician, or lawyer. Rachel de Queiroz, a notable Brazilian author, writes as vigorously and independently today, denouncing political corruption or social abuse, as did a brilliant mulatto publicist, Antonio Torres, a few years ago, when as Brazilian consul in quasi-Nazi Germany, he gained the respect of even the Germans in spite of the independence of his views on a number of questions.

Probably the Itamarati—the Brazilian Foreign Office—remains the last great fortress of Brazilian "racism" or "aryanism," as well as of Brazilian belief that public office is an exclusive privilege of men. But even the Itamarati has surrendered to the pressure of the Brazilian tendency toward equalization of opportunity for all. Mulattoes, Torres, for example, have been appointed consuls, and women have been admitted to the Brazilian foreign service and have risen as high as consul or minister.

Women have been members of the Brazilian Parliament and of the Municipal Chamber of Rio de Janeiro. A woman has been the very capable director of the National Museum of Natural History of Brazil. There are a number of colored men in high public office, though Brazilian courtesy would describe them, not as "Negroes" (as even near-Nordic individuals with a drop of African blood are described in the United States), but as *morenos*—that is, people of dark complexion. Even during the Empire, a number of distinguished statesmen, members of the Imperial Cabinet and of the Imperial Senate, diplomats, judges, and national deputies, were *morenos* in this sense.

It is said of the Emperor Dom Pedro the Second that he was a strict puritan as regards the private and public morality of statesmen, whose rise in office depended somewhat upon his approval. He used a red pencil to mark out names of men of whose conduct as private individuals or as public officers he disapproved. But he probably never used his red pencil against a man simply because he was *moreno* in the sense of Negroid or had a drop of African blood. On the contrary, he had among his best personal friends men like the Rebouças, who were dark mulattoes. It is said that once, at a very elegant court ball, one of the Rebouças was present, but felt rather out of place among a predominantly "Aryan" aristocracy. Dom Pedro then asked his own daughter, Princess Isabel, to dance a quadrille with Rebouças. It was Princess Isabel who signed the 1888 Abolition Law in the absence of the Emperor, who was then in Europe in very bad health. She was the wife of Prince Gaston d'Orléans, Count d'Eu, and would have succeeded her father on the throne of Brazil had not the Republic been established in 1889 by a group of Brazilians eager for up-to-date political "democracy."

The fact is that the Imperial regime in Brazil was a happy combination of monarchy with democracy, together with a system of aristocratic selection based not so much on birth, race, color, or class as on individual capacity. The Empire gave Brazil a tradition of quality as opposed to the mere power of quantity characteristic of both plutocracy and demagogism. That tradition seems to explain why even today public life attracts or retains some of the most refined and cultured Brazilians in the highest positions, whereas in other American countries, capable men tend to become business and industrial leaders. Although pessimistic critics think that men of quality are being defeated as a general rule by men whose power comes from money or from the votes they can command, pessimists always exaggerate the dark side of facts, and for years the Republic has remained loyal to this typical tradition of the Monarchy. But one should always remember that such a tradition was never incompatible with a broad tendency toward equality of opportunity for all. Hence the considerable number of men of humble birth who, during the Empire, became barons, counts, and viscounts, and have also reached high office during the Republic. This perhaps unique combination—certainly unique in America—of democracy with aristocracy explains why Brazil is, as an American nation, at the same time so "old" and so "new," so conservative and so liberal, so attached to its past and yet so ready to make experiments in social and technical progress.

For Brazil may be in certain respects one of the most picturesquely archaic countries of the American continent—with *gauchos* or cowboys who have still Moorish customs of dress and of dealing with horses; with mulatto and Negro women sweets vendors dressed, as in Bahia, in somewhat Muslim or African styles; with sugar cane planted as in the sixteenth century and carried from the most archaic sugar mills to the coast in primitive boats or in oxcarts of the most rustic type; with two pretenders to the national throne, one living like a prince in a palace in Petropolis and ready to become the third emperor of Brazil under the name of Pedro the Third. Despite all this, Brazil is, also, in certain other respects, one of the most socially, culturally, and technically advanced countries in the world.

In aviation, architecture, music, science, art, and literature, Brazil can hold her own in the modern world. Santos Dumont, a Brazilian, was a pioneer of aviation, one of the first men, if not the first man, to fly a plane of his own invention, a feat that the French have recognized by dedicating a public monument to his honor. Today commercial aviation is developed far more highly in Brazil than in any other part of Latin America.

Brazil is a pioneer also in modern functional architecture. Public buildings, factories, and private residences recently built in São Paulo and Rio are considered by foreign architects to be examples of a really new method of building and happy solutions of a number of problems facing a modern architect in the tropics. In Heitor Villa-Lobos,[1] Brazil has a composer as modern and experimental as any in Europe. His work is typically Brazilian, combining, as it does, the gaiety and the sadness of his country.

On the American continents, Brazilian painting—with Portinari, Dias, Cardozo Ayres, Brennand, the Monteiro brothers, Pancetti, and others—is considered by some critics, both foreign and Brazilian, to be second only to Mexican painting in its expression of advanced artistic feeling; and Brazilian sculpture, inspired by the vigorous work of an eighteenth-century mulatto sculptor whose monumental statues and decorations can be seen in the churches of Minas Gerais, is becoming equally original in execution.

From the point of view of artistic vigor and human significance, Brazilian literature is probably second to none in Latin America. The poet Manuel Bandeira is great by any standard, his only deficiency being that he writes in the Portuguese language, a language that Brazilian pessimism sometimes describes as "clandestine." Another modern Brazilian poet of rank is Carlos Drumond de Andrade. Great, too, were Machado de Assis and Lima Barreto, Brazilian prose writers of the late nine-

[1] Recognizing the relevance of the regional in the ecological approach to the interpretation of Brazil, Villa-Lobos has invited me to collaborate with him on a musical and literary interpretation of Brazilian culture as this culture expresses itself in the various regions from the Amazon to Rio Grande do Sul. This would be an alliance of interpretative music and interpretative literature, of a psychological rather than a sociological character, as an attempt to create a synthesis of Brazil in which both unity and diversity would be considered. I have had the collaboration of plastic artists in some of my interpretations of Brazilian life and culture, as the map drawn along lines I suggested by Senhor Cicero Dias, the painter, for my book *The Masters and the Slaves*. The Villa-Lobos project would, with my collaboration, include suggestions for a ballet that would be representative of Brazil as a culture at once unitary and diversified.

I 3

teenth and early twentieth century, who are today followed by such novelists as José Lins do Rego, Graciliano Ramos, Jorge Amado, G. Cruls, A. Callado, P. Asfora, Rachel de Queiroz, Guimarães Rosa, Erico Verissimo, and Mario Palmerio. Both Assis and Barreto were mulatto, Assis never expressing himself as such, Barreto sometimes dramatizing his condition of "Negro" and "plebeian" in a somewhat un-Brazilian way. The Brazilian essay—of which Assis, Joaquim Nabuco, Euclides da Cunha, and Ruy Barbosa were masters—is considered by foreign critics the most original expression of Brazilian literature. For it combines philosophical and social preoccupation with the artistic and literary, becoming therefore more than *belles-lettres*, a tradition that originated with the Luso-Brazilian of the seventeenth century, Father Antonio Vieira—a real genius—whose sermons were more like modern essays than like orthodox sermons.

Brazil is also proud of its achievements in industry, and, indeed, much has been accomplished during the last half-century. It is interesting to observe that during the Empire the modern industrial development of Brazil had a remarkable pioneer in Viscount de Mauá, a man of great creative energy; today he is succeeded by the well-known editor and industrialist Assis Chateaubriand, whose activities are amazingly widespread.

It would not be accurate, however, to take these dynamic figures in art and industry as truly representative of the Brazilian rhythm of activity, which expresses itself more typically in a combination of toil and leisure (the number of civil and religious holidays for which Brazil is famous well illustrates this point).

For Brazilians, being Latins, are free—perhaps too free—from the Protestant conception of leisure as a vice, and recognize, apparently instinctively, its importance as an antidote to those money-making activities which reduce man to a mere economic entity.

The too-hard-working people of today (with special reference to the United States and Russia) think of leisure as something to be achieved in the future. But why leave the enjoyment of leisure to the future? Why not more machines, but at a rate that will not break up the Brazilian tradition of leisure? When Elihu Root, the well-known North American Secretary of State, first arrived in Brazil in 1906, he was delighted with Salvador, with its suave rhythm of existence as well as its hospitality; and the people of Salvador themselves, in their capacity to enjoy leisure without being indolent, may well be considered the most civilized in Brazil.

In this happy combination of toil and leisure, an optimist might see that Brazil has a contribution to offer to the happiness of mankind. But some aspects of the Brazilian attitude toward leisure are not entirely happy, one being the assumption that the state exists to provide them with leisure. It is a common thing for governmental departments, for instance, to have a staff greatly in excess of the work to be done, the surplus manpower being nothing more than parasitical.

The systematic combination of these two extremes, toil and leisure, is one of the tasks of social legislation in Brazil as the country changes over from an agrarian to an industrial economy. Work for all and leisure for all would be the ideal solution, but this can be achieved only gradually, for Brazilians in particular despise violent solutions. One should not forget that both capital punishment and dueling were abolished in Brazil many years ago as too barbarous to be tolerated by so humane a people. Revolutions, either for independence from Portugal or for the Republic in 1889, have tended to be "white" rather than bloody, and even the abolition of slavery was carried through without violence. Brazil has also managed to solve her boundary disputes with neighboring Spanish-speaking republics by arbitration rather than war.

It is true that recently Brazil surprised the world not with a revolution *à la Latin American,* but with the violent death—by suicide—of its President. The suicide of Getulio Vargas may be considered somewhat un-Brazilian. An explanation of it may be that he was born and grew up too near Spanish America, and though very Brazilian in spirit and feelings, seems to have been influenced by certain Spanish-American dramatic methods of playing politics. Until recently such methods included dueling, suicide, and assassination in a way almost unknown in Brazil—that is, among the leaders of politics in Brazil. In this, as in other aspects of political and social life, monarchy seems to have preserved Brazil from the excessive romanticism of Spanish America: including the *mystique* of violence which seems to be a romantic rather than a classic method used by statesmen or peoples for dealing with critical problems— though there are situations that man has to face tragically, no matter whether his predominant inclinations are classic or romantic. After all, Greek tragedy is classic and not romantic; and Vargas's end seems to have been marked by a touch of Greek tragedy rather than to have been caused entirely by a latent romanticism hidden in so sober, silent, and apparently cold a man. Some even think that he was led to suicide not so much by his political opponents as by some friends and relatives who, having his full, absolute confidence, acted disloyally toward their patriarchal chief.

In any case, the Brazilian reaction to so unexpected and un-Brazilian an event as Vargas's suicide was classic rather than romantic. The army, the air force, and the navy acted in a way that seems fantastic in relation to Latin America, but which were taken not from the Portuguese or from any European language, but from the Amerindian language dominant among the real natives of Brazil. Names of rivers, mountains, trees. Telluric names. Tropical names. And there was no hesitation, from the very beginning of Brazil as an independent nation, over extending titles of nobility to the descendants of Amerindians. On the contrary: when they were the descendants of Amerindian chiefs or *caciques*, they were considered to be essentially noble. Even during the colonial days the Portuguese had thought so. This explains why the Marquis of Pombal, a man with Amerindian blood, became the most powerful man in the Portuguese world of his time—the eighteenth century—without any restriction to his position as a nobleman on account of his Amerindian blood. It explains also why the Pope's selection to be the first Latin American cardinal of a man who was a member of an old aristocratic family of Brazil—an old family with Amerindian noble blood—was so well received by Brazilians. It was as if the Roman Catholic Church, by this choice—which took place half a century ago—was approving the Brazilian policy of attempting to develop a civilization in the tropics, at once European and Amerindian, boreal and tropical, and consequently really universalistic in its main designs and techniques.

I say in its techniques because what is happening to cattle raising and agriculture is happening in Brazil with other human activities that are parts of a civilization or a culture: such activities as the art of gardening, for instance. Through the use of the same methods or techniques of combining tropical experience with European science, Brazil is also developing its own styles of ornamental gardens complementary to its own styles of architecture. Here, as in other matters, Brazilians agree with modern European scientists who have discovered that European men, despite their skill and power over nature, have learned only how to cultivate European soils in a European climate.

This is why some modern students of these and other problems in the expansion of civilization think that a new science has to be developed to deal with these very complex problems from a tropical point of view complementary to the European or boreal one that has been overdominant in science and technology. Why not a special science to deal with the adaptation of European science and technology to tropical situations, and even with the invention of new techniques to solve problems peculiar to the tropics? Problems not only of cattle raising, agriculture, architecture, urbanization, and regional planning, but also of psychology connected with education, with political organization, with mental hygiene. For it seems that the behavior of man in the tropics has to be considered, in some of its aspects, in relation to situations and conditions peculiar to tropical environment; to the fact, for instance, that the tropical weather is favorable to easy, informal contact, in public squares, of crowds with political leaders—without the need of party meetings inside buildings that have a distinctly party atmosphere. Music, the drama, theatrical performance, religious rites may be affected in a similar way by tropical weather or climatic conditions, may develop new forms through an immediate psychological and social relation among the artists or the religious leaders and large crowds, and not through the radio and television, whose importance is probably to become greater in boreal than in tropical environments.

A German phytopathologist who was in Brazil during the second decade of the present century, Professor Konrad Guenther of the University of Freiburg, wrote a fascinating book about his experiences, the English edition of which is entitled *A Naturalist in Brazil*. Professor Guenther writes that all the time he was in tropical Brazil he was impressed by the splendor of the blossom, "such splendor of blossom as I had never seen," to quote his own words. And there were always—he adds— the sunlight, and the blue sky, and the people in the streets, who enhanced the charm of the picture "not only by their white or brightly colored clothes, but also by the alternation of white, brown, and black faces. . . ." Such an atmosphere—a combination of nature and culture in effects of tropical brightness—is bound to affect men in their behavior, in their character, in their art, in their philosophy of life.

The same German scientist writes: "The thing about the tropics, in my opinion, is that one is always, by day and night, in touch with nature. Just as the lightly clad body is in immediate contact with the air, so that one always feels free and comfortable, so in the tropics there are no closed rooms." Professor Guenther tells of a lady, apparently from northern Europe, who once told him that she could no longer live in Europe, because "the rooms were so oppressive: she often had the feeling that she could not breathe." I have known northern Europeans who after years of residence in Brazil have failed to re-adapt themselves to Europe for exactly the same reason: they seem to develop a sort of claustrophobia, known to psychologists and psychiatrists as a morbid exaggeration of an attitude that most men and women have toward oppressive rooms or oppressive situations. Perhaps some day there will be sanatoria in such tropical countries as Brazil for the treatment, or possibly the cure, of boreal Europeans and Americans who no longer can live a healthy life in boreal Europe or boreal America— the word "boreal" is used here in its broadest sense—on account of climatic and other factors that make rooms and life too oppressive to some men and women, and also to some children.

Children in Brazil were for centuries, when they belonged to the higher class of Brazilians, the victims and even the martyrs of the idea that European civilization should be preserved in Brazil just as it is kept or preserved—as if in ice—in boreal Europe. They were dressed as if they were European and the weather was European winter weather. Scottish dresses both for boys and girls became fashionable for some time in nineteenth-century Brazil, and you can imagine what this meant for children eager to be free and comfortable, and also how this developed in some of them what modern psychologists call a complex—an anti-Scottish complex—that in not a few men has been cured by the fact that they have come to develop a high esteem for other Scottish values. I may add in this connection that Brazilians have adopted one combination of European civilization and tropical nature which seems to be unknown in tropical areas of Asia and Africa which I have visited. I refer to the combination of Scottish whisky and coconut milk.

European and Anglo-American scientists such as the German Professor Guenther and the Anglo-American Dr. Marston Bates are bringing a valuable contribution to the foundation of a possible special science for the intensive, systematic study of tropical men, tropical nature, and tropical cultures in places where they have stabilized or are stabilizing themselves in total and complex situations through the intimate contact, and even fusion, of culture and environment. For these scientists are adding to studies of these situations by scientists or analysts born in the tropics, though educated in Europe and the United States, the comparison between their European or Anglo-American background and their experiences in the tropics; and also the comparison between their experience in Brazil, for instance, and their experience in India or tropical Africa.

"No one can get out of his skin," writes Professor Guenther, adding: "Even at the Equator the European is still a European; at first he feels an alien in the tropics, and unrelated to tropical nature." Speaking as a European, he generalizes: "Only by a strenuous and exhausting effort is one able to see into the alien nature of the tropics and realize its essential character." And as if he were willing to contribute with his experiences and his science to the creation of that special science for which I have suggested the somewhat pedantic denomination of "tropicology," Professor Guenther summarizes his knowledge of tropical situations in these very significant words:

> *"While traveling in two different tropical countries will prevent one from drawing general conclusions from observations that hold good of one country only, it also makes one realize that there is a definite tropical character common to all countries astride the Equator, and which differs fundamentally from the character of the more temperate latitudes."*

By including himself among those who consider it their task "to determine this difference and to explain it in a scientific manner," the German phytopathologist may be considered, together with Wallace, Gourou, the two Bateses—the British one and the Anglo-American—a pioneer of a possible modern science, required by modern problems and their impact on the relations of modern Europe with non-European cultures and peoples, which might become known as tropicology.

I have suggested the convenience, as a sub-science of this special science, an equally intensive and systematic study of the various developments of European forms—forms more than substances or contents, though the two are hardly separable—of civilization in tropical areas, carriers of which have been men and women from Spain and Portugal, particularly from Portugal. For it seems that the Iberians have been able to identify themselves with tropical surroundings and to assimilate values from tropical nature and tropical cultures and to mix with tropical races or populations in a way characteristic only of them, especially of the Portuguese, and of no other European peoples, whose activities in the tropics have been mainly political, commercial, industrial, military, and not ethnically and culturally symbiotic as the relations of the Portuguese and the Spanish peoples with the Amerindians, the Africans, the Orientals of tropical areas have been.

I am one of those who think that the advantages of Iberians over other European peoples in developing such symbiotic relations with tropical nature, tropical men, and tropical cultures are mainly owing to the fact that since their beginnings as national and quasi-national societies Spain and Portugal have been only partly European: their climate and situation allowed them to adopt numerous values and techniques from non-European civilizations whose origins were tropical. This explains why, during the early days of Brazil, the Portuguese began to build not only according to their European science, but also according to what they had learned from the Arabs, the Moors, the East. When the Dutch conquered northern Brazil and established themselves with Recife as their capital, they introduced in this town and this particular Brazilian region a type of architecture which proved to be an unsuitable import, with few or no concessions to tropical climate. It was characterized—a characteristic that seems to have affected architecture in Recife until a comparatively recent time—by what specialists in architectural technique call "a prototype designed to keep out snow and let in sun," with eaves too high and too narrow to be "protective" of human habitation in the tropics. A modern student of "housing for the humid tropics," Professor Douglas H. K. Lee, whose article "Thoughts on Housing for the Humid Tropics," with photographs by Professor Robert L. Pendleton, appeared in the January 1951 number of the *Geographical Review* of New York, points out that equally unsuitable types of house, apparently adapted from the European "villa," are to be found in the modern Belgian Congo.

While the Dutch and the Belgians have behaved this way, the Portuguese have taken an entirely different attitude. Verandas were adopted from the East by the Portuguese and became a characteristic of architecture in Brazil, being used even around churches and chapels, in the same way as in India. The word "veranda" seems to have been introduced in European languages by the Portuguese.

Much more than any other architecture, Brazilian architecture was affected by the close contact of the Portuguese with the East: not only were gardens filled with Chinese pavilions and pagodas, but also the Oriental roof became characteristic of houses in Brazil. These influences emphasized the "Moorish" rather than the "Roman" traits of Brazilian domestic architecture: a double and sometimes antagonistic influence always present in the development of architecture in Brazil, as I shall attempt to suggest in a special chapter on a sociological interpretation of that development.

Roman traits were emphasized in Brazilian architecture, as in that of the United States, when a new economic and political order began to develop in Portuguese America with the expansion of monarchy from royal to imperial. Old colonial plantation lords became barons, viscounts, *comendadores* in an imperial nobility that also expanded from feudal agriculture into industry and trade. Consequently, as in the United States with the beginning of the phase that Mr. Lewis Mumford characterizes in his *Sticks and Stones,* in which the name "millionaire" became "the patent of America's new nobility," there arose in Brazil a scale of living and a mode of architecture with something imperial in it, and this emphasized the Roman element in architecture, as against its Eastern and Eastern-tropical elements. The main effort of the architects of patrician domestic buildings of this phase, in Brazil, in such places as Rio, Recife, and Salvador, was to give façades of "big houses"—then called *palacetes* and even *palacios*, like the Cattete Palace in Rio, built by a coffee baron of the Empire days, and now the official residence of the President of the Republic—the effect of "dignity" and "permanence" which Mr. Mumford points out as characteristic of the "Imperial" or "Roman" period in the history of United States architecture. This occurred not only in domestic, but also in other forms of architecture. For one of the aspects of the period, perhaps more in the United States than in Brazil, was its unity. "In government, in industry, in architecture, the imperial age was one," Mr. Mumford writes, referring to the United States. And he goes on to the last consequences in his analysis of this unity: the imperial or "Roman" impulse in the United States expressed itself also in monumental tombs or temples, mausoleum architecture very characteristic of the period. In Brazil even tombs ceased to be predominantly "Moorish"—hidden in private chapels in the patriarchal country houses or in town churches—to become almost as public, "Roman," and imperial as the façades of the new aristocratic or plutocratic residential buildings in towns like Rio, Recife, and Salvador.

How could an Empire's or Emperor's baron, viscount, marquis, or *comendador* be buried in an almost secret place, when his imperial condition or almost Roman, consular dignity made it imperative that his remains be kept in a sort of temple or mausoleum? During this period in the history of Brazilian architecture, its "Moorish" private, intimate element lost a great part of its importance under the impact of the "Roman," "imperial," public element. Some of the aspects of this era in Brazilian social and architectural history are studied in my book *Sobrados e Mucambos*. Here I wish to emphasize the fact that in recent years a characteristic of the development of Brazilian civilization has been a greater integration between its Roman and Moorish elements, which has meant also a greater integration of its European and tropical elements. This tendency is clearly suggested by developments in building, thus showing that architecture is almost always a significant expression of integrative or disintegrative trends in other aspects of a civilization.

Although Brazilian architecture, as far as it means a system of general architecture—church, military, official, domestic—is, from the north to the south of Brazil, Portuguese or Iberian architecture adapted to a tropical space, it has received, in different phases and different regions of its pre-national and national development, non-Portuguese influences, some of them contrary to tropical ecology. The influence of the Swiss *chalet*, for instance, neutralized by the influence of the East Indian bungalow, partly owing to the efforts of some British railroad builders with an Asiatic experience in British India to introduce into Brazil that Oriental type of residence considered ideal for the tropics by some. The influence of the violently anti-tropical Norman style—so prominent in the Rio de Janeiro's most *parvenu* domestic architecture when Rio began to be a "modern city" in the early part of the nineteenth century. German and Italian influences in the building of country houses and even urban houses—in Blumenau, for instance—owing to the presence of considerable numbers of German and Italian colonists in some areas of southern Brazil. Fletcher and Kidder even tell us, in their book *Brazil and the Brazilians*, of a "perfect Yankee house" that, in about 1870, was to be found in Brazil: the house of an Anglo-American owner of a cotton factory at Saint Aleixo. Fletcher and Kidder inform us that "both [factory and house] were actually framed in the United States, brought out in pieces and put together in Brazil," the pine used for the house having, "in spite of predictions to the contrary, proved superior in durability to Norwegian pine."

A number of foreign observers, and Brazilians as well, agree on recognizing that "the Dutch influence gave Recife, the capital of the State of Pernambuco (for some time, during the seventeenth century, occupied by the Dutch), its particular character." These are the words of Peter Fuss, the German author of a book entitled *Brazil* published in Berlin in 1937. Like many other foreign observers, Herr Fuss based his remark on the fact that in Recife, as late as 1937, he found that "old, high-gabled houses . . . still recalled the early activities of the Dutch colonists." These old houses were not the ones originally built or rebuilt by the Dutch themselves, but their high-gabled structure showed a building tradition that Herr Fuss and many other foreign observers of Recife architecture have identified as north European, rather than Portuguese.

Fletcher and Kidder, without specifying a "Dutch" influence—as many other observers do—write in their always reliable book that "many of the houses of Pernambuco [by Pernambuco they meant Recife] are built in a style unknown in other parts of Brazil." As a specimen of this style, they give the description of a house six stories high (first known by Kidder) which, being Luso-Brazilian in its patriarchal functions, seems to have been the result of a neat north European, or "Dutchman"—"Dutch" and also commercial or progressively bourgeois—upon the building habits of this part of Brazil. The same authors—Fletcher confirms Kidder, who was the pioneer of the two, in the discovery of Brazil with Anglo-American eyes—state that when Kidder first knew the most ancient district of the city of Recife, in 1833, the buildings still exhibited "the old Dutch style of architecture," to which the Portuguese, after having regained the place from the invaders, had added their very Moorish "latticed balconies or *gelouzias*."

Introduction

What happened, then, was absorption of "Dutch" architecture by the Luso-tropical one. This was to be expected in regions like Pernambuco, as the "Dutch" architecture was artificial, brought in pieces—bricks and all—from Europe, just as the Santo Aleixo "Yankee house" was brought from the United States, whereas the Luso-tropical architecture was an ecological system of building which specialized in using local materials —stone, woods, *etc.*—and in adapting itself to tropical conditions.

In Brazil, as in New Amsterdam, the Dutch seem to have "copied the styles of old Amsterdam, and as the crowded conditions of old Amsterdam had induced the narrow Dutch front with the terraced gable-end, the unimaginative Dutch burghers reproduced the narrow buildings in New Amsterdam. . . ." According to a United States historian, Professor Max Savelle in his *Seeds of Liberty* (New York, 1948), this is how the Dutch behaved in the area that is now New York. Their behavior in tropical Brazil was characterized by a still more unimaginative attitude in regard to architecture in particular and to the art of adapting European values and European techniques to the tropics in general. This explains why they were so rapidly swallowed by the tropical China that Brazil is or has been in relation to European or Anglo-American values not well adapted to its tropical location. The success of the Portuguese in Brazil is to be explained, to a large extent, in terms of a constant disposition on their part to adapt European values and European techniques to tropical conditions, going so far as to repudiate some of the European values and techniques and to adopt tropical ones instead. This they did in matters not only of architecture, but also of food, as the replacement of wheat by manioc in the most tropical areas of Brazil clearly indicates.

Only recently it was pointed out at the 1953 Conference on

Tropical Architecture held in London that modern Brazilians have rediscovered values in tropical art, hygiene, and town-planning which, though known by ancient peoples, had not been recognized by Europeans or Anglo-Americans in their attempts to develop modern civilization in tropical areas.

Thus Mr. O. H. Koenigsberger remarked in his paper "Tropical Planning Problems" (published in *Conference on Tropical Architecture*, London, 1954) that "it is already becoming clear that the virtue of wide streets is not as uncontested and axiomatic as the sanitary engineers of the earlier decades of this century believed. The arid tropics, for instance, have a tradition of narrow, arcaded, and sometimes even covered streets which provide shade and relief from heat and glare." This tradition, brought to Brazil by the Portuguese, has affected Brazilian architecture in its most genuine expressions, both "colonial" and "modern." Modern buildings in Brazil are returning to the old Eastern-Iberian style of arcaded streets through a sort of co-operation between architecture and urbanism.

Mr. S. O. Jaiyesimi, from Nigeria, speaking at the same Conference on Tropical Architecture in London, pointed out that "the use of new materials to build in the Western style will lead to the spread of modern civilization through the tropics, but a local architectural idiom will never evolve if architects fail to take the initiative in the use of local materials and crafts." At the same conference Mr. R. S. Colquhoun from Great Britain pointed out that "the Brazilians have rediscovered the pierced screen of Mogul architecture as a sun break. . . ." It is interesting to note that the modern Brazilian movement to "rediscover" this and other Oriental values in architecture, some of them brought to Brazil by the Portuguese in the colonial days, started with the Conference on Regionalism that met in Recife in February 1926, organized for a Society for the Defense of Regionalism (in architecture as well as in other arts, literature, recreation, cookery, planning, urbanization, education, *etc.*) founded in Recife as early as 1924, having Professor Odilon Nestor as president. This has been recently recognized by one of the leading modern architects of Brazil, Senhor Henrique E. Mindlin, in what is probably the best book on the new Brazilian architecture: *Modern Architecture in Brazil* (Rio de Janeiro, Amsterdam, 1956), with a preface by Professor S. Giedion. He states that the Regionalist Manifesto of Recife (1926) is a document of "positive significance" for the development of a Brazilian architecture at once modern and regional, its ideas finding expression in "recent attempts at integrating contemporary elements with regional and traditional ones." The same, in regard to this anticipation by the Recife Regionalists, has been pointed out by the professor of architecture at the School of Architecture of the University of Rio de Janeiro, Senhor Paulo Santos. A similar anticipation of the Recife regionalists in regard to mural painting and its themes as developed by Senhor Candido Portinari and other modern Brazilian painters has been noted by Professor Robert S. Smith. This anticipation seems to be generally recognized in literature; and in regard to social studies the Regionalist Manifesto seems to mark a distinct beginning for modern anthropological and sociological studies in Brazil on an ecological or regional basis.

Another "Brazilianism" in the art and science of building was recognized by the architects who met in London in 1953, when it was pointed out by one of them that standards for indoor spaces have to be or can be reasonably lower in the tropics than in Europe. This subject was considered in a very intelligent way by the London Conference. One of the architects present, Mr. G. Anthony Atkinson, in a paper on "Tropical Architecture and Building Standards," remarked that medical and public health requirements usually adopted for architecture in the tropics are copied from European laws and—in the case of tropical territories under British control or influence—"seem to have little scientific validity, being based in British territories on English and Scotch regulations of the time." Moreover, in the tropics, "many activities can take place in the open air. A roof alone might be good enough to give protection against the sun and the rain, and against the dew on cool, cloudless nights. . . . It is most desirable to reconsider the basis of space standards and to think in terms of social rather than only of health requirements," he added, thus recognizing the social or sociological importance of modern efforts toward a scientific treatment of tropical problems of housing, as well as of town-planning and agriculture, according to tropical conditions.

Mr. A. Adedokun Adeyemi, from Nigeria, remarked, following the same line of thought:

> *"Modern planning schemes in Africa often fall into the error of designing for sophisticated Africans who attempt to lead a life based on a false conception of Western standards. The real need is to plan to raise the general standard of living of the mass of the people, and this can be done by accepting what is good in the old traditional way of life."*

This is exactly what is being done in relation not only to architecture and town-planning, but also to music, agriculture, sculpture, literature, sociology, and cattle breeding by a number of Brazilians who have become deeply tropics-conscious, and who were awakened to this by the insistence, since 1924, of the Recife Regionalists, on the importance of Brazil's developing its civilization on the basis of a tropical ecology.

Even in regard to dress, Brazilians are showing a disposition to break with a too-passive submission to European patterns and fashions, and to develop styles that will correspond from both hygienic and aesthetic points of view to tropical conditions. In connection with this, a recent experiment by Senhor Flavio Carvalho of São Paulo must be considered a pioneer attempt toward a scientific solution of the problem, not only for Brazil, but also for other modern civilizations situated in tropical areas. His idea is that of a bold modernization of suggestions taken from the East Indians, the Africans, and other tropical peoples. Specialists in nutrition in Brazil are doing the same in regard to traditionally tropical foods that had ceased to be elegant; their virtues as foods adequate to a tropical clime are being rediscovered. Hats and shoes in Brazil, or for a considerable number of Brazilians, have ceased to be orthodox European. There are distinguished Brazilians who do not wear either shoes or hats, but appear in the streets hatless and with sandals. The use of slacks and pajamas is becoming possible outside of strictly domestic or informal circles.

The traveler who more than a half-century ago wrote that "in their ambition to copy European and North American fashions, the gentlemen of Rio utterly disregard the eternal fitness of things, wearing broadcloth suits of black, with tall stovepipe hats, neither of which articles should be adopted for a moment in their torrid climate" and boldly stated that "linen clothing and light straw hats are the true costume for the tropics," can hardly have imagined how the situation would change in a few decades.

It would have been equally difficult for Europeans and Anglo-Americans who visited Brazil at the end of the nineteenth century to foresee that absorption of non-Iberian immigrants by tropical Brazil which is making such anticipations as the Italianization of São Paulo or the Germanization of Santa Catharina appear almost ridiculous. It is a fact that these non-Iberian immigrants have introduced a number of valuable

Italianisms and Germanisms into the Portuguese language of Brazil, as well as into the food habits and other customs of the Brazilians. The same thing is true of other non-Iberian immigrants who have established themselves in Brazil, the Japanese included. But most of them have been Brazilianized as they have become adapted to the tropics. The tropics and Brazilian civilization seem to have a secret alliance against all possible enemies.

Writing of European immigrants to modern Brazil, Professor Arthur Ramos says in the chapter "Social Pioneering" in *Brazil*—an excellent book edited by Professor Lawrence F. Hill and published in 1947—that "from the point of view of racial contacts" the Italian colonist in Brazil has been "the most adaptable after the Portuguese." From the first generation on, he becomes "completely acculturated." Of the German colonists in Brazil, Professor Ramos points out that "in the plateau regions" of southern Brazil they established small farms "as opposed to the vast estates of the Portuguese-Brazilian system." Writing of the non-Portuguese or non-Iberian European colonists in general (Italians, Germans, Slavs), Ramos says that they changed "the character" or the "social structure" of a few of the sub-regions of southern Brazil, where they have established themselves specially through "small holdings," basic to their agricultural activity. He admits, with Professor Emilio Willems, the "marginality" of some of the German colonists in relation to Brazilian traditional national culture. But he also agrees with Professor Roquette Pinto, Brazil's greatest modern anthropologist, on the desire of German immigrants to become assimilated by that culture, as expressed by the fact that "numerous German-Brazilian horsemen, mounted in the *gaúcho* manner, with silver spurs, broad-brimmed hats, breeches with silver buttons, lassos" are seen in southern Brazil. In an essay,

Introduction

"*O Mundo que o Portugues Creou*"—a summary of lectures delivered in European universities in 1937—I have pointed out less evident signs of the same desire of European colonists of non-Iberian origin in Brazil to become assimilated into the traditional national culture of Iberian or Portuguese origin, a culture that some of them feel to express a longer and deeper harmonization of European ways with conditions in a tropical or quasi-tropical space.

In recognizing this, they have recognized the fact that Brazilians have solved a number of problems in connection with civilized life in the tropics in a way that places Brazilian civilization among the creative civilizations that man has developed in the tropics. If the Brazilians have been creative, credit should be given them for a quality not generally associated with the tropics. Lafcadio Hearn, though enthusiastic about tropical life and tropical peoples, seems to have thought that the tropics were not fit for men of ideas. Men should avoid thinking in the tropics. The warm climate did not seem favorable to creative intellectual life of a higher order.

Tropical Brazil does not seem to favor this and similar generalizations about the tropics. Its intellectual life has been a surprise to Europeans and Anglo-Americans. Teixeira de Freitas —a jurist whose influence reached Argentina and Chile—was a creative thinker born and raised in tropical Brazil. Brazilian was also Santos Dumont, an inventor, considered by authoritative European—British and French—historians of aviation to have preceded the Wright brothers in the invention of the modern airplane. Brazilian is the physics researcher Senhor Cesar Lattes, considered in the United States one of the creative young scientists of our day. Brazilian were Oswaldo Cruz, the Almeida brothers, Vital Brazil, famous for their research on tropical problems of medicine, research illuminated

3 7

by new ideas on these problems. Brazilian literature, Brazilian architecture, and Brazilian social science have all showed signs of creativeness.

It was during a long residence in tropical Brazil that Alfred Russel Wallace developed ideas about biology which made him a rival of Darwin. Other European and Anglo-Americans have lived in Brazil a life of intensive and productive thought as scientists in different branches of national or cultural science: Lund, a Scandinavian geologist; Grivet, a philologist born in Switzerland; Hartt, from the United States, also a geologist; Sigaud, a Frenchman who was a pioneer in tropical medicine, which he studied in Brazil; Patterson, an Englishman, who was a pioneer in the same field; Max Müller, a German, a naturalist. Jewish literature on the American continent was born in tropical Brazil with a poem written by Rabbi Aboab da Fonseca, for long years a resident of Recife. It seems also that Protestant theological and social thought about problems created by the contact of European Christians with natives of the tropics began in Brazil with the French and Swiss Protestants who established themselves in Rio de Janeiro as early as the sixteenth century.

Brazil may be a tropical China for its power of absorption of exotic elements. But considered in some aspects of its civilization, it is a positive contradiction to the classic idea both of "China" and of "tropics" as spaces where human life is characterized by inertia in its most passive forms.

[I]

The European Background
of Brazilian History

Brazil, which was discovered and colonized by the Portuguese, is sometimes called Portuguese America. As Portuguese America it is generally considered an extension of Europe, and in its main characteristics it remains Portuguese and Hispanic, or Iberian. It is also Catholic, or a branch or variant of the Latin form of Christianity or civilization.

But the facts that its origins are mainly Portuguese or Hispanic and that its principal characteristics are Latin Catholic do not make Brazil so simple or pure an extension of Europe as New England was of old England and as New England was of Protestant or Evangelical Christianity in North America. For, as everyone knows, Spain and Portugal, though conventionally European states, are not orthodox in all their European and

Christian qualities, experiences, and conditions of life, but are in many important respects a mixture of Europe and Africa, of Christianity and Mohammedanism. According to geographers, the Hispanic peninsula is a transition zone between two continents; it is a popular saying that "Africa begins at the Pyrenees"—a saying sometimes used sarcastically by Nordics.

For eight centuries the Hispanic, or Iberian, peninsula was dominated by Africans. Arabs and Moors left their traces there. Although some of the modern Spanish and Portuguese thinkers—as during a certain phase of his life, Unamuno—would have Spain and Portugal Europeanized with all speed, others, following Ganivet, have maintained that Spain and Portugal must look south to Africa for their future and for the explanation of their ethos. The same conflict of opinion is to be found among foreign students of Hispanic social history and cultural problems: some—the German, Schulten, for instance—believe that one of the tasks of modern Europe should be to annex Spain definitely to the European system of civilization; others—the Frenchman, Maurice Legendre, for instance—go so far as to say that the African element is one of the best original ingredients of Spain, not to be repudiated with shame, but to be cherished with pride.

Legendre is one of the authors who point out the similarity between the Spanish peninsula and Russia in that each is a transition zone between two continents: *"Elle* [Spain or Iberia] *est à la rencontre de deux continents comme la Russie."* [1] And not only between two continents, one might add, but also between two climates, two types of soil and vegetation, two races, two cultures, two conceptions of life, two ecological

---

[1] Maurice Legendre: *Portrait de l'Espagne* (Paris, 1923), p. 49. The situation of the Hispanic peninsula as a transition zone is certainly similar in many important respects to that of Russia, described by Professor Hans Kohn as "a meeting place of the East and the West by her history and by her nature" (*Orient and Occident*, New York, 1934, p. 76).

complexes. Also between Euro-Africa and Hispanic America.

As in Russia, such antagonistic conditions and conceptions of life as are to be found among Spaniards and Portuguese have not come together without violent conflict. But amalgamation, accommodation, assimilation have been more powerful than conflict. The result is that the Portuguese, like the Spanish and the Russians, are, in more than a cultural and social aspect, a people with the "split" or Dr. Jekyll-Mr. Hyde personality that psychologists have studied in certain individuals, and sociologists have perceived in certain social groups. In other aspects, however, they are made not only more dramatic, but also psychologically richer and culturally more complex than simpler peoples by the fact that they have developed a special capacity to maintain contradictions and even to harmonize them. This capacity is now being demonstrated impressively by the Russians; and it has been demonstrated by the Spanish and the Portuguese during the most creative phases of their history, through one or another of the classical methods by which individuals and groups solve their inner conflicts of personality. According to modern American sociologists and social psychologists such solutions are, fundamentally, three: (1) the rejection of one element or interest, usually by repression, and the selection of another, opposing one; (2) the splitting of the personality into two or more divisions, each looking toward some interest or objects; (3) integration, or balance, of contending elements.

If I am not mistaken, each of the three classical solutions could be found as a dominant factor in any of the various phases of the social and cultural development of the Spanish and Portuguese peoples. Of these phases, we are concerned most directly with the one that immediately preceded the discovery of the American continent and its colonization by Spanish and Portuguese. But the truth is that the social and psychological preparation—unconscious preparation—of the Spaniards and the Portuguese for that tremendous task seems to have taken the entire eight centuries of close contact of the Spanish and Portuguese Christians with the Arabs and Moors who dominated the peninsula. For such centuries were not all, or only, centuries of war, conflict, intolerance. As Professor Fernando de los Ríos reminds us, there were epochs of struggle and intolerance, but also "marvelous periods of understanding and co-operation." "To stress the latter we have only to remember," he writes, "how in the thirteenth century the three cults—Christian, Moorish, and Mosaic—were celebrated in the same temple, the mosque of Santa María la Blanca de Toledo." [2]

On the other hand, the periods of Castilian and orthodox Catholic domination over the so-called "Hispanic totality" seem to illustrate the solution—or attempt at a solution—of co-existent ethnic and cultural antagonisms through rejecting or repressing various elements and selecting one stock or group and one culture or religion as the perfect or orthodox one. The Inquisition was perhaps the most powerful instrument used in Spain and Portugal to accomplish this. But neither Castilian centralization nor the Inquisition was able to repress differences or entirely neutralize the process of accommodation in the cultural field and the process of amalgamation in the biological and ethnic one. The *mozarabes* (Christians living under Mohammedan rule), the *mudejares* (Moors living under Christian rule), and the *New Christians* (Jews completely or superficially converted to Christianity) had in Spain and Portugal become too powerful, too penetrating, too plastic, too fluid, and too complex to allow Spanish or Portuguese social and cultural life to be controlled by a single, definitive, clear-

[2] "Spain in the Epoch of American Civilization," in *Concerning Latin American Culture* (New York, 1940), p. 24.

cut group considering itself biologically pure (*sangre limpia*) or culturally perfect by either European or African standards. There were dramatic conflicts between those who had Christianity and Latin as their ideal of perfection and those who were fanatical followers of Mohammed or Moses. But the general result of the long contact of the Spanish and Portuguese peoples with the Arabs, the Moors, and the Jews was integration, or balance, of contending elements rather than segregation or sharp differentiation of any of them or violent conflict between them.[3]

The Arabs added to the Spanish and Portuguese languages a rich vocabulary of Arabisms by means of which some sociological conclusions may be reached. One of these is that in both languages Arabisms seem to outnumber Latinisms among old scientific and technical terms of importance related to agriculture and land industries. And some popular expressions, as "to work hard like a Moor," seem to explain why certain parts of the peninsula are considered "fertile soil" by Arabian au-

[3] Recent research seems to indicate that Jewish blood among Catholic Iberians is even more abundant than had been thought. According to a recent discovery by Señor Pedro Sainz Rodríguez, Francisco de Vitoria, a famous Catholic thinker and scholar, considered the Spanish founder of modern international law, descended from Jews. The same is now thought of Torquemada himself. This made Don Luis Araquistain remark in a recent article in *Cuadernos* (Paris, May–June 1957) entitled "*¿Cual era la religión del Greco?*"—for El Greco is also considered by some to have been a Jew: "*Todos los días se hacen nuevos descubrimientos de españoles que descienden de judíos . . . ¿Que español está seguro de no llevar sangre judía o árabe en sus venas?*" (page 16). See also on the subject *El Greco y Toledo*, by Dr. Gregorio Marañon (Madrid, 1956); *España en su Historia*, by Don Americo Castro (Buenos Aires, 1948); and *Aspectos del Vivir Hispánico*, also by Castro (Santiago de Chile, 1949). Dr. Laín Entralgo, in his *España como Problema* (Madrid, 1956), though thinking that Castro overestimates the "Semitic contribution (Arabic and Jewish)" to the "Hispanic life," considers Castro's reinterpretation of the Hispanic past, putting emphasis on this contribution, "fundamental" (II, 495). I myself placed a similar emphasis on the Iberian origins of the Brazilian people and Brazilian culture in books anterior to those of Professor Castro.

thors and "arid land" by Christian ones. A significant detail is that in the Portuguese language the word for olive tree, *oliveira*, is of Latin origin whereas the current word for the commercial product of the same tree—*azeite*, oil—is of Arab origin. Other examples might be added to suggest how Arabs and Latins, Christians and Jews, Catholics and Mohammedans have formed the Spanish and Portuguese culture (for it is really *one* culture composed of various sub-cultures), the Spanish and Portuguese languages, and the Spanish and Portuguese ethnic types—more or less harmonious, more or less contradictory products of a sort of competitive co-operation among different human (and perhaps ethnic) capacities and culturally diverse specialized talents and antagonistic dispositions.

Regional diversity in peninsular conditions of soil, of geographical situation, and of climate should also be taken into consideration by the student of the European background of Brazilian history, a background that is not purely European, but also African; not purely Christian, but also Jewish and Mohammedan; not only agrarian (as illustrated by the importance of the farmers in the earlier days of Portugal), but also military; not only industrial (as developed by the Arabs and the Moors), but also maritime and commercial (as developed by Nordics and Jews); marked not only by the capacity for hard, continuous, monotonous work and by the inclination toward sedentary farm life, but also by the spirit of adventure and romantic chivalry. As a key to understanding why such tremendous forces for absolute uniformity of culture, character, and life as a violent centralization of political power in Lisbon (or Madrid), the Inquisition or the Society of Jesus, and as, after the discovery of Brazil, so brutal and efficient a one-man dictatorship as that of the Marquis of Pombal in Portugal, were not able to destroy differences, variety, spontaneous popular vigor among the Portuguese, the diversity of physical conditions is only less important in Spanish and Portuguese history than is the dramatic diversity of ethnic and cultural values.

These forces for uniformity were probably essential to the development not only of Spain, but also of Portugal as efficient colonizing powers; but it is certainly a good sign of social vitality in each that neither of them became strictly orthodox or Catholic in the religious and social sense desired by the Jesuits or the Inquisition; that neither of them lost its regional and cultural diversity under the pressure of strongly centralized government. For the preservation of such healthy differences or antagonisms, it was a good thing that the forces for uniformity did not always act together, but were sometimes competitive or antagonistic: the Crown against the Church, for instance; the Society of Jesus against the Inquisition. There was a period when the Jews themselves had the Jesuits as their protectors against the powerful Inquisition. And the fact is that, though nominally expelled, the Jews did not disappear from Portuguese life.

As a very competent student of Portuguese cultural history, Aubrey F. G. Bell, has reminded us, Sobieski, a Polish traveler, wrote in 1611: "There are in Portugal very many Jews, so many that various houses in Portugal have a Jewish origin. Although they have burned and expelled them, many live hidden among the Portuguese." [4] When it became fashionable in Portugal during the seventeenth and the eighteenth centuries for gentlemen to wear glasses in order to look wise and learned, shrewd Sephardic Jews were able to disguise their Semitic noses under spectacles. And Christians and Jews alike seem to have used rings set with precious stones to show their disdain for manual labor—a custom that survived in Brazil. The display of nobility by Portuguese aristocrats, both Christian and

[4] *Portugal of the Portuguese* (London, 1915), p. 4.

Jew—for the Jews in Portugal and Spain were an aristocracy rather than a plutocracy—sometimes assumed grotesque forms, as when three gentlemen formed a partnership in the use of the same silk suit, two of them having to stay at home when the third went out. A traveler tells us of Jewish physicians, disguised as Christians, in Portuguese America in the seventeenth century who prescribed pork so as to lessen the suspicion of Judaism. And they all were noted for their attention to dress, even when working as carriers or engaging in other humble occupations, like the Sephardic sellers of *"pan de España"* in Smyrna.

Sometimes the king of Portugal himself protected the Jews of his kingdom against a too-strict enforcement of laws against them, laws based on an ideal of religious rather than of racial purity. Such an ideal would have considerable political importance in the foundation and development of Brazil as a politically orthodox colony of Portugal. There was a time in Brazil when friars came to meet newcomers in their boats, not to ascertain their nationality or inspect police papers or examine their physical health, but to inquire into their religious health. Were they Christian? Were their parents Christian? How orthodox were they? As immigration authorities at the service of the State as well as of the Church, the friars were guarding against the danger, not of contagious disease or a criminal disposition, but of infidelity or heresy. The heretic was considered a political enemy of Portuguese America: if he was a Jew, he had to disguise himself as a New Christian; if a Protestant, he had to disguise himself as a Catholic. It seems, however, that there was considerable accommodation in the adjustment of such differences as far as the rich Jews were concerned.

The Jews were an important element in Portugal's social and cultural life, not only for their commercial activity and their capacity to establish cosmopolitan contacts for the Lusitanian Christian adventurers when their maritime enterprises began, but for other things as well. One should not forget that for such enterprises the Portuguese were particularly favored by their geographical situation; or that from their remote beginning on, they were greatly influenced by the sea. Some authors refer to that portion of the Atlantic Ocean which lies between the west coast of Portugal and a line drawn through the Azores to Madeira as "the Lusitanian Sea"; and Dalgado, a specialist in climatic geography, reminds us of the fact that, taken as a whole, the "Lusitanian Sea" has more currents than any other sea near Europe—a fact that explains, he adds, "the quantity and the variety of fishes to be found in it." [5] Another specialist in the subject, Kohl, more than half a century ago styled Portugal the "Netherlands of the Iberian Peninsula," a comparison likewise made by Fischer, the creator of a map showing the configuration of the Hispanic peninsula. Dalgado describes Portugal as "the western inclined plane of the Iberian peninsula, for it is the exposure of the large portion of its surface to the oceanic winds on the western side which gives it its distinctive climate." [6] Not only, one might add, its distinctive climate from the point of view of physical geography, but also its distinctive historical and cultural climate. For the ethnic and cultural history of Portugal, the heterogeneous ethnic composition of its population, and its commercial and urban cosmopolitanism in opposition to its agrarian or rural conservatism are all connected with Portugal's being the "western inclined plane of the Iberian Peninsula."

Certain anthropologists consider the Iberians to have been the original inhabitants of the Hispanic peninsula, and some describe them as Mongoloid. But so many intruders have settled in Portugal—the Ligurians, the Celts and the Gauls, the Phoe-

[5] D. G. Dalgado: *The Climate of Portugal* (Lisbon, 1914), p. 33.
[6] Ibid., p. 42.

nicians, the Carthaginians, the Romans, the Suevi and the Goths, the Jews, the Moors, the Germans, the French, the English—that it would be difficult to find a modern people whose recent and remote ethnic and cultural past is more heterogeneous. It should be added that before Brazil was discovered and its colonization begun, the population of Portugal had been colored by the introduction of a considerable number of Negroes,[7] used as domestic slaves, and of some East Indians, noted for their talent as wood carvers and cabinetmakers.

With such a heterogeneous ethnic and cultural past, the diversity shown by the Portuguese as both anthropological and cultural types is not surprising. Some students of the Portuguese ethos regard the Phoenicians, the Carthaginians, and the Jews as the source of the spirit of maritime enterprise that flourished in Portugal from the fourteenth to the seventeenth centuries. They also point out that the Romans gave the Portuguese the bony structure of their language and of some of their social institutions; and that the Moors left many a trait or influence, not only in social institutions and in the language, music, and dances of Portugal, but also in its material culture—architecture, industrial technique, cuisine, and popular dress. The presence and influence in Portugal of French and English Crusaders with their spirit of adventure and their disdain for agricultural labor; the presence and influence there of the Jews, with their commercial spirit and (as they were Sephardic Jews) their disdain for all kinds of manual labor and their excessive enthusiasm for the intellectual and bureaucratic professions; the Portuguese victories over the Moors; the Portuguese conquests in Asia and in Africa and the opportunity to employ Negroes, East Indians, and Moors to work in the fields

[7] L. S. Silva Rebello: *Memoria sobre a população e a agricultura de Portugal desde a fundação da monarchia até 1865* (Lisbon, 1865), p. 60.

and in the manual arts—all these factors seem to have developed in a large part of the Portuguese population the spirit of adventure and the aristocratic prejudices that appeared among some of the first men to come from Portugal to America.

In Portuguese America these prejudices took the form of love of military action, of show and grandeur, and of bureaucratic occupation or parasitism, along with slave-making activities, directed first against the Indians and concentrated later on the importation of Africans to work on the almost feudal plantations that some Portuguese were able to establish in Brazil. Fortunately for both Portugal and Brazil, such acquired tastes did not destroy entirely in the Portuguese of the old, rural stock—in the so-called *portugueses velhos* who would be the basic human element of the agrarian colonization of Brazil —their traditional love of agriculture. Men like Duarte Coelho and the Albuquerques brought from Portugal to Brazil, in addition to the spirit of adventure, a feeling for social continuity and a capacity for long, patient, and difficult labor. They loved trees and rural life. They were, by tradition, gentlemen farmers or planters. Duarte descended from the agricultural nobility of the north of Portugal, as did his wife, Dona Brites, who became the first woman governor in America. From the same region there migrated to Brazil a number of families who followed Duarte and Dona Brites, some related to them. The Portuguese peasants of that region—the North Atlantic region—are generally considered rather dull of intellect, though religious, musical, occasionally gay, patient, and hardworking.

But the Portuguese of the old rural stock who came to Brazil in the sixteenth century would have been incomplete or one-sided without the so-called "enemies of agriculture," whose predominating traits were their spirit of adventure, their love of novelties, their cleverness, their commercial and urban spirit, their genius for trade. The farmers with a deep love for the land and a thorough knowledge of agriculture were sometimes abused or exploited in Brazil by those of their fellow countrymen whose passion was for commercial adventure and for urban life—most of them probably Jews. But this antagonism was, in more than one respect, beneficial to Portuguese America. Urban Jews with a genius for trade made possible the industrialization of sugar-cane agriculture in Brazil and the successful commercialization of Brazilian sugar.

This antagonism, however, must be regarded by the student of early Brazilian history not only as an evil—for it was an evil—but also as a stimulus to differentiation and progress. One of the most capable interpreters of Portuguese economic history, Senhor Antonio Sergio, has made sufficiently clear that the commercial class in Portugal, the businessmen of the coast line, became more important than the aristocratic proprietors of the hinterland in shaping, with the king's co-operation, a national, or rather an international, policy that neglected the hinterland to foster maritime adventure. The process has been carefully studied by J. Lucio de Azevedo, the best authority on the economic history of Portugal.[8]

I hardly do more than summarize what Sergio suggests and Azevedo explains when I say that the early rise of the commercial classes in Portugal is a fact never to be overlooked by the student of the European background of Brazilian history. As Sergio reminds us, Lisbon became the seaport where the commerce of the north of Europe met that of the south; it was owing to this tendency toward maritime commerce and the concentration of attention on the seaports that the problem of peopling the southern part of Portugal, where agriculture has always depended on expensive irrigation, began to be neglected at an early stage. Because the chief aim of European commerce

[8] *Epocas de Portugal Economico* (Lisbon, 1929).

at this time was, as everyone knows, the acquisition of Oriental products, the Portuguese businessmen of Lisbon, some of them Jews or connected with Jews, took advantage of the geographical situation of their town, and also of the fact that feudalism was not so powerful in Portugal as in other parts of Europe, to become masters of the national policy and to transform it into a bold cosmopolitan, commercial, and at the same time imperial adventure through scientific and quasi-scientific efforts to discover new routes for commerce, new lands and new markets to be exploited, and pagan populations not only to be converted into Christians, but also to be subdued into Portuguese subjects or slaves. The king of Portugal himself became "the Merchant of Merchants" and the state officials also turned traders.[9]

It is well known that in the fourteenth and fifteenth centuries, with the irruption of the Turks into the eastern seaports of the Mediterranean and because of other difficulties, the need for a sea route to India became acutely felt in Europe. No European nation was in a more advantageous position to solve this grave problem than semi-European Portugal, a nation so precociously maritime and commercial in its political program that, as early as the latter part of the fourteenth century, laws were enacted by King Dom Fernando which gave special protection to maritime commerce and encouraged naval construction; which gave more assistance to such a cause than to the noble proprietors of latifundia, especially of lands regained from the Moors—lands that needed irrigation, then considered a matter of royal aid or something above the economic capacity of the not very wealthy proprietors. It seems that such aid was never given. In not assisting the aristocratic proprietors of latifundia, the kings of Portugal perhaps had in view the defi-

[9] Antonio Sergio: *A Sketch of the History of Portugal*, translated from the Portuguese by Constantino José dos Santos (Lisbon, 1928), p. 88.

nite and efficient development of centralized royal power, which might be endangered by a strong landed aristocracy.

The policy of disdain or neglect of the Portuguese hinterland followed by some of the most influential kings of Portugal like Dom Fernando explains why so many noblemen began to go to Lisbon as candidates for government appointments. As such, even they grew enthusiastic over maritime adventure, trade, naval construction; they became co-operators, rather than enemies, of the merchant princes of the seaports when the sea route to India was opened and parts of the East became colonies or semi-colonies of Portugal. Some of these aristocrats went to Brazil, appointed by the Portuguese Crown to high bureaucratic positions or military posts or sent on special missions that required from them the best of their military experience and their capacity as leaders. There they encountered such mutually antagonistic, but also co-operative, forces as the king, the Church, the Jews, the common man, the heretic, and the political or common criminals forced to leave Portugal and go to Brazil.

It seems to me that some authors—Sombart is one of them—overemphasize the importance of the Jews in Portuguese maritime and colonial enterprises, including the development of Brazil as a sugar-producing colony. Nevertheless one should not go to the opposite extreme: that of overlooking the part played by the Jews in the cultural development of Portugal and in the definitely cosmopolitan shape taken by its economic policy after the days of Dom Fernando. For Portuguese kings and Jewish princes of finance understood each other so well that Jews had been royal tax-collectors since the early days of the Portuguese monarchy; and under some of the best kings Sephardic Jews were ministers of finance, royal physicians, royal astrologers. Under Portuguese royal protection Jewish merchants are said to have become proud and conceited; to have adorned their horses with tassels; to have indulged in luxury. And one can imagine what powerful rivals of the Catholic chaplains, confessors, advisors, and educators they became as royal physicians, astrologers, and tax-collectors. For in those days a man's body was becoming again almost as important as his soul, and shrewd astrologers seemed to be able to guide a king or a queen, a prince or a captain, through mysterious regions of this world and of the next—regions entirely unknown to Catholic masters of theology and divinity.

For those who study the history of Portugal from a Brazilian point of view, it is interesting to follow Jewish activities in connection with the maritime and commercial enterprises that had sugar-producing in Brazil as their by-product, if not their chief product. From the reign of Sancho II, who was interested in the development of the Portuguese navy, the Jews were obliged to pay a navy tax: for each ship fitted out by the king they had to provide "an anchor and a new anchor-row sixty ells long or instead to make a money payment of 60 livres." They controlled, among other branches of commerce, the food supply, and more than once we are reminded by such students of the history of Jewish activities in Portugal as Azevedo that they were accused, with or without reason, of holding up supplies in order to raise prices—a practice not peculiar to Portuguese Jews of the fourteenth and fifteenth centuries.

At the root of the ability of the Portuguese to acclimatize themselves in various parts of the world better than almost any other Europeans, some writers find the great admixture of the people of Portugal with the Semitic race; and not the Jews alone, but the Moors also would have contributed to that special capacity. Against such a generalization there stands a fact of considerable importance: that "New Lusitania"—the northeastern part of Brazil—was settled mostly by men and women from northern Portugal, a population noted for its Romano-Visigothic blood and "Nordic" characteristics. Such men and women, some of them from the agricultural nobility, could adapt themselves well to the tropical climate of that Brazilian region where sugar cane was made the basis for a revival of feudal social organization, with Africans as slaves. Perhaps the Portuguese climate itself—a climate more African than European—best explains why the Portuguese adapt themselves better than other Europeans to tropical climates. And one should not forget that during the first generations of settlers of the tropical parts of Brazil this adaptation was based on slave work; the Portuguese did not do the hardest work in the fields, but had Indians, and later Negroes, as plantation slaves.

It is to be noted that it was not Brazil that made the Portuguese masters in the art of living and sometimes of fortunes based on slavery: when the colonization of Brazil began, Portugal itself was full of African slaves—though this, of course, was only a miniature of what was to develop in Brazil on a large, almost monumental, scale. When they reached Brazil, most of the Portuguese already had a love of display and grandeur and a distaste for manual work which are to be explained, in large part, by their having had, for nearly a century, most of their domestic work done by Negro slaves and, for many centuries, some of the most difficult agricultural labor provided by the Moors.

To the Portuguese, the Moors had been not only the efficient agricultural workers who knew how to transform arid lands into gardens as if by a miracle, but also a dark race who had not always been the serfs, but sometimes had been the masters of a large part of the Iberian peninsula. Portuguese of the purest Nordic blood had found in brown Moorish women, some of them princesses, the supreme revelation of feminine beauty. As more than one student of Brazilian history has pointed out—in particular the American Mr. Roy Nash, whose book *The Conquest of Brazil* is one of the best ever written on Brazil from a sociological standpoint—the first contact of the Portuguese or the Spanish with a darker-skinned people had been "the contact of the conquered with their brown-skinned conquerors." And "the darker man was the more cultured, more learned, more artistic. He lived in castles and occupied the towns. He was the rich man and the Portuguese became serfs upon his land. Under such conditions, it would be deemed an honor for the white to marry or mate with the governing class, the brown man, instead of the reverse." [1]

Through the sociological study of the famous Portuguese legend of the *moura encantada*, I reached years ago the same conclusion as Mr. Roy Nash: that the idealization, by the Portuguese people, of the brown woman, or the Moorish girl or woman, as the supreme type of human beauty had probably a very important effect on the direction taken by their relations with Indian (Amerindian) women in Brazil. Mystic, poetical, given to dreams about their past, lovers of beautiful plants as well as of useful and commercial ones, the Portuguese have peopled some of their woods and fountains with fascinating legends of Moorish princesses. The boy who is fortunate enough to discover and treat well the animal or the plant that is only a disguise for some beautiful Moorish princess of the past will marry her and be rich and happy. And in all such stories and legends the Moorish brown girl is regarded as the supreme type of beauty and of sexual attractiveness; the Moors are considered superior, and not inferior, to the purely white Portuguese.

Such legends are still active among the Portuguese peasants, a large majority of whom are illiterate. Portuguese children of all classes grow up under the spell of such non-European or

[1] *The Conquest of Brazil* (New York, 1926), p. 37.

non-"Aryan" legends and myths. One can imagine how active the pro-Moorish legends were among the Portuguese who, in the sixteenth century, first came into contact with the Indians in America, another brown race. Their historical experience, their folklore, their popular literature in prose and verse—all these voices from their past told the Portuguese who first arrived in Brazil that brown people are not always inferior to white people.

Legends are a living force among illiterate peasants such as those of Portugal and may express a truth more effective and enduring than some of the ever-changing half-truths taught by pedants rather than by scholars. Illiteracy among peasants with a rich folklore or folk heritage like that of Spain and Portugal does not necessarily mean ignorance, but may be intimately connected with wisdom, imagination, and humor. From their legends most of the Portuguese who discovered and colonized Brazil knew that a brown people may be superior to a white people, as the Moors had been in Portugal and Spain; and from their long contact with the Moors, considered in that part of Europe not an inferior, but a superior, race, the Portuguese assimilated many mores and conceptions: the Moorish ideal of feminine beauty (a fat woman), the Moorish taste for concubinage or polygamy, the tolerance and consideration of both races for mixed-bloods, their conception of the domestic slave as almost a sort of poor relation kept at home. The Portuguese in Brazil retained many marks of Moorish influence in their not very strictly European or very strictly Christian moral and social behavior. This was especially true of the common men, though in general it applies to Portuguese of all classes.

I wish to say more about the illiterate peasants of Portugal, to whom Brazil owes so much. Since the early days of the sixteenth century they have been the continuous basic element for the development of a real new culture—not a merely sub-

European or colonial one—in that part of the American continent. As James Murphy [2] and more recent foreign observers in Portugal have found out, the illiterate peasants are the flower or the cream of that nation; and from more than one point of view they—and not the noblemen, the bourgeois, the finely educated—have been the flower and the cream of the Portuguese colonization of Brazil.

A number of Brazilian anecdotes and jokes are directed at the Portuguese peasants: about how naïve or rustic they are; how ignorant of technical progress; how stupid or dull some of them are by contrast with other Europeans or with the native or mestizo Brazilian—the *carioca*, the *caboclo*, the *amarelinho* (who is, of course, the supreme hero of many Brazilian stories). In these anecdotes the Portuguese peasant is not necessarily the villain—indeed he never is really the villain. But, being generally represented as stout, naïve, and childlike, and also as sexually potent as primitive men are supposed to be in contrast with the too-civilized ones, he is made by Brazilian legend a sort of ridiculous but lovable Falstaff. The caricature merely emphasizes his ignorance in the face of an urban and technical progress naturally strange to men from a predominantly pastoral and agricultural country like Portugal.

Since the sixteenth century Portuguese peasants have brought with them to Brazil a wealth of legends, of incantations, of folksongs, of popular literature in verse and prose, of popular arts; and it is mainly through them—illiterate peasants and artisans—rather than through the erudite or the learned, that similar popular or folk values from the Indians and the Negroes have been assimilated by Portuguese America and have become a source for a new culture: the Brazilian culture.

Some students of modern cultures tend to exaggerate the importance of literacy. Reading and writing are very useful

[2] *Travels in Portugal* (London, 1795).

means of communication for industrial civilizations and for merely political forms of democratic organization—though, at that, they are apparently being superseded by the telephone, the radio, and television. Such countries as China, India, Mexico, and Brazil will probably not have the same need for literacy as a means of achieving modernization as had the vast masses during the nineteenth century and even Soviet Russia earlier in this century.

Aubrey F. G. Bell, who knew Portugal familiarly, wrote that "thrice fortunate" are they who "can associate and converse with the Portuguese peasants during the summer *romaria* or village *festa*, or as they sit round the winter fire (*a lareira*), or gather for some great common task, a shearing (*tosquia*) or *esfolhada* (separating the maize cob from its sheath), for they are certain to glean a rich store of proverbs, folklore, and philology," and goes on to state that "it may be said without exaggeration that the Portuguese people, for all its colossal ignorance and lack of letters, is one of the most civilized and intelligent in Europe." [3] In saying this, he is paying the greatest tribute that the son of a highly industrial and mechanical civilization such as the British can pay to a people often ridiculed for its backwardness. That this backwardness is no evidence of low intelligence or inferior race is the opinion of the most careful students of the Portuguese people and Portuguese history.

Noblemen, kings, merchant princes, doctors of philosophy, law, and medicine, priests, Sephardic Jews, scholars, and scientists have contributed brilliantly to the Portuguese colonization of Brazil. But it should be repeated that the most constant creative force in it has probably been the illiterate peasants, some of them men with North African blood: Arabian, Moorish, and even Negro. It is the result of their work that may be presented today to the world as one of the most successful col-

[3] Op. cit., p. 15.

onizing efforts, not so much of Europeans as of semi-Europeans, in tropical America.

The Portuguese common man was present in the first Portuguese colonizing efforts in Brazil. A recent careful study of documents of that period has showed that a number of Portuguese founders of *paulista* families in southern Brazil—families later famous for their pioneer work in central, northern, and the extreme parts of southern Brazil—were artisans or peasants. Portuguese artisans seem to have come in a considerable number in the sixteenth century to Bahia, the first town of importance built in Brazil; some of them were paid very high wages. They soon became numerous in Pernambuco as small-town merchants and artisans, rivals of the second- and third-generation descendants of the noblemen and gentlemen farmers from the north of Portugal who, with the help or assistance of rich Jews, had founded the sugar industry in Brazil. Later, in 1620, two hundred Portuguese families arrived in Maranhão from the Azores. In 1626 others came to Pará, and in the eighteenth century a large number established themselves in Rio Grande do Sul. They were not noblemen but peasants and artisans, common men whose mediocre success in agricultural colonization is explained by the fact that the feudal system prevailing in large areas of Portuguese America made it almost impossible for common men to prosper as farmers.

If Portuguese agricultural colonists established in Pará (Nossa Senhora do O and other places), in Bahia (Sinimbú, Engenho Novo, Rio Pardo), and in Rio de Janeiro did not succeed remarkably as agriculturists, it must be pointed out that even less successful were the Irish peasants established also as farmers in the interior of Bahia and the German families located early in the nineteenth century in the interior of Pernambuco; indeed, these were magnificent failures. But as soon as they were able to escape from a feudal system of land domination in which there was hardly any place for a genuine farmer or an independent agriculturist, most of those Portuguese agriculturists found jobs as artisans or prospered as traders in coast cities, where so many of them have been strikingly successful as merchants and founders of new industries.

In his very interesting *New Viewpoints on the Spanish Colonization of America*, Professor Silvio Zavala tells us that Philip II permitted Portuguese farmers to emigrate to Spanish America [4]—perhaps, I venture to suggest, because the conditions were more favorable to farmers in some areas of Spanish America than in most areas of Portuguese America. According to Professor Zavala, colonization of a military character had spread over Spanish America; but a large part of Portuguese America was dominated from the sixteenth century to the nineteenth by a feudal type of colonization even more alien to the ordinary European farmer than was the purely military one. And in both Hispanic Americas, the Portuguese and the Spanish, there developed another type of privileged colonization whose interests did not coincide with those of the ordinary colonists—that of the Jesuits, whose policy it was to segregate the Indians and even to compete agriculturally and commercially with the ordinary colonists through using Indian (Amerindian) labor that most of the civilian community did not obtain so easily or freely as the Jesuits, though it was taxed to support them.

Privileged as they were under most of the kings of Portugal and Spain during the most decisive phase of colonization of America, the Jesuits did extraordinarily valuable work in Brazil as missionaries and educators, but their excessively paternalistic and even autocratic system of educating the Indians ran counter to the early tendencies of Brazil's development as

[4] *New Viewpoints on the Spanish Colonization of America* (Philadelphia, 1943), p. 110.

an ethnic democracy. This point—so clearly seen, from the Spanish-American democratic point of view, by Bartolomé de Las Casas when he wished to utilize colonization by farmers "who should live by tilling the rich lands of the Indies, lands which the Indian owners would voluntarily grant to them," lands where "the Spaniards would intermarry with the natives and make of both peoples one of the best commonwealths in the world and perhaps one of the most Christian and peaceful" [5]—was also clearly seen, from a Brazilian point of view, by José Bonifacio, leader of the movement for the independence of Portuguese America. He realized the danger of a native policy of isolation such as the one followed for some time by the Jesuits in Brazil—danger to the development of Brazil as a democratic community—and he therefore advocated the practice of racial crossing and cultural interpenetration until, under the inspiration of his ideas, a comprehensive plan for dealing with the Indians was adopted by the Emperor of Brazil in 1845. Following a tradition rooted in ideas held by the Portuguese kings and statesmen, sometimes in opposition to the Jesuits, the plan included the promotion of intermarriage between the Portuguese and the Indian, of instruction, and of assistance in the form of housing, tools, clothing, and medicine. It also included the right of natives to acquire title to land outside reservations.

If privileged types of colonization have prevented the majority of Portuguese common men who have emigrated to America from becoming conquerors and owners of virgin areas of good agricultural lands, they seem to have found compensation for this repression of their "possessive" rather than "creative" instincts in their really extraordinary procreative activity as polygamous males. Some of them became famous, like João Ramalho in the sixteenth century, for their many children by

[5] Ibid., pp. 110–11.

Indian women. As such they became the rivals, the equals, sometimes the triumphant competitors of Portuguese *fidalgos*, or noblemen like Jeronymo de Albuquerque whose addiction to polygamy marks them as inheriting Moorish rather than European and Christian traditions of sexual morality. Such excesses, profitable to Brazil from the point of view of a purely quantitative colonization, were not always beneficial to the development of a Christian family life in Portuguese America. Against them not only the Jesuits, but Church authorities as well, more than once made their voices heard.

Every student of the social history of Brazil knows that for an adequate knowledge of this subject (as for that of the social origins and social development of other modern nations), the gathering of sufficient information on the life, the activity, and the influence of the masses of the people is a task still remaining to be done. Information on the basic social and cultural contacts among human groups producing modern civilization is still incomplete. As has been remarked by an American student of social history, Professor Dwight Sanderson, the available sources have often emphasized political structures and documentary evidence, while students of mythology and folklore not infrequently go to the other extreme in their evaluation of cultural survivals and of the common people's contributions to the development of modern culture or civilization. Hence the need of a re-study of some problems of European and American history from a sociological standpoint.

Portugal and the Portuguese colonization of Brazil need such a re-study based on a new evaluation of the Portuguese contribution to modern civilization. This contribution was perhaps made in larger part by the merchant, the missionary, the common man, the intellectual, the scientist, and the woman who followed her husband in his overseas adventures, than by the *conquistador*, the military leader, the statesman, the bishops, or the kings—even though Portugal, in its most creative phase (that is, during the fifteenth and the sixteenth centuries), was remarkable for its far-seeing, energetic, and capable kings, princes, and statesmen.

During the fifteenth and sixteenth centuries the Portuguese —most of them engaged in trade—enriched European civilization with a number of plants and cultural values and techniques assimilated from Asia and Africa. Portuguese America was also benefited by these, for it was Portuguese merchants who introduced into Europe (or were among the first Europeans to introduce or reintroduce) a taste for the following things: sugar, tea, rice pudding, pepper, and cinnamon; the guinea fowl; the parasol, the umbrella, and the palanquin; porcelain and Arabian tiles; the veranda (of the East Indies); concave roofs, rounded cornices, and pagoda-like summer houses; Chinese gardens and fans; Oriental rugs and perfumes. And as early as the sixteenth century the same merchants took to Brazil some of these tastes and luxuries, as well as silks and jewels. They were the pioneers of modern international trade between the Orient and the Occident, between the Old World and the New.

North Europeans, who have made of the daily bath a supreme technique in modern domestic comfort, scorn the Portuguese peasant for not taking as many baths as they do; but Portuguese navigators and traders were among the first Europeans to bring from the East the almost un-Christian (and certainly un-European) habit of the daily bath—which in Europe was at first, and to some extent is still, a luxury reserved to ladies and gentlemen. Though the Portuguese are ridiculed today for using toothpicks at the dinner table, it was probably a Portuguese who brought from China to Europe the first porcelain for the tea of the sophisticated. The Portuguese were also probably the first Europeans to bring East Indian cotton textiles, especially calicoes, to Europe, thus revolutionizing social habits and cultural behavior in the European Christian countries. For, as every student of modern European civilization knows, the cheap East Indian cottons increased the use of underclothes, thereby "improving both health and cleanliness."[6] And the Portuguese started yet another social and cultural revolution, this one in the Orient, when they introduced into Japan the European Jesuits (including the great Francis Xavier), European muskets, and possibly syphilis.

The Portuguese also made their new colony known in Europe for its beautiful plants like the evening primrose, its useful woods like Brazil-wood and rosewood, its delicious fruits like the pineapple, its fine Bahia tobacco, its Pará or Brazil nuts, its Amazonian rubber, its hammocks made by the Indians, and its plants with medicinal properties like ipecacuanha. Soon after the discovery of Brazil, the Portuguese began to study Brazilian plants and animals, and especially Indian or Amerindian customs and foods, with an accuracy that has been praised by modern scientists. They also began to build in tropical America houses of a new type and with extra-European characteristics, houses whose architecture exhibited a combination

[6] Shepard Bancroft Clough and Charles Woolsey Cole: *Economic History of Europe* (Boston, 1941), p. 263. See also Adolphe Reischwein: *China and Europe* (London, 1915), pp. 61–7. James Edward Gillespie: *The Influence of Overseas Expansion on England (1500–1700)* (New York, 1920); Ramalho Ortigão: *O Culto da Arte em Portugal* (Lisbon, 1896); Edgar Prestage: *The Portuguese Pioneers* (London, 1934); and Gilberto Freyre: *O Mundo que o Portugues Creou* (Rio, 1940) also discuss the subject and point out aspects of the Portuguese influence in the social and cultural life of Europe as a result of Portuguese contacts with Africa, the Orient, and America.

of Asiatic and African modes with traditional European styles. They began to develop a Luso-Brazilian cookery based on their European traditions adapted to American conditions and resources, and also on their experience with the plants and culinary processes of Asia and Africa.

The Portuguese are also associated not only with the introduction into or popularization in Europe of Brazilian sugar, under the name of *mascavado* or *muscovado*, but also with the dissemination of the use of tobacco as an aristocratic custom among Europeans. As a result of the use of tobacco—from Brazil and other parts of America—it seems that the Europeans in general, and the Portuguese in particular, began to spit more than before; and it is significant that the English word *cuspidor* comes from the Portuguese verb *cuspir*, to spit. But this is not the only word that has moved from the Portuguese, or through the Portuguese, from East Indian, African, Asiatic, and American languages into the English and other European languages. Numerous words of Portuguese origin or first Europeanized by the Portuguese indicate how important a part Portugal played in the pioneer days of modern international trade: *bamboo* (the tree); *veranda* (for porch); molasses (from *melaço*); *palissander* (palissander wood), from *pau santo;* bossal (the African-born slave) from *boçal; marmelade; caravel* (a type of vessel); *tapioca* (the starch of *mandioca*); *pagoda* (a tower-like structure); *kraal* (a type of African village); *cobra* (snake); *cobra-de-capelo* (an East Indian snake); *jararaca* (a serpent); *jacaranda* (Brazilian rosewood); *caste* (a hereditary and endogamous social group); *palanquin* (the Asiatic sedan chair widely used in Brazil); *cashew* or *cajou* (a nut); *jaguar* (a large feline of Latin America); *samba* (an Afro-Brazilian dance); *mango* (an East Indian fruit now very common in Brazil); *Port* and *Madeira* (types of wine); *canja* (a thick soup of chicken and rice, highly praised by Theodore Roosevelt),[7] *cruzado* (a Portuguese coin mentioned by Shakespeare), and *valorization*, a "Portuguesism" in the English language denoting a technique for the commercial protection of a product, a technique used first by Brazilians in connection with their coffee, and since then by other peoples in connection with various other commodities. And it is my belief that *pickanniny* comes not from the Spanish, as generally stated by dictionaries and by H. L. Mencken in *The American Language*, but from the Portuguese word *pequenino*. *Formosa* (the name of the important island off the coast of China) is also a Portuguese word, not Spanish. Most of these words are evidences of Portuguese ubiquity prior to or contemporaneous with the colonization of Brazil.

In dealing with the European background of Brazilian history from a sociological standpoint, one is led to the somewhat paradoxical conclusion that it was not an entirely European background: it was also Asiatic and African. Even China had a direct influence in the development of Brazil as a new type of civilization in the tropics. For from China the Portuguese brought to Brazil architectural values and techniques that would become Brazilian. And for years it was from China that elaborate gowns were imported to be used in Brazil by judges and doctors in law or jurisprudence.

[7] *Through the Brazilian Wilderness* (New York, 1914), p. 165. Theodore Roosevelt introduced also into the English language a number of Portuguese-Amerindian names of animals such as *tamanduá-bandeira* and *piranha*.

[II]

Frontier and Plantation
in Brazil

From its very beginning, the history of Brazil was marked by two apparently contradictory tendencies that were in fact complementary to each other. I refer to the mobility of those groups of men who expanded Portuguese America toward the north, south, and west in contrast to the permanent settling, with satisfaction or delight, near the Atlantic sea coast, from Maranhão to São Vicente, by other social and perhaps biological types of men: those who came from Portugal with enough capital to establish themselves as slaveholding sugar-cane planters and to live on their plantations almost like feudal lords.

These sugar-cane planters, even more than the men who dug the soil for gold, were the *vertical* founders of Brazil in the sense that some of them rooted themselves deeply in the land and built for themselves and their families, and sometimes for their slaves, not cabins or huts, but solid stone or brick houses. These mansions soon took the name of "big houses." The slave quarters were given an African name: *senzalas*. The planters also built their churches or chapels and their sugar mills of the same noble, enduring material as their mansions, and sometimes surrounded them with noble, long-lived trees imported from Asia, Africa, and Europe: palm trees, mango trees, jaca trees; and by noble and useful animals also imported from older civilizations: horses, cows, cats.

The *horizontal* founders were the continuously migratory men. Though heterogeneous, these were mostly men whose spirit of adventure and love of individual freedom were too strong to let them settle down on the coast and live comfortably in the neighborhood of churches and official buildings, where taxes soon began to be collected by representatives of the Portuguese Crown. Nor did they like to live in the shadow of schools maintained by puritanical priests and of ecclesiastical courts presided over by representatives of the Holy Inquisition —courts eager to detect and punish religious heresy and sexual irregularity among the colonists.

By pushing on to the extreme south or the extreme north, by going to the west in search of gold and of Indians to sell to the planters as slaves, the migratory men escaped the influence of the feudal social organization established on the coast by the sedentary men. These latter had brought from Portugal a social status that in Brazil was not only maintained, but also improved by them, with the rapid prosperity of the cane agriculture and the sugar industry in that part of America.

Whereas the majority of the migratory men, or frontiersmen, were simple and even rustic in their social tastes and habits and had no stable form of domestic architecture—only huts almost as primitive as those of the Indians, whose diet and methods of nomadic agriculture they also copied—some of the sugar-cane planters developed or maintained in Brazil lordly manners, able as they were to support aristocratic establishments and to enjoy a diet almost entirely European; indeed, a number of them persisted for years in importing from Portugal their wines and much of their food, as well as fashionable dress for both sexes.

While the migratory men, like all bold pioneers, enjoyed in the wilderness a freedom of action that included a remarkable and most un-Christian liberty to have many women, the plantation master was at no disadvantage with the frontiersman in this respect, for without leaving his own lands he could have as many women as he wished in addition to the legitimate one he had brought from Portugal or to whom he had been properly married in Brazil. It is true that orthodox priests, especially the Jesuits, denounced such abuses or irregularities and preached against them. But it should not be forgotten that one of the characteristics of the feudal, aristocratic plantation system that developed in Brazil was the almost absolute power of the sugar planters. Privileged as they were by the King, they were able to become real feudal lords and, as such, to defend the cause and the interests of Portugal against savages and rival European powers. Every time that a planter acted *pro domo sua*, he was acting also in favor of Portuguese power in America. For the white mansions, or "big houses," became, even more than the public buildings, symbols of Portuguese stability in the coastal areas of Brazil. They became also the physical expression of a new type of feudal or patriarchal power that through isolation and self-sufficiency was to develop into a strong spirit of independence, a spirit of republicanism and even rebellion against the Crown.

The Crown privileges explain why the "big houses" became

not only more important than most of the public buildings, but also more important than the cathedrals, the individual churches, and the purely religious monasteries. I say "individual churches" because each big house or mansion had its own church or chapel as part of its architectural and social complex, with a chaplain dependent upon the plantation master or *senhor*—more dependent upon him than upon his bishop; and I say "purely religious monasteries" because some monasteries rivaled the "big houses," being established less for purely religious purposes than for the economic exploitation of the land through the cultivation of sugar cane by large numbers of slaves owned by monks or religious orders. Indeed, some of the powerful religious orders that took an active part in colonizing Brazil, rather than condemning the plantation regime for its un-Christian abuses, admitted it as the dominating force in colonial life and economic structure and adapted themselves to it.

Another evidence of the adaptation of the religious lords to the plantation regime and, sometimes, of recognition of its superior power, is the fact that, unlike Spanish America, Portuguese America never became noted for magnificent cathedrals. These would have symbolized powerful bishops, a powerful Church, a strong clergy. But there was never in colonial Brazil a really powerful Church or a strong clergy; nor were there domineering bishops, as each important sugar planter, though a devout Catholic, was a sort of Philip II in regard to the Church: he considered himself more powerful than the bishops or abbots.

This explains why the plantation system and the Jesuit system were in conflict most of the time. The Jesuits did not easily admit the supremacy of the plantation system over their own. Their supreme dream in Brazil seems to have been that of a rigidly theocratic system or regime like the "republic" they founded in Paraguay; and in such a system the "big house," with its harem and other abominations, would be a blot on a green valley. As, however, they were unable to destroy or undermine the powerful plantation system, the Jesuits concentrated their energy on developing an educational system that would bring under their influence the rich colonists' children as well as the Indian children. In their schools, which soon became famous, white and Indian youths were taught Latin and rhetoric. As blacks and mulattoes, however, were not usually admitted, the Jesuits are not to be accounted among the influences that favored race amalgamation and ethnic and social democracy in Brazil. This type of democracy was a direct product of frontier life and pioneering and a by-product of the aristocratic plantation system, in which miscegenation developed freely.

From what has been said of Brazil's plantation system and of its contrasting frontier activity, a student of Anglo-American social history might conclude that the development of Portuguese America was not greatly different from that of the United States. And the fact is that a number of Brazilian tendencies and developments may be equated with the two most important systems in American industrial society in the light of what is said of them by an American scholar, Professor Ulrich B. Phillips: that they form a large part of the American past from which the present, with its resources, its industrial and social constitution, and its problems, has resulted. What he writes about the plantation system in the United States describes Brazilian conditions also: "The plantation system was evolved to answer the specific need of meeting the world's demand for certain staple crops in the absence of a supply of free labor. That system, providing efficient control and direction for labor imported in bondage, met the obvious needs of the case, waxed strong, and shaped not alone the industrial regime to fit its requirements, but also the social and commercial system and the political policy of a vast section." [1]

Just as Negro slavery and cotton or tobacco grew up together in the Old South of the United States, so Negro slavery and sugar and, later, coffee grew up together in that vast section of Brazil where the planters were the political lords. There, as in the United States, the one-crop system moved westward to newer land, carrying with it slavery and other institutions until, in some parts of the country (Matto Grosso, Pará, and Rio Grande do Sul), frontiersmen and planters met and developed hybrid forms of social organization. As in the United States, so in the Brazilian plantation areas more orthodox in their feudal characteristics, one-crop agriculture frequently vitiated the soil, deprived the population of food crops, and necessitated a terribly ill-balanced diet.

The Brazilian frontiersmen were more obedient to the laws of tropical nature than were the planters. Though there was no refinement on the frontier, the life, though nomadic, was more healthful than that of the sedentary planters. For example, some of the latter ate food procured from Portugal in an age when food brought from Europe seldom reached Brazil in good condition.

Unlike the first generations of planters, of whom many had brought wives from Portugal, and whose descendants intermarried among themselves, most of the frontiersmen of Brazil were not pure Portuguese but Portuguese-Indian hybrids: the *bandeirantes*, the *paulistas*, later the *cearenses*—descendants of Portuguese and Spaniards who had taken Indian women as their companions, and a type of pioneer that has hardly any North American counterpart except the Canadian *métis*. Because of the prominence of this type in the exploration of new

[1] *Plantation and Frontier, 1649–1863* (Cleveland, 1909), *Documentary History of American Industrial Society* (Cleveland, 1910), I, 71–2.

areas, colonization soon ceased to be strictly European and became a process of auto-colonization—a process that has recently become nationwide in Brazil. J. F. Normano called "the adjustment of existing territories to the economic life of the nation" the "internal national colonization." And he seems to be right in considering this new phase of Brazilian colonization of Brazil an aspect of the phenomenon described by Turner as "the moving frontier." [2]

Judged by what they were able to accomplish, the *paulistas*, the *bandeirantes*, and the *cearenses* have been a more brilliant expression of hybrid vigor than any other to be found in America. Some time ago Professor Earnest A. Hooton, the American anthropologist, wrote me from Harvard that as a student of hybridization he had been enormously interested in the history of the *paulistas*. Professor Hooton was one of the leading anthropologists of our day who do not think that the notion of the physical and constitutional inferiority of the hybrid can be seriously entertained. He points out in his lectures and essays that mixtures of widely differing races produce in some instances hybrids resembling one or other of the parental stocks, but more often types displaying a combination of features drawn from all the races involved in the cross. Occasionally, according to Professor Hooton and other anthropologists, the combinations blend into new and apparently stable types. This seems to have been true of the *paulistas*, a result of the cross-breeding of Spaniards, Portuguese, and (to a very small extent) Negroes with Indians. They seem to have developed into a new and stable type of man or race, known for their vigor, their endurance, their fighting capacity, and the qualities or virtues of pioneers. This seems to be true also of the *cearenses* and other regional types of Brazil.

[2] J. F. Normano: *Brazil, A Study of Economic Types* (Chapel Hill, 1935), p. 2.

The *paulistas* first became noted for their slave-hunting expeditions—*entradas*—from which they brought back pure Indians as slaves for the plantations. They went over the Chaco, across the Paraguay River, as far as Bolivia. One party penetrated to the neighborhood of Quito, on the Ecuador plateau, and a small expedition is said to have crossed the Andes.

It is easy to see why the *paulistas* came into conflict with the Jesuits, whose policy it was—in Brazil as in Canada—to segregate the Indians under a very artificial system of perpetual parental tutelage and to prevent or discourage intermarriage of whites with the natives, on the theory that "the Indian mind was incapable of high development." On this point a few modern anthropologists agree with the Jesuits: the Whethams (William Cecil Dampier and Catherine Durning), for instance, in *The Family and the Nation* (London, 1909), praise the Jesuits for their "considerable scientific insight and wisdom" as champions of racial purity on the American continent. But anthropologists who have carefully studied the problem of the American Indian and of the half-breed from a biological as well as from a social point of view—such men as Franz Boas, Roland B. Dixon, Hooton, Manuel Gamio, Mendieta Núñez, and E. Roquette Pinto—if asked to pass a judgment on the subject, would probably find less "scientific insight and wisdom" in the segregation policy followed by the Jesuits than in the establishment of joint schools for natives and whites alike, which was the policy of the Portuguese Crown in Brazil and even of the Jesuits under the pressure of some of the Portuguese kings and statesmen.

The first generations of *paulistas* were not the result of any deliberate policy; they were the consequence of the scarcity of white or European women in that part of sixteenth-century

Brazil. The old Lusitanian spirit celebrated by Camões in his famous poem took some of the most ambitious and bold Portuguese men into the jungle or the hinterland of tropical South America, where Indian women were easy and polygamy was one of the compensations for hardship. Of the typical *paulista* or *bandeirante* it has been pointed out, by more than one interpreter of his personality, that his first virtue was a resignation described by some as "almost fatalistic." Many *paulistas* or *bandeirantes* never returned from the hinterland; they remained there, multiplying themselves in mestizo children and founding towns in what were to be the states of Minas Gerais, Matto Grosso, Goyaz, and Bahia. Santo Amaro, for instance, was founded by a João Amaro who was for years the bravest man known in that region. For soon the *paulistas'* aim expanded from the mere capture of Indians for slavery to the conquest of the interior, the establishment of settlements and towns, the search for mines of gold and precious stones, and the repression of Spanish attempts at entry from the south and from Peru—a rather complex activity that has been studied by a number of Brazilian historians and geographers concentrating on the fascinating question of how Portuguese America became such a vast part of the American continent: Theodoro Sampaio, João Ribeiro, Alcantara Machado, Affonso de E. Taunay, Basilio de Magalhães, Paulo Prado, and Cassiano Ricardo.

An Anglo-American author, L. E. Elliott, writes that the *bandeira*, "in its greatest phase, was a traveling city," "a commune linked by common interest"; [3] and Senhor Cassiano Ricardo, who has recently written an overenthusiastic but stimulating and penetrating essay about the *bandeiras*, remarks that they, more than any other institution, promoted the ethnic and

[3] *Brazil: Today and Tomorrow* (New York, 1917), p. 28.

social democracy so characteristic of Brazil. While the plantation system was aristocratic in its structure—though democratic in its by-product, the mestizo, as I have said—the *bandeira* is praised by Senhor Cassiano Ricardo and others of its
admirers for having been thoroughly democratic. Mr. Roy
Nash attempts to explain the success of those democratic
"traveling cities" or "communes" by saying that the *bandeirantes*, "like the Bolsheviki," formed a militant minority that
could co-operate and did not lack cohesion or social solidarity.[4] The work accomplished by the *paulistas* and by Brazilians
from other regions who have distinguished themselves in the
history of the "moving frontier" in Brazil remains a very im-
pressive example of the hybrid's capacity not only for action,
but also for co-operation. In Brazil the "moving frontier" has
meant the creation of ways of life and new combinations of
culture—a capacity that some eloquent "Nordic" enthusiasts
would like to identify exclusively with their purely white
idols.

But, fascinating as were the first frontiersmen of Brazil, the
bandeirantes, one should not forget that while they were adding vast tracts to the colony, the first generations of sugar-cane
planters of the coast were not having an entirely easy task.
Attacks from Indians, from English and French pirates, and
especially from the Dutch, disturbed the planters' agricultural
routine. They had also to deal with revolts of Negro slaves,
though these do not seem to have been so numerous or violent
as in other areas of America, perhaps because the treatment of
slaves by the Portuguese, and later by the Brazilians, was less
provocative of rebellion. This is the conclusion that Brazilian
students of the social history of their country have reached
through what seems to be as objective and impartial a means
as possible: the opinion of foreigners who knew slavery condi-

[4] *The Conquest of Brazil* (New York, 1926), p. 104.

tions in various regions of America.⁵ One of these foreigners was an American missionary, the Reverend Mr. R. Creary, whose notes on the plantation system of Brazil were never published, but remain in manuscript in the Library of Congress. His opinion is particularly valuable because it comes from a very unsympathetic critic of Brazilian customs in plantation days. Nevertheless, he remarked that Brazilian slaves in the southern part of the Empire were "fairly treated and generally had much more liberty than was compatible with very efficient service." ⁶ As to the northern part of the Empire, Alfred Russel Wallace, the famous British scientist and abolitionist of the nineteenth century, found them generally well treated and "as happy as children." ⁷ And Mme Ida Pfeiffer, who visited Brazil in the late 1840's, and who was one of the most intelligent travelers of her age, wrote: "I am almost convinced that, on the whole, the lot of these slaves is less wretched than that of the peasants of Russia, Poland, or Egypt, who are not called slaves." ⁸ But it is an English clergyman, the Reverend Hamlet Clark, who strikes the most radical note about slavery in the plantations of nineteenth-century Brazil: "Nay indeed, we need not go far to find in free England the absolute counterpart of slavery: Mayhew's London Labour and the London Poor, Dickens' Oliver Twist, Hood's Song of the Shirt and many other revelations tell of a grinding, flinty-hearted despotism that Brazilian slave-owners never can approach." ⁹ Another traveler who knew Brazil during the full maturity of the Brazilian slave system—the first half of the

⁵ Gilberto Freyre: "Social Life in Brazil in the Middle of the 19th Century," *The Hispanic American Historical Review*, V (1922), 597–628.

⁶ R. Creary: "Brazil Under the Monarchy" and "*Chronicas Lageanas*," 1886 (Ms. in Library of Congress).

⁷ *A Narrative of Travels on the Amazon and Rio Negro* (London, 1852), p. 120.

⁸ *Voyage autour du Monde* (Paris, 1868), p. 18.

⁹ *Letters Home from Spain, Algeria and Brazil* (London, 1867), p. 160.

nineteenth century—was W. H. B. Webster. He found the
slaves of Brazil happier than most philanthropists considered
them.[1] An investigation of conditions of work on Brazilian
plantations conducted by a British committee—a committee
eager to find abuses—revealed in 1847–8 that lenient laws were
favorable to the good treatment of the slaves; that holidays,
which amounted to about thirty-five days a year, were allowed
them for feasting or for earning money to free themselves
(manumission); that in contrast with conditions on the West
Indian plantations, where slaves were hired out for profit, the
typical Brazilian planter had a patriarchal feeling for his slaves.
José Cliff, who appeared before that British committee (Select
Committee on Coffee and Sugar Planting), said that in Brazil
—a country he knew well—human nature ruled against the
separation of small children from their mothers.[2] Henry Koster, an English merchant who lived in northern Brazil for years,
wrote that the European planter was likely to have purchased
his slaves on credit, whereas the Brazilian inherited his, and had
nothing to urge him on to get greater profits;[3] and Robert
Southey, in his famous *History of Brazil*, refers to the laws by
which the situation of the slaves was mitigated.[4] Such evidence
seems to show that the slave on Brazilian plantations was generally well treated and that his lot was really "less wretched"
than that of European laborers who were not called slaves. As
my old teacher at Columbia University, Professor Carlton
J. H. Hayes, more than once reminded his students, audiences
in England wept at hearing how cruel masters "licked" their
cowering slaves in Jamaica; but in their own England little

[1] *Narrative of a Voyage to the South Atlantic Ocean* (London, 1834), p.
43.
[2] *British Foreign and State Papers*, LXII, 622, XXXII, 126; *Reports from
Committees* (House of Commons), *Session of 1847–1848*, p. 201.
[3] Henry Koster: *Travels in Brazil* (London, 1817), II, 183.
[4] *History of Brazil* (London, 1822), p. 674.

Englishmen and Englishwomen ten years old were whipped to their work—even in factories owned by the anti-slavery orators.

I have no doubt that some of the anti-slavery orators in Brazil saw in their old age, on plantations belonging to some of the modern, highly commercialized sugar factories, labor conditions much worse than those which they knew in their youth under the horrid name of slavery. Were they now living, they would probably agree with the modern students of Brazilian social history on this point: that, taken as a whole, slavery on nineteenth-century Brazilian plantations seems to have been less despotic than slavery in other American areas; and less cruel—if one admits degrees in cruelty—than the regime of labor in industrial Europe during the first terrible fifty years of economic *laissez-faire* which followed the Industrial Revolution. Less cruel, also, than the regime of labor in latter-day Brazil, where the worker's condition in fields and factories is still a problem very difficult to solve.

Of course, one is always under the risk of becoming sentimental about the old days; that is, indeed, the attitude of some Brazilians in regard to the plantation system as well as to the monarchical system of government which, for nearly a century of Brazil as an independent nation, maintained the same political tradition as that under which the colony had lived from the sixteenth century to the beginning of the nineteenth. "Ideal coloring" is sometimes given by authors in Brazil, just as in the United States, to plantation life in the old days; in Brazil "ideal coloring" distorts also the picture of political conditions during the Monarchy or the Empire.

The best evidence indicates that there was much suffering in those days; that social conditions were far from being ideal; that public hygiene or sanitation was a myth. But no careful student of the subject should go so far as to dismiss entirely the legends of the Brazilian plantation and the Brazilian Monarchy as nothing but sentimental or literary fancy. For both of these made possible the development of human and cultural values that remain among the most characteristic traditions of Brazil. It would be foolish for Brazilians to desire to return to the days when those values were not only active, but also powerful and exclusive. But it would be equally foolish to deny that from them the Brazilians acquired distinctive qualities—not simply a feudalistic social and psychological complex that seems to make most of the descendants of the lordly class arrogant and even sadistic and most of the descendants of slaves too unambitious and too obsequious and even childish and masochistic in their behavior and in some of their attitudes.

One should never forget, however, that neither the plantation system nor the monarchical system ever meant, in Brazil, hard social gradations; it was possible for men of exceptional talent, no matter how socially inferior their origin, to rise to the highest positions in the Brazilian aristocratic and monarchical system. And it was customary for plantation lords to have their illegitimate brown children, when brilliant, as well educated as the legitimate ones. W. H. B. Webster observed that in nineteenth-century Brazil some of the most intelligent Negroes owned by kind masters were educated with the masters' children and that some attained great success after their liberation.[5] This means that in Brazil neither the plantation system nor the monarchical system was rigidly closed to social or political democracy; the present anti-democratic tendency is a very recent development and is contrary not only to our republican avowals, but also to our monarchical and plantation traditions.

Each of the traditions, taken as a whole, was a combination

[5] Op. cit., p. 43.

of democratic and aristocratic tendencies rather than a pure expression of immoderately despotic, autocratic, dictatorial trends. Such trends were possibly more characteristic of some of the Spanish American republics in their *caudillo* phases than of monarchical and aristocratic Brazil, where the plantation system acted as a powerful republican opposition to any autocratic excess on the part of the Crown, and where the Crown served as a permanent limit to autocratic excesses on the part of plantation lords. The result was that Brazil developed a healthier democratic (or pre-democratic) condition from the rivalry among almost equal powers, which neutralized—yet respected—each other, than did the Spanish American republics in which, as presidents, *caudillos* and dictators, generals and adventurers were able to exercise absolute power during years and years of sometimes sadistic rule.

I do not mean to belittle the Spanish American republics that have had *caudillos*, or to overpraise Brazil for the fact that a monarchy, combined with an aristocratic plantation system, prevented Portuguese America from having *caudillismo*. For some of those Spanish American republics have a right to laugh at Brazil—a Brazil that knew no real *caudillos* during the nineteenth century, but has known *caudillismo* since the Republic was established there in 1889: Pinheiro Machado, for instance, was a *caudillo*, and a very recent one. Even during the monarchical days Brazil, exceptionally it is true, had a deluxe *caudillo* as prime minister; though he wore a frock coat and not a military uniform and made no attempt to close the Imperial Parliament, he was intolerant of political differences and reduced the political parties to insignificant groups. I refer to the Marquis of Paraná, who was more imperial in his activities than the Emperor himself. But he was an exception, and, though an autocrat, a very elegant one; he was not an ordinary *caudillo*.

As a rule, the leaders of the Brazilian government during the Monarchy came from the oldest plantation areas—Bahia, Pernambuco, São Paulo, Rio de Janeiro—and some of them were statesmen, not mere politicians. Some became champions of great democratic reforms: Joaquim Nabuco, for instance. More than once, popular opinion expressed itself through them. This is what makes me say that, though it sounds like a paradox, one finds in monarchical and aristocratic Brazil as it was during the great days of the plantation regime a healthier pre-democratic condition than in some of the nineteenth-century Spanish American republics dominated by *caudillos* and harassed by revolutions.

The student of the Brazilian plantation system is tempted to compare it with the plantation system in other areas of America, especially the South of the United States. The system in Anglo-Saxon America probably had a more rigid aristocratic structure, from the point of view of race superiority and inferiority, than in Brazil, where race prejudice was never so strong as among Anglo-Saxons. There was race prejudice among plantation-area Brazilians; there was social distance between master and slave, between white and black, just as between old and young, man and woman. But few Brazilian aristocrats were as strict about racial purity as the majority of the Anglo-American aristocrats of the Old South were. Family pride was stronger than race pride. And women were probably more oppressed by men in the Brazilian system than in the Old South. There were, however, exceptions; occasionally women were the heads of the houses or plantations. My grandfather knew one when he was a young boy. Her name was Dona Felicia, and her slaves, her children, and also her husband were known as Dona Felicia's slaves, children, and husband. She carried a whip with her to punish children, slaves, and even her husband. But such situations were exceptional.

The elements that composed the plantation ensemble in Brazil were practically the same as those which characterized the plantation ensemble in the United States; plantation cooking is certainly one of them. The "trinity of figures" suggested by former Governor Taylor of Tennessee for a monument to the Old South of the United States might be used by a Brazilian sculptor for a similar monument to the old north of Brazil. And instead of being restricted to a regional glorification, the idea might indeed be expanded to a glorification of the "Old Plantation" on the American continent, to embrace not only the north of Brazil, but also other areas or regions of the Hispanic, Anglo-Saxon, French, and Dutch Americas. For such "a trinity of figures" as the one suggested by Governor Taylor —consisting of "the courtly old planter, high bred and gentle in face and manner . . . the plantation uncle, the counterpart in ebony of the master so loyally served," and "the broad-bosomed black mammy with vari-colored turban, spotless apron and beaming face, the friend of every living thing in cabin or mansion"—corresponds to a tradition common to all aristocratic plantation areas of America. There may be over-simplification, besides an excessive idealization of the past, in Governor Taylor's idea for this monument, for the plantation system in America was a complex one and its harsh aspects were probably as numerous as its pleasant ones. But the "trinity of figures" existed—in Brazil as well as in the Old South of the United States.

Professor Francis Pendleton Gaines, in his book *The Southern Plantation*, published in New York in 1925—three years after the publication of my first attempt to characterize the Brazilian plantation—mentions other equally important types of the Southern system of complex: "the gay girl from Dixie"; "the young cavalier"; "the prototype of Negro minstrelsy." [6]

[6] P. 15.

8 3

Professor Thompson mentions "the driver"; [7] Professor Cotteril refers to "the overseer universally detested by the slaves." [8] All these personality and social types established by the "isolation of plantation life" existed in Brazil. From a Brazilian point of view, I should like to see included in a monument to the plantation the plantation mistress; the field slave; the *muleque*, or Negro boy, who was the white boy's patient and sometimes masochistic companion; and the mulatto young woman who had in Brazil the African name of *mucama*, "the white mistress's companion." Such a monument would perhaps become too crowded to be an effective glorification of heroes of the past—though according to some architects and social philosophers this is what most monuments should be: the glorification of groups and not of individual heroes.

As in the South of the United States, so in Brazil not all plantation masters were "courtly," "high bred," and "gentle in face and manner." The distinction established in the United States by Professor Gaines's scholarly essay referred to above —the distinction between the Southern plantation as it appears in legend and as it really was—is one that should be made also in relation to the plantation area of Brazil; its literary apologists paint its past as too rosy. As I have suggested in one of my essays on the rural past of Brazil, not all plantation houses, but only a minority of them, were really mansions from an architectural point of view, or places where good, abundant food was the rule instead of the exception; not all sugar-cane planters were honest and noble—some mixed ordinary sand with their sugar, some were heavy drinkers, not of fine or old wines, but of ordinary rum, or *cachaça;* not a few were gamblers,

[7] Edgar T. Thompson: "The Plantation: the Physical Basis of Traditional Race Relations," in *Race Relations and the Race Problem* (Durham, 1939), p. 214.

[8] R. S. Cotteril: *The Old South* (Glendale, 1939), p. 268.

and some were always in debt and as ignorant of business detail, amount of income, and number of slaves as was Colonel Dangerfield, the hero of James K. Paulding's *Westward Ho!* As for the sons of the great families, not all of them became statesmen, orators, authors, bishops, generals, or admirals; a number reached old age with no higher interest than a passion for horses, Negro women, and cockfighting. In the plantation area of Brazil, as in the South of the United States, informal horse racing was not a mere sport, but an almost religious institution. Hunting was another. And as in the Old South as described by Phillips, Gaines, and Thompson, so in the Brazilian plantation area, the economic basis of feudal social life was precarious or uncertain. There, as here, the prevailing economic condition among slavery-age planters, first of sugar, later of coffee, was characterized by extravagance, despoiling of soil fertility, ignorance of scientific methods in agriculture, and ineffective labor; a condition that here, as in the Old South, culminated frequently in what Professor Gaines calls "bankruptcy with the break-up of an estate and sometimes westward migration." What ordinarily happened in Brazil when a man lost his plantation was that he went to one of the seacoast towns, where he would live a commonplace life as a secondary public employee. Sons of once very wealthy planters became lawyers, judges, and doctors in frontier towns.

Festive occasions drew together many rural families in the plantation area. St. John's Eve, in June, was probably the greatest day of the year on Brazilian sugar-cane plantations, at least on the oldest and most typical of them. There were European dances in the interior of the mansions, where silver —a common luxury—and shining glass appeared in all their glory, while outside, the Negroes danced their African dances, especially the samba, around large bonfires built to honor St. John and to keep the Devil away. Food was abundant. Special cakes, particularly of corn, were made for the occasion. As a feast day St. John's Eve was the Brazilian equivalent of Christmas on the Southern plantations.

One of the Portuguese traditions connected with St. John's Eve as celebrated in old Brazil was that of bathing and washing: one should take a special bath. I say a special bath because Brazilians have always been fond of baths, sometimes bathing more than once a day, as nineteenth-century European travelers noticed in the plantation area. John Esaias Warren, an American who was in Brazil in the middle of the last century, says that the first spectacle that arrested his attention on his landing there was that of a number of persons of both sexes and all ages—persons of the common people—bathing in the waters of a river. He observed among them "several finely formed Indian girls of exceeding beauty dashing about in the water like a troop of happy mermaids." [9] The aristocrats were not so pagan; they had private baths constructed of palms in rivers that were almost private rivers, almost private plantation property. And there the ladies bathed daily, swimming also like happy mermaids. For swimming was one of the characteristic sports of the plantation area.

Wedding days were also among the great feast days of plantation life in Brazil, just as in the Old South of the United States. But to weddings one should add, in regard to Brazil, the days when white children were baptized and the day of the year when one's sugar mill began to operate. For the latter it was the custom to have an important religious and social celebration; then the plantation chaplain or an outside priest or friar would sprinkle with holy water the first sugar cane to be crushed in the mill.

[9] John Esaias Warren: *Pará; or Scenes and Adventures on the Banks of the Amazon* (New York, 1851), p. 9. See also Freyre: "Social Life in Brazil in the Middle of the 19th Century," p. 626.

Hospitality was customary. It is probable that in Brazil, as in the South of the United States, the pride of the big planters in keeping a good table at which travelers were generously fed was not only an expression of "conspicuous waste" of the type so well described by Thorstein Veblen, but also a manifestation of the so-called gregarious instinct intensified by isolation. Visitors of all kinds had a right to sit at the table of a plantation lord or baron and to occupy a bed in one of his guest rooms. A peculiar personality type developed in Brazil under such an excess of generous entertainment was that of the *papa-pirão;* that is, men who went from one plantation to another, being regaled with everything that each afforded and doing nothing but gossip, smoke cigars, and play cards. There were parasites of this type who ceased to be absolute parasites; they were also jesters or men famous for their humor, jokes, and anecdotes. Some Brazilian planters, like kings of the past, had their own private jesters or jockeys; some maintained clowns and acrobats, besides a plantation band of Negro boys.

An institution of Brazil's plantation system for which I find no equivalent in the South of the United States is the private chaplain. He was a member of the patriarchal family, with the rank of a bachelor uncle or an old and widowed grandfather, rather than that of a priest rigidly under the control of his bishop. He was under the direction of the planter, who sometimes paid him generously for his good services. He not only took care of the religious or devotional activities of whites and slaves, but was also the private tutor of the boys, the one who taught them grammar, Latin, and sacred history and prepared them to enter military or naval school (or simply the army or the navy), law school, seminary, or medical school. Under the Brazilian patriarchal system, these were gentlemen's careers: the army or the navy, government, diplomacy, public administration or law, the Church or priesthood, and, for the most

progressive, medicine. Stimulated by the Emperor, the Imperial
Academy of Medicine became a school that bestowed as much
social prestige with the degrees it gave as did the two traditional law schools, Recife and São Paulo. Every generation in
a family had to have a priest; it was almost a social disgrace not
to have one. As families then were large—ten, twelve, even
fifteen children to a single mother, or twenty or more when
the aristocrat married more than once, as often happened—it
was not uncommon for parents to have at least one boy who
was really inclined to enter the priesthood or to be a monk in
one of the many monasteries. But if no one of the children was
born with this inclination, the youngest son was sometimes
made a priest or a monk against his will. This explains the large
number of priests and monks in patriarchal Brazil who had no
predilection for the priesthood or the monastery. The situation was not so much the fault of the Church, which accepted
such entrants in order to maintain a clergy made up of sons of
the aristocracy, as a consequence of the aristocratic plantation
system.

Though families are not so large today among descendants
of the old plantation or aristocratic stock as they were during
the slavery period, they continue to be big. An American
sociologist recently concluded, through a study of vital statistics, that in Brazil the trend in family size "is exactly opposite
to the trend generally reported in the United States and Western Europe. The families of the well-to-do and educated are
substantially larger than those in lower levels." [1] According to
the same investigator, not only is the number of living children
of the typical planter in Minas Gerais nearly double the number of the common laborer's (the chief cause being the higher

[1] John B. Griffing: "A Comparison of the Effects of Certain Socioeconomic Factors upon Size of Family in China, Southern California, and Brazil" (dissertation); "Natural Eugenics in Brazil," *Journal of Heredity*,
XXXI (1940), 13–16.

mortality rate of children in the poorer class), but the rate of fecundity of Brazilian mothers is also very high. One point should be made clear: the large number of priests and monks from well-to-do plantation stock did not always mean that they were childless; some had children, and more than one prominent Brazilian has been the illegitimate descendant of a priest or a monk.

Only in the latter part of the nineteenth century was there a diminution in the sacrifice of youth, not so much to organized religion as to an organized patriarchal regime that had both youth and religion under its control. Nevertheless, the inclination of Brazilians toward those careers long considered the only decent or proper ones for gentlemen—government, diplomacy, law, public administration, medicine, priesthood, army or navy—is still to be found as a survival of the plantation system. Not only decadent aristocrats or decadent descendants of aristocrats, but also social upstarts eager to imitate the decadent aristocracy have followed that tradition until recently or are still following it. The reaction against the tendency is now strong, but is not winning an easy victory against such deep prejudices. There seems to be no doubt that the plantation system in Brazil, with its whole structure based on slave work, developed in many Brazilians a peculiarly aristocratic attitude toward manual labor and also toward trade, business, and commercial or industrial activity. This explains, to a certain extent, why the Portuguese peasant became in Brazil the successful grocer; the Frenchman, the fancy-goods dealer; the Englishman, and later the German and the American, the wholesale importer, the engineer, the expert in industrial and mechanical work, in railroad construction, and in transportation; the Italian, the German, other Europeans, and the Japanese, the successful farmer; whereas the Brazilians of the old stocks (and those who are not of the old stocks, but find it elegant or convenient to imitate them) remain—as bachelors of arts or doctors of law, of philosophy, or of medicine —a sort of bureaucratic or intellectual caste whose hands are too delicate for ignoble work and who are altogether too superior to compete with materialistic foreigners.

This gentleman complex is considered by some observers to be one of the most harmful survivals of the plantation system in Brazil. Feeling themselves above all the drudgery of life, a number of Brazilians have sought in lottery, gambling, expensive cardplaying, and adventure a substitute for work. Cardplaying was intimately connected with the plantation system of Brazil—as I conclude, from what I have read about the plantation system in the South of the United States, it was there also. Not many years ago I found a document in a Brazilian archive which seems to indicate that the first thing printed in Brazil, in colonial days, was not a newspaper or a book, but a set of playing cards.

There were bullfights in colonial Brazil, but they never became so important in Brazil as in Mexico or Ecuador. Perhaps rich planters thought too much of their horses, if not of their cattle, to let them die in bullfights. For Brazilian planters, just like Southern planters in the United States, were especially fond of horses. The well-to-do were almost as proud of the number of fine horses they owned as of the number of their children, legitimate and illegitimate, and of their slaves, field and domestic. Some of them were such lovers of riding that they learned to perform acrobatic stunts on horseback. Others were too lazy or too dignified even for that; when they traveled, they were carried by their Negroes in hammocks or palanquins like Hindu princes.

There were two other points of similarity between this regime and that of the Old South in the United States—the prevalent swearing by the masters and their excessive individualism. What Colonel Allston said of Southern planters—that "they were the least given to acting together in combination" —might be said of Brazilian sugar-cane lords and even of coffee planters, though the latter eventually learned to co-operate.

As to the effect of the plantation on intellectual life, it seems that the Brazilian system, perhaps because it was more powerful, surpassed that of the Old South in producing talented authors and scholars, statesmen, orators, and diplomats. The best dictionary produced in Brazil was written by a plantation master, and early in the sixteenth century an ethnological treatise was composed in Bahia by another. The Brazilian mother of Thomas Mann came from the plantation area. A number of Brazilian poets, essayists, and artists were born on plantations. As in the Old South, many mansions could show creditable libraries, and some planters sent their boys to study in Europe.

There was a time when students emphasized the bad effects of the whites' contact with Negroes on the plantations, and slavery did undoubtedly stimulate, in the whites most directly touched by it, a despotic individualism, as well as indolence and an aversion to manual labor. On the other hand, Brazilian culture was deeply enriched through the association of white boys with old Negro men and women who told them stories full of a humanity and sweetness that sometimes surpassed the humanity and the sweetness of the stories found in conventional schoolbooks. Slavery afforded the ruling class a leisure that enabled a number of its talented men to study the best methods of destroying feudalism and developing democracy in Brazil—a democracy based on a knowledge of the so-called biological superiorities and inferiorities of race or class. Some of the men who have become real democratic forces in Brazilian life and art—men such as Joaquim Nabuco, Sylvio Romero, José Lins do Rego, and Cicero Dias—have been the products of the old plantation system. Every one of them seems to know how true for Brazil are the remarks of U. B. Phillips concerning the plantation system in the United States: in the plantation system there was "little of the curse of impersonality and indifference which too commonly prevails in factories of the present-day world where power-driven machinery sets the pace, where the employers have no relations with the employed outside of work hours." [2] Strange as it seems, most of the despots, *caudillos*, and anti-democratic leaders that Brazil has had did not derive from its plantation area, but came from other sections.

[2] U. B. Phillips: *American Negro Slavery* (New York, London, 1918), p. 307.

[III]

Brazilian Unity and Brazilian Regional Diversity

Professor Glenn R. Morrow of the University of Pennsylvania not long ago pointed out that the first Congress of Regionalism in Brazil—perhaps the first in America—met in Recife in 1925. Recently, at Yale University, the subject of Brazilian Regionalism was discussed at the Inter-American Conference of Philosophy, where I fear that it was not entirely understood by some members, though all comments were sympathetic and generous. Regionalism as understood and described by Brazilian regionalists is a social philosophy; and one of the main objections voiced at the Conference was that philosophy, being "a work of reason," cannot "accept regional data, forms of thought and of sentiment of local content, unless it corrupts and destroys itself." The view was therefore advanced by one critic that, as regionalists, my friends and I put too much emphasis on the regional aspect of Brazilian culture.[1]

Before attempting to discuss the two antagonisms of Brazilian life and culture—unity and regional diversity, or unitarism and regionalism—I wish to make as clear as possible the idea of regionalism as understood by modern Brazilian regionalists. They distinguish regionalism from nationalism, and also from mere sectionalism—to use Frederick Jackson Turner's word for sterile or self-sufficient regionalism. A region may be politically less than a nation. But vitally and culturally it is more than a nation; it is more basic both as a condition of life and as a medium of expression or creativeness. To be a genuine philosopher a man has to be super- or supra-national; but he can hardly be supra-regional in the sense of ignoring the regional condition of the life, the experience, the culture, the art, and the thought that he is considering or analyzing.

As Mr. Joseph E. Baker writes in his analysis of regionalism: "The regionalist who ignores the universal is at fault, of course; the life of his region is his medium of expression, not his message, and he should not make his thinking a mere search for the curious, the odd, and the picturesque—that was the error of the local-colorist. But the internationalists (to which, indeed, our present brand of nationalism must be referred) recommend to us a literature which gives neither the universal ideal of humanity at its best, nor the subtle essence of a local culture; but rather those elementary physical and economic interests which are common to man at his crudest in Atlanta, Manchester, and Hamburg—the lowest common denominator, not the profoundest human potentialities. We are much more likely to rise to a conception of man as fully human by con-

[1] Afranio Coutinho: "Some Considerations on the Problem of Philosophy in Brazil," *Philosophy and Phenomenological Research* (1943), IV, 191.

templating his achievements as they flower in different regions
—of America, and of Europe." [2]

The regional point of view, considered as an approach to the
study of history or sociology, seems to some of us Brazilian
regionalists as philosophical as any other. This is also the conclusion reached by a South African student of regionalism, Professor J. W. Bews. He defines regionalism—under the name of
"human ecology"—as "a special way of regarding the ultimate
reality of life," as a "philosophy of life," [3] and not merely as a
science or a technique. One may object to Professor Bews's
philosophical regionalism by saying that a strictly regional
"philosophy of life" has a tendency to be incomplete. But it is
a philosophy; it is a philosophical attitude or point of view. It
is perhaps incomplete without its antagonistic point of view:
universalism or cosmopolitanism. I agree with those who think
that these two currents of thought—by some called localism
and internationalism—mutually enrich each other. I agree
with those who expand to the cultural sphere the well-known
idea of Professor Moritz Bonn concerning economic life: that
there is a process of counter-colonization, as opposed to that of
colonization.

It is as counter-colonization that regionalism seems to us
Brazilian regionalists to be a healthy tendency in Brazilian, as
well as in continental American, life, a tendency opposed to
excessive national, as well as to exaggerated international or
cosmopolitan tendencies. But the three types of cultural influence—the indigenous or regional, the national (probably the
most transitory and artificial of all), and the supra-national, or
cosmopolitan—enrich each other; and the ideal is apparently
to secure, through a combination of the three, the constant and

---

[2] "Regionalism: Pro and Con. Four Arguments for Regionalism," *Saturday Review of Literature*, XV (1936), 14.

[3] J. W. Bews: *Human Ecology* (London, 1935), p. 284.

stimulating interaction of all their antagonisms. As a political scientist wrote recently: "The principal task of the student of international organization is not to waste more time debating over regionalism versus universalism, but to study the ways in which, in concrete cases, the two principles can be utilized in combination and the standards to be applied in the dosage of each to be adopted." [4]

Some students of the social international situation that has developed in the world since the Industrial Revolution in Europe—industrial world-conquest based on ideals of standardization of all places according to the standards of the most powerful capitalistic states—have recognized the need for a creative regionalism in opposition to the many excesses of political centralization and unification of culture stimulated by politically and economically imperial interests and forces. It is the basic theory of such students that a growing number of separate cultural units will contribute to the stability of the world by preventing the formation and the expansion of imperialisms and of empires. [5]

The regionalist movement that a group of authors, artists, and scientists started in Brazil in 1925, and that was perhaps the first systematic movement of its kind in America, was and continues to be an effort to encourage a more spontaneous cultural life in Brazil through a freer expression of culture by the people of the various regions. The northeast, where the movement started, is a region with a particularly rich history, and is noted for its human potentiality. That region was losing consciousness of the values of its history as well as of its possibilities; the loss was occurring not only because of general standardizing influences originating in industrial world-con-

[4] Pitman B. Potter: "Universalism Versus Regionalism in International Reorganization," *The American Political Science Review*, XXXVI (1943), 862.
[5] Quincy Wright: *A Study of War* (Chicago, 1942), II, 1334–5.

quest, but also because of similar influences originating inside America and within the Brazilian nation itself.

The danger of cultural monotony or excessive unification of culture within America sprang from the influence of North American capitalistic industrialism, largely dominated by the idea that what is good for the people of the United States should be good for every other people of America. Some of the American manufacturers, inclined toward world uniformity, would repeat, with probably the best intentions, the same excess in that direction as was manifested by those British manufacturers who were the first to take control of the Brazilian colonial or semi-colonial market early in the nineteenth century. We are told by an Englishman [6] that so avid was the speculating in England then as regards the South American markets that everything was sent to Brazil with no consideration for the fitness or adaptability of English products to the climate or to the wants of the Brazilians. Implements useful only for Europeans, comforts and conveniences fit only for Britons, Scandinavians, Russians, Germans, and inhabitants of the Alps, were sent in abundance to tropical Brazil: warm blankets, warming pans to heat them, and even ice skates. True, most of the blankets were adapted by the Brazilians to the purpose of gold washing in the rivers of the Minas Gerais region; most of the warming pans were used in the sugar mills of the northeast regions; and even the skates were turned to a new use: wrought iron for shoeing mules and horses being scarce in Brazil then, the more intelligent Brazilians altered the British skates and put them on their horses' hooves. But I have no doubt that a few of the most colonial-minded actually tried to use the blankets, the warming pans, and the skates so as to look European, Nordic, or civilized.

I have known a number of Brazilian ladies who in Brazil

[6] R. Walsh: *Notices of Brazil in 1828 and 1829* (Boston, 1831), I, 245-6.

wear such furs as are fashionable on winter days in Paris, London, and New York; and a number of wealthy Brazilian men have built themselves residences not fitted to the tropical or near-tropical conditions of most of the country, but designed in rigid Scandinavian, Dutch, or Norman style. And more than once Brazil has copied its constitutions so closely from European ones or from that of the United States that the Brazilian political situation has been as artificial, as ridiculous, and as absurd as the use by a tropical people of ice skates in order to appear as civilized or fashionable as the Swiss, the Scandinavian, or the British.

The sending of ice skates and furs to Brazil by European or American manufacturers—whose ideal world would be one in which every people would have a polar or near-polar winter with plenty of ice for the universal use of skates and furs, to the benefit of large-scale industrial production—illustrates the ideal and the interest of manufacturers of goods and ideas who think in imperial terms. For them the world is divided into two areas: the imperial area, where goods and ideas are manufactured according to the manufacturers' needs and regional culture standards, and the colonial area, where people are expected to live, not according to their own needs and regional conditions, but according to standards imposed on them by those manufacturers.

As a reaction against this type of cosmopolitan standardization based on an almost divine right of colonization of areas technically less advanced by peoples who happen to be the most powerful ones from a technical and military point of view, a movement directed toward counter-colonization has been developing among nations, regions, or populations whose cultures are the most diverse—the Mexicans, the Arabs, the East Indians, the Brazilians, to mention only a few—but whose "consciousness of kind" (to use Franklin Giddings's expression) is the same. They all feel that their colonial or semicolonial status is doing harm to their creative capacity and their human potentiality. Under such a status they have become pure imitators instead of creators of culture. And as John Dewey said: "Since we can neither beg nor borrow a culture without betraying both it and ourselves, nothing remains save to produce one."

The problem of Brazil as a culturally creative nation has not been only that of resisting outside imperialistic attempts to maintain countries like those of Latin America as cultural colonies under various pretexts and so-called reasons or needs for strict unity or unification—as a Pan American unity sometimes used for the sole benefit of the United States or a Hispanic unity meant to be an instrument of domination by Spain over its former colonies of America; it has also been and is the problem of combining sub-regional diversity and national unity.

Ecologically Brazil is a region, to a large extent a natural region—so clearly so that it is considered by some geographers a "continental island." It is also a cultural region, a population whose predominating cultural values and standards are of Portuguese origin, in contrast to the Spanish, Dutch, English, and French values and standards of its American neighbors.

But Brazil is not simply one natural and cultural region; inside the almost continental immensity of that part of America, nature and culture have their own subdivisions. Therefore Brazil needs to defend itself permanently against internal enemies of its organic regionalism. For Brazil has more than once in its history had leaders whose ideal or whose mystical conception of a Brazilian Nation or Empire or Power has been that of Philip II in regard to Spain: the absolute supremacy of some Castile—I use the name Castile as a symbol of the tendency to overemphasize unity above diversity—over the other regions of the country.

Castilianism in Brazil, as I see it, has not meant only a region striving, through some Philip II, to dominate the other regions. Nor has it been only a state—technically a federal state with no more rights than any other, but actually an imperial power—striving to dominate the remaining states. This happened during the first republican period of Brazil: more than once a state—an almost entirely artificial political state—dominated the other states of the union through quite mechanical or quantitative advantages, such as a larger number, not so much of people as of voters or votes, and through a larger number of banks, factories, and manufactures.

Castilianism in Brazil—again as I see it—may mean and has meant other forms of domination by brutally powerful majorities over minorities whose rights should be respected to a larger extent than those majorities are willing to admit—that is, if we are to have really creative cultural diversity instead of a mere imitation of it. It may mean and has meant other forms of domination by technically powerful minorities over abused or exploited majorities. An example of the first type would be the excessive zeal of certain members of the vast Portuguese or Luso-Brazilian majority for the cultural uniformity or unity of Brazil so far as Portuguese or Luso-Brazilian values are concerned; they consider any opportunity for creative expression given to non-Portuguese European groups or to non-European or mixed groups a menace to Brazilian unity. Of course, here we are not concerned with interregional antagonisms of a strictly geographical configuration, but with interregional antagonisms or conflict in social and cultural realms rather than in physical space. Most of the Brazilian cultural sub-regions, however, have natural or physical sub-regions as their main bases:

the purely white minority of Brazil, for instance, is located more in the south than in the north. That is also true of the non-Portuguese or non-Luso Brazilians; their sub-regions are more in the extreme southern part of Brazil than in any part of the north.

Obviously a healthy minimum of cultural basic uniformity is necessary if Brazil is to remain a confederation instead of becoming a vast boarding-house—the "boarding-house" of Theodore Roosevelt's famous metaphor in regard to the United States. And that minimum is traditionally composed, in Brazil, of Luso or Hispanic basic values and cultural means of interregional and interhuman communication. The most important of these means is the Portuguese language. That minimum is made also of values and even techniques predominantly European, and not Amerindian or African—predominantly, but not exclusively.

The entire subordination of historical and geographical differences to a rigid ideal of uniformity would be too narrow an ideal of unity for such a complex cultural "continent" as Brazil. Oversimplification of the problem of Brazilian complexity through its subordination to mere political convenience was one of the weaknesses of the Empire in Brazil, noted for its excess of centralization. Some students of Brazilian problems think that it was one of the defects of the political regime that prevailed in Brazil from 1937 to 1945 under the name of *Estado Novo* (New State). That regime went too far in its reaction against the excess, not of creative regionalism, but of "state rights" developed in Portuguese America during the so-called "first Republic."

"State rights" was one of the Anglo-American political theories imported by Brazilian republicans from the United States without a previous careful study of Brazilian geographical and historical conditions. The result was that national parties almost ceased to exist in Brazil; populous and powerful rival states like São Paulo, Minas Gerais, and Rio Grande do Sul developed into something like political parties. Each one of them had as its real political program not so much the solution of national, or Brazilian, problems of social and human interest as the promotion of narrowly sectional or state interests, industrial, commercial, and agricultural. A railroad—most of it with double track—built in one of the powerful states with federal or national money was an almost luxurious enterprise for Brazil, while there were Brazilian regions in which transportation needs were entirely neglected. Descendants of Germans were allowed liberties or privileges entirely incompatible with Brazilian cultural basic unity (such as the right to have schools where Portuguese was not taught) by politicians who needed German votes in order to dominate or control their particular state.

Other politicians were interested in making of their particular state the economic Castile or the political and even military Prussia of Brazil—power politics within the national sphere. There was a time when the police force of São Paulo was nearly as powerful as the Brazilian Army. It had its own French military instructors and other features characteristic of a national army. The same, or almost the same thing, has happened in Rio Grande do Sul and in Minas Gerais. I once came from Minas Gerais with the vivid impression that I had been in a Brazilian Prussia. A vast amount of public money was being spent, not on public works or for the permanent benefit of the people, but to maintain a police force almost as powerful as the national army. What for? Apparently for the defense of state rights—really, perhaps, for the defense of the political group then in power in that particular state. Whatever the reason, the fact was not an expression of healthy or creative regionalism, but a horrid caricature of it. American students of the problem of regionalism are right when they establish a fundamental distinction between regionalism and sectionalism. Some of the pages written by Turner about sectionalism in the United States might have been written about the same problem in Brazil.

Under a regime like the so-called *Estado Novo*, which some describe as an "authoritarian democracy," the prevailing *mystique* in Brazil—that is, the *mystique* that official propaganda then emphasized through its radios and newspapers as the only basis for orthodox patriotism—was the opposite extreme of the doctrine of "state rights" as known from 1889 to 1930. It was the dangerous *mystique* of Castilian unity or Castilian uniformity. "Castilian" in this case does not mean, as it did in old Spain, the supremacy of one Brazilian region over the others. It means centralization: political centralization. It means the excessive subordination of a country as vast as Brazil to its political capital: to Rio de Janeiro.

One cannot deny that Getulio Vargas and other "unionists" or "centralists" have done away with excesses or abuses of "state rights." For the fact is that the 1889 Republic in Brazil was marked by "a tariff war between the states—between them and the Union." [7] But some have reached an extreme point in their ideal or their policy of political centralization and national uniformity—a point at which the cure may do more harm than the disease to the politically sick nation. The disease was an excess of state rights, so prominent and harmful in Brazil before the 1930 Revolution; the cure was the excess of uniformity stimulated by the so-called *Estado Novo*, with the central power directing everything in Brazil. There were exceptions: states like Pernambuco became in 1937 almost independent from Rio in the semi-Fascist or para-Fascist characteristics that they developed. Such exceptions seem to show

[7] J. F. Normano: op. cit., p. 123.

that the regime practiced in Brazil as the *Estado Novo* needed modification, not only for the sake of a freer local life, but also for the sake of a more effective control of national affairs by a vigilant, independent, and critical public opinion and press.

"Unionism" or "centralism" is not an innovation in Brazil. The Brazilian Empire, as I said, was noted for centralization. That was one of its defects. But it did probably less harm to Brazilian regional and cultural diversity than the *Estado Novo* system of centralization and uniformity did from 1937 to 1945. For during the Empire, centralized power was in the hands, not only of a constitutional emperor, whose abuses, or attempts at abuse, of centralized power were sharply criticized in Parliament and in a free press, but also of the intellectually and morally best and ablest public-minded men of Brazil. Most of these reached supreme power after having given public evidence, in their own provinces, of their capacity and honesty, and not (like most of them today) through a strictly personal choice by the president or chief of the nation. Some of them rose to power from very humble origin. At least two of them, André Rebouças and Saldanha Marinho, were almost jet-black and of slave descent, and several were mulattoes, the descendants of slaves. For the Empire in Brazil was remarkable for its combination of politically aristocratic methods with ways and customs as democractic as those of any republic that the continent has had. It was remarkable for its tendency toward an ethnic and social democracy—not only a Brazilian tradition, but a Portuguese tradition as well.

The men who founded the Federal Republic that in 1889 replaced the Empire had been impressed by the excesses of centralized power in their vast country. They adopted a constitution which copied that of the United States. Instead of seeking to combine unity with regional diversity, they borrowed from the United States the principle of state rights, thus putting such an emphasis on a political state autonomy derived from merely quantitative conditions and advantages held by one state over the others that many abuses became possible. The problem of combining diversity with unity—perhaps the most fundamental problem in organizing Brazil as a community—seems to have suffered as much from the political methods of combining them adopted by the Federal Republic of 1889 as from the centralization methods followed by the Empire. The solution of the problem appears to be not a narrowly political one, but a social one, whereby states are reduced to a minimum of importance, and natural and cultural regions are treated as organic realities, each with its own characteristics, but all vitally interdependent in their economic interests and needs; all vitally interdependent for the solution of their social and cultural problems and aspirations. Diversity will then become creative as never before; and unity will be less of a problem than now, with regions co-ordinated by an interregional organism, but not oppressed or exploited by the region or sectional group economically or technically most powerful at the moment.

It seems to some of us, as students of regionalism, that countries with a regional past, like Brazil, ought to keep constantly in mind the example of Spain, where centuries of systematic Castilianization did not succeed in imposing Castilian regional culture on all Hispanic regions as their only or sacred culture. From the point of view of unity, Brazilians are fortunate in having a single language. Differences of pronunciation have never been significant in Portuguese-speaking America, though a Congress met recently in São Paulo—a *paulista* initiative, not one by the central government of Rio—at which some of the best philologists, authors, composers, musicians, historians, and sociologists of Brazil were present to study the problem of the Portuguese language in Brazil. There it was decided that the Portuguese spoken in Rio by the so-called *carioca* (the inhabitant of the capital of Brazil) is the most agreeable to the ear and the best adapted to music, to song, to the theater, to the cinema, and to public speaking. Its adoption as the Portuguese to be used by composers, dramatists, and professional speakers was a unanimous decision of the São Paulo Congress, and was well received by all Brazilians. This does not mean that regional linguistic peculiarities are to be avoided by writers, or in the theater, the song, and the drama when regional characters appear: far from it. It means that one of the Brazilian regional ways of pronouncing the Portuguese language—the *carioca* way—has been chosen by a very representative group of Brazilians as the official language for the Brazilian theater, Brazilian song, and the Brazilian cinema when regional characters do not appear in them.

So reasonable and sensible a measure is a good example of the possibilities of combining unity with diversity in a country almost continental in its extension. And a significant thing about it is that it came from São Paulo—a sort of Catalonia of Brazil: a manufacturing region that has no equal in Latin America, with a capital that is the most European and at the same time the most "Yankee" of the Brazilian cities, and a people whose cult of efficiency and love of toil are in sharp contrast to the almost Chinese indifference and resignation to poverty of certain Brazilian groups of other regions. Like the Catalans of Spain, some *paulistas* feel that their industry is helping to maintain others in idleness; one *paulista*—a *paulista* not by birth, but by adoption—has compared São Paulo to a locomotive pulling the rest of Brazil, twenty mere cars—possibly sleeping-cars. But, also like the Catalans, *paulistas* tend to become proud arrogant, and even prone to exaggerate when they contrast their brilliant economic achievements with those of Brazilian Andalusians: Brazilians from Bahia, Pernambuco, and Rio Grande do Sul, who are, according to *paulista* critics, exuberant conversationalists, speechmakers, and poets rather than hard workers.

In spite of this *paulista* attitude, however, not only Brazil generally, but also São Paulo particularly, owes much to Brazilians from the regions more famous for their delicious oranges, their fine cigars, and their poets, diplomats, and writers than for their factories, modern industries, and skyscrapers. For some of the industrial leaders of São Paulo have been Brazilians from the north or from Rio Grande do Sul who found life too sleepy or too archaic in their native regions. The men from Ceará—an arid region—are particularly noted for their ability to migrate to populous cities or to pioneer areas of Brazil and become prosperous in some region characterized by one of two extremes: overpopulation or wilderness. A number of men from Ceará—men of Portuguese origin, with Indian blood and perhaps the Indian nomadic tradition—have made good in São Paulo and Rio as industrial and commercial leaders and innovators; many have been the pioneers of Brazilian colonization in the vast Amazon region. They are, in more than one respect of ethos and activity, the modern *bandeirantes* of Brazil, successors of the old *paulistas*.

If one accepts Mr. Waldo Frank's generalization, the *paulistas* are now bourgeois under "planless industrialism"; bourgeois "out from the workers, who are poor and spiritless and also directionless at the moment." Though this is somewhat exaggerated, there is some truth in it. The *cearenses*, or men from Ceará, also, fall into "planless industrialism" when they become bourgeois and prosperous in the big cities of Brazil. But most of them are going west. A number of them and of other Brazilians of the arid and semi-arid areas of Brazil—regions known for their cattle raisers, rebels, wanderers, mystics, troubadours —are going west, or going to the Amazon, or are in the army and the navy. They are men eager for adventure. They are as warlike in spirit as the old *paulistas*, who, in contrast to the modern ones (whose presence in the army and the navy and in the risky pioneering colonization of the Amazon and the west is insignificant by comparison), fought in their day against the most belligerent Indians of the southern continent, against the Jesuits, and against the Spaniards.

The Brazilians from northeastern Brazil—the arid, semi-arid, and coastal parts—are, like the original *paulistas*, typically *caboclo*, or indigenous, and more tellurically and traditionally Brazilian in spirit and behavior than any other regional type. Most of them are—or, what has sometimes the same socio-psychological effect, imagine themselves to be—the descendants of some near or remote Indian brave; though sometimes this sort of "ethnocentrism," to use Sumner's word, is contradicted by the almost Scandinavian blond hair and blue eyes of the self-styled *caboclo*, or by the strong evidences of African blood in his not entirely Indian body.

As telluric and at the same time as traditional as the Brazilians of the northeast, Bahia included, are the old *paulistas* of São Paulo. One of them became the interpreter of his group when he expressed his pride in his ancestors' having been *paulistas* or Brazilians for more than four hundred years. But the old *paulistas* of São Paulo are becoming scarcer and scarcer, deeply affected as they have been in their anthropology and psychology by their increasing contact with growing numbers of Europeans and of Brazilians from other regions who have been attracted to São Paulo by its industrial prosperity. Almost as telluric and as traditional as the Brazilians of the northeastern region are those of Rio de Janeiro, of Minas Gerais, and of certain areas of Rio Grande do Sul, Pará, and other regions of Brazil.

Still other aspects of Brazil, in point of regional diversity, make the comparison with Spain relevant. For Spain is the clas-

108

sic—the most dramatic—example of a country in which a stupid policy of centralization and of extreme unification has resulted in emphasizing the invincible power of regions and regional cultures. And, developing Senhor Ribeiro Couto's suggestion, Minas Gerais is in some ways the Castile of Brazil, and Ouro Preto its Toledo. Like the Castilian of Spain, the *mineiro* (inhabitant of Minas) is distinguished by his austerity and tendency to introspection, though he is far from having the intense mysticism and individualism of the real Castilian. Though apparently very simple, he is complex, subtle, and even sophisticated—as shown in the sense of humor which makes him smile at himself when necessary. This is not true of all *mineiros*. I have known *mineiros* with no sense of humor who always take themselves seriously. But some of the deepest, driest, most sophisticated humor of Brazil comes from Minas Gerais. I never saw the *mineiro* poet Carlos Drumond de Andrade laugh; but he is a Brazilian master of dry humor, and as such he characteristically comes from Minas Gerais. The same thing is true of a typical *mineiro* whom I knew well when he was in Lisbon as a political *émigré* in 1930 after having been a very important man in Brazil. As an *émigré*, he kept his magnificent sense of humor. He was the supreme realist of the entire group of *émigrés* with whom I came daily into contact, a group that included men who had occupied the most important positions as political leaders in Brazil. Some of them had fantastic ideas about what would happen in Brazil with the development of the Revolution of 1930, but that old *mineiro*, cigarette in mouth, had no illusions. He knew that a shrewd politician of a new type was to rule Brazil for many years, not just for a few months. He even outlined some of the contradictory but politically clever tendencies that the new regime would probably follow. Of himself and some of his political colleagues, he said: "We are politically dead." He was right in his psychological knowledge of Brazilians. He was prophetic without assuming the air of a prophet; he was too shy to do that, and had too much humor, too.

Because of a similar psychological knowledge of Brazilians displayed by Getulio Vargas, some observers have written that he was only by accident from Rio Grande do Sul: that in reality he was a *mineiro*. I think such observers are wrong. They appear not to know Rio Grande do Sul well. Vargas was the psychological, if not the logical, product of the obscure but very interesting area of the Rio Grande do Sul where he was born—the *missionera* area. It is true that there is a real antithesis between this area and the frame of mind one generally associated with the gaucho of the Rio Grande do Sul region. The men of the *missionera* area are not typical gauchos in behavior, but, having more Indian blood than the typical gauchos, and being the descendants of Indians educated and oppressed by Spanish Jesuits, they have in them something of their Jesuit masters: they are silent, introspective, subtle, realistic, distant, cold. They have also something of their brave ancestors, the "mission" Indians, whom the Jesuits were never able to dominate entirely. They are telluric, instinctive, fatalistic, proud, dramatic, almost tragic in their reactions to crises.[8] Getulio Vargas seems to have been a sort of Dr. Jekyll and Mr. Hyde in that he had in him something of the Jesuit, but something also of the Indian. He was avid for power and domination, but he also stood for the common people and for revolt against sterile conventions and powerful plutocratic groups. Characteristically, he gave his first child the name of Luther; and the first thing he ever wrote as a young man was an article in de-

[8] This was first written in 1944, at a time when Getulio Vargas was generally considered to belong to an extrovert and even merry type of Brazilian. Count d'Aurora, a Portuguese magistrate and writer who was in Brazil when Vargas committed suicide, pointed out the anticipatory character of this unusual characterization of Vargas.

fense of Zola. On the other hand, the Dr. Jekyll in Vargas made him behave sometimes as a politician whose only endeavor seemed to be to remain in power.

A few years ago I suggested that a psycho-sociological characterization of Brazilian regional types might be based on the various Brazilian ways of dancing their Carnival dances. Carnival is enthusiastically celebrated in Brazil, and the celebration lasts for three days. People dance in the clubs and theaters and in the squares and streets. In some areas classes, races, sexes, and ages mingle as they do not do on ordinary days, with such free democratic exuberance and joy in fraternizing that one does not know how pagan it is, or how lyrically Christian; though largely pagan, it seems to have something Christian about it. But Carnival dances are only superficially the same throughout vast Brazil. In some areas they are "Dionysian," to use the old word revived by an American anthropologist to denote a well-known type of human behavior; in other areas they are "Apollonian" or of an intermediate type.

Based on the assumption that Carnival for the Brazilians is only an exaggeration—sometimes, I admit, a morbid exaggeration—of their ordinary and characteristic behavior, I have suggested that through a careful study of the ways in which they dance their Carnival dances it is possible to classify their regional and sub-regional differences of temperament, ethos, and personality, as well as to recognize their Brazilian unity of behavior and their universality of human personality. The first results of such a study seem to indicate a considerable difference in the temperament or personality of such close neighbors as the gauchos and the *missioneros* of the Rio Grande do Sul region. Along with this study, I have suggested also a study of the characteristic Brazilian way of playing the very Anglo-Saxon game of association football, or soccer. The Brazilians play it as if it were a dance. This is probably the result of the influence of those Brazilians who have African blood or are predominantly African in their culture, for such Brazilians tend to reduce everything to dance, work and play alike, and this tendency, apparently becoming more and more general in Brazil, is not solely the characteristic of an ethnic or regional group.

Since I published my first notes on these two subjects—the regional ways of dancing and of playing football, as a dance with something African to it—I have read Mr. Waldo Frank's brilliant comment on the tango, "a *sculptural* dance-music"; and elsewhere he tells us that, watching a group of men in Brazil playing soccer, he observed that they played "weaving the ball intricately (like the melodic line of a *samba*) to the goal." [9] It is almost the same remark that I had made in an article written in 1938, which I am sure Mr. Frank never saw, just as he never saw the one I published in 1940 about the Brazilian ways of dancing Carnival dances. I rejoice at the coincidence of his observation with mine, for I consider the author of *South American Journey* one of the few Americans who have written really illuminating pages on Brazil—illuminating for outsiders and for the Brazilians themselves. I know that sometimes he turns bombastic; but in his best pages he is enlightening, and we should be thankful to him for them, and thankful also for his realization of Brazilian complexity and diversity, his respect for what regions and provinces mean in an intricate culture such as that of Brazil. Too many foreign observers tend to see only what is metropolitan or picturesque, what is very progressive or very primitive or archaic: São Paulo or Rio, naked savages or the Amazon River. But it is between these antagonistic extremes that the real Brazil lies, with its variety of regional situations.

Now, as under the Empire, there is a tendency to repress re-

[9] Waldo Frank: *South American Journey* (New York, 1943), p. 50.

gional and provincial diversity to the advantage of political centralization and unity. On the other hand, there are reformers who are against all centralization; they favor the total effacement of national as well as regional differences. In Brazil regional energies seem to be too powerful to be easily repressed by mere political coercion or mere ideological wish. Getulio Vargas, for some time so powerful in Brazil, was too shrewd a politician to wish to be a new Philip II; and today there are fewer reformers impatient or intolerant of regional differences than some years ago. Some of them see that even the Soviet Union is returning to an intelligent policy of combining internationalism with regionalism.

The study of Brazilian social history and social conditions seems to show that there, as in other vast and complex nations, each man should be allowed to develop a particular loyalty to his basic community, region, or province. Though in his transnational attachments he may go so far as to become a true citizen of the world, yet his status as member of a primary locality group seems essential to his personal and social health.

[IV]

Ethnic and Social Conditions in Modern Brazil

As I showed in Chapter I, the "European" background of Brazilian history was itself only partially European. It was also African and Asiatic. It was complex. Portuguese ethnic and cultural complexity seems to have been, from the most remote beginning of Brazil, a stimulus to its differentiation from Europe and its independence from a strictly colonial or sub-European status.

Geographically, Brazil is more closely related to Africa than to Europe. According to some plant and animal ecologists—one of them Professor Konrad Guenther—South America is in reality a continent distinct from North America. North America's climate and botanical and zoological characteristics remind one of Europe, while in the same respects South America's show a certain degree of independence and individuality. We must think of Brazil, Professor Guenther writes, referring to the marks of successive geological periods on the South American continent, as inhabited by a rich, diverse fauna, "which during all these long ages had time to develop in independence." [1] Such independence and diversity are interpreted by some authors as being perhaps the consequence of South America's having once been a number of islands, each evolving its own flora and fauna.

A different explanation is suggested by other geologists and ecologists: the age-long isolation of the continent and its division into many different topographical types. From the point of view of animal ecology, another ecologist—this one a Brazilian of German origin, Professor Rudolf von Ihering—distinguishes six regions in Brazil: the Amazon region; the country to the south of Pará; the Sertão of the northeast; the interior of the southern states; the northern coastal zone, originally forest-clad; and the southern coastal zone, characterized by high grassy plains. These are only the regions; the sub-regions are many. As ecologists tell us, multiplicity of form is the essential characteristic of nature, especially of tropical nature, and if a European gardener tries to lay out a garden in Brazil he must follow "nature as a teacher" in the way suggested by Professor Guenther, and his garden must display the chief characteristic of the tropical vegetation, namely variety.

Tropical nature and the complexity of European background should have led the Portuguese pioneers who established themselves in Brazil as planters to practice variety in agricultural activity and production. But this did not happen, human behavior never being logical. One-crop agriculture, es-

[1] Konrad Guenther: *A Naturalist in Brazil: The Flora, the Fauna, and the People of Brazil*, translated from the German by Bernard Miall (London, 1931), p. 160.

1 1 5

pecially sugar cane, became the characteristic of the Brazilian natural and social landscape in the areas first dominated by Portuguese invasion. Sugar was later to be replaced by coffee, but with the same unhealthy consequences for nature and for human society. In both spheres, essential harmony in the relations between living creatures was broken when one-crop agriculture was adopted instead of diversification. Tropical nature, being essentially many-sided, was perverted when only one particular plant was grown predominantly or exclusively over wide areas. And on the human side, as has been said, one type of social organization, a feudal or quasi-feudal one, was allowed to dominate.

Fortunately for Brazilians, tropical nature itself seems to have rebelled against the uniformity imposed upon it by European one-crop agriculture. Small islands of secondary crops developed in the midst of the vast oceans of sugar cane; tobacco, corn, and manioc were among the native and almost spontaneous forms of agriculture adopted from the Amerindians by the Portuguese, or cultivated only by nomadic Amerindians. And somewhat the same thing happened in the sphere of human ecology: the Indians, for instance, rebelled against the imposition upon them of the plantation-slave status. Some became collaborators only with frontiersmen, and most of them developed into fierce enemies of the one-crop planter who wanted them as his slaves. But the Brazilian Indians were nomadic in habit and taste. Sedentary life, agricultural routine, the monotony of labor on the plantations meant death for them. This explains why Negroes from Africa were imported in such large numbers to Portuguese America, and why their descendants are today such an important element in the ethnic composition and social structure of Brazil.

If the equilibrium of Brazilian nature was dramatically disturbed when sugar cane was made the single basis of Portuguese domination, the introduction of the African Negro into the sugar regions is regarded by some historians and sociologists as an even greater disturbance—the Negro being introduced into areas in which he did not rightly belong. It may not, however, have constituted so serious an ecological disturbance as these authors believe. Henry Bates, a British scientist who spent a number of years in Brazil during the middle of the nineteenth century, came to the conclusion that the Negro was happier than the Indian in tropical America. Bates contrasted the Indian's "constitutional dislike of the heat" with the Negro's perfect adaptation to it. His reasoned judgment was that the Negro, not the Indian, is "the true child of tropical climes," [2] the true child of tropical Brazil as well as of tropical Africa.

From the standpoint of man's relationship to nature, the Negro's adaptation to the climate and other physical conditions of Brazil seems to have been perfect. From the social standpoint, he was culturally better prepared than the nomadic Amerindian to adjust himself to the status of slave—plantation and domestic slave—in Portuguese America. His adaptation to American conditions was as happy as that of the sugar-cane plant, his symbiotic companion in the task of changing the Brazilian landscape from an area of virgin forest to one dominated by plantation colonization and one-crop agriculture.

Some of the millions of Negroes imported to Brazilian plantations were obtained from areas of the most advanced Negro culture. This explains why some African slaves in Brazil—men of Mohammedan faith and intellectual training—were culturally superior to some of their European, white, Catholic masters. More than one foreigner who visited Brazil in the nineteenth century was surprised to find that the leading French

[2] *The Naturalist on the River Amazon, Humboldt Library of Science* (New York, [n.d.]), I, 725.

bookseller of the Empire's capital had among his customers Mohammedan Negroes of Bahia; through him these remarkable Negroes, some of them ostensibly Christian but actually Mohammedan, imported expensive copies of their sacred books for secret study. Some of them maintained schools, and the Mohammedan Negroes in Bahia had mutual-aid societies through which a number of slaves were liberated.

In the province of Minas Gerais, too, the slaves had mutual-aid societies. And the American Thomas Ewbank, while in Brazil (1845–6), once dined with a Bahian planter who told him that the slaves of Salvador (capital city of Bahia, and formerly the capital of colonial Brazil) preserved their own language, organized clubs, and nurtured revolutionary schemes that their Pernambuco brethren repeatedly attempted to carry out; some Bahian slaves were able to "write Arabic fluently" and were "vastly superior to their masters." [3] I have been fortunate in finding evidence confirming what Ewbank was told, and proving that, besides the merely strong slaves good only for field work, many culturally advanced Negroes were brought to Brazil. Perhaps no other American colony had, among its Africans imported for labor, so large a number of the latter type. And this importation of culturally advanced and aesthetically attractive Negroes from the African areas most influenced by Mohammedan civilizing power explains why in Brazil, probably more commonly than in any other American colony, beautiful Negresses became the famous mistresses of wealthy and prominent Portuguese merchants in Bahia, Ouro Preto, Rio, and Recife. Some of them surpassed their white or Amerindian rivals in prestige. In Minas Gerais, more than one became rich and married her daughters to so-

[3] Thomas Ewbank: *Life in Brazil, or The Land of the Cocoa and the Palm* (London, 1856), p. 441.

cially important young men, European or Brazilian white. One such was Jacintha de Siqueira, whom I found named in an interesting genealogical document in some family archives of that region; many a Brazilian now prominent in political or professional life has her blood in his veins.

Negroes are now rapidly disappearing in Brazil, merging into the white stock; in some areas the tendency seems to be toward the stabilization of mixed-bloods in a new ethnic type similar to the Polynesian. Although this tendency is usually found among peasants and immigrants, there have been other Jacinthas in the history of aristocratic Brazilian families; they are rare, but they have existed, and they are the subject of gossip. Ewbank wrote, in his book on Brazil at the beginning of the reign of Pedro II: "I have passed black ladies in silks and jewelry, with male slaves in livery behind them. Today one rode past in her carriage, accompanied by a liveried footman and a coachman. Several have white husbands. The first doctor of the city is a colored man; so is the President of the Province." And he describes the Viscountess of C—— as "tinged." [4]

There has been, and still is, social distance between different groups of the population. But social distance is—more truly today than in the colonial age or during the Empire (when slavery was central in the social structure)—the result of class consciousness rather than of race or color prejudice. As the Brazilian attitude is one of large tolerance toward people who have African blood, but who can pass for white, nothing is more expressive than the popular saying: "Anyone who escapes being an evident Negro is white." Sir Richard Burton observed in imperial Brazil that "here, all men, especially free men, who are not black, are white; and often a man is officially white, but naturally almost a Negro. This is directly opposed to the sys-

[4] Ibid., p. 266.

tem in the United States where all men who are not unmixed white are black." [5] Visiting Brazil half a century after Burton, Bryce included it among the countries where the distinction between the races is a distinction "of rank or class rather than of colors." [6]

Even during colonial days, if a person was politically or socially important, the fact that his or her ethnic past had some direct contact with Africa was robbed of significance by present position: he or she passed for white. I have examined this Brazilian process of sociological "Aryanization" in more than one book in which the Brazilian solution of the problems arising from race contact is contrasted with other solutions and is explained in the light of the peculiar social and cultural experience of the Portuguese as a transition people between Europe and Africa.

Another transition people, the Russian, is now revealing to the world a new and in some ways successful type of social organization which includes miscegenation (especially Euro-Asiatic race mixture) among its solutions of social problems. In more than one aspect of its ethnic and social situation, Brazil reminds one of Russia; it is almost an American Russia.[7] The experiment in ethnic and cultural bi-continentalism begun in Portugal centuries ago took a new dimension in Brazil: three races and cultures are fused under conditions that, broadly speaking, are socially democratic, though as yet productive of only a very imperfect social democracy defective both in its

[5] *The Highlands of Brazil* (London, 1867), I, 393.

[6] James Bryce: *South America, Observations and Impressions* (New York, 1913), p. 470.

[7] This comparison of Brazil to Russia was made prior to the same comparison by Count Keyserling. It is here repeated from the author's essay, "*Aspectos de um seculo de transicão,*" published in *Livro do Nordeste* (Recife, 1925). Recently, other observers have insisted on another comparison: that of Brazil with China. Mr. John Gunther, when in Brazil, told the author that he was impressed with some of the similarities of Brazil to China.

economic basis and in its political forms of expression. All imperfections admitted, however, Brazil stands today as a community from whose experiment in miscegenation other communities may profit. Probably in no other complex modern community are problems of race relations being solved in a more democratic or Christian way than in Portuguese America. And Brazil's experiment does not indicate that miscegenation leads to degeneration.

Professor Charles R. Stockard's conclusions—that "mongrelization among widely different human stocks has very probably caused the degradation and even the elimination of certain groups"; that "the extinction of several ancient stocks has apparently followed very closely the extensive absorption of alien slaves"; and that "if one considers the histories of some of the South European and Asia Minor countries from a strictly biological and genetic point of view, a very definite correlation between the amalgamation of the whites and the negroid slaves and the loss of intellectual and social power will be found" [8]—do not obtain their best support in the Luso-Brazilian experience. It is true that Portugal has not today the intellectual and social power that it had four centuries ago; but this is also true of "Aryan" Holland and "Aryan" Denmark.

According to Professor Stockard's theory, Brazil, where miscegenation proceeded more freely than in Portugal or Spain, should be vastly inferior in intellectual and social power, not only to Portugal, but to quasi-white South American nations like Argentina and Chile. Objective studies of Latin American national or regional variety in achievement and cultural development do not seem to confirm the inferiority of mestizo Brazil to its more "Aryan" neighbors. It is in Brazil, not in the more "Aryan" countries of Latin America, that one

[8] *The Genetic and Endocrine Basis for Differences in Form and Behavior* (Philadelphia, 1941), pp. 37–8.

finds today the most vigorously creative group of young architects, young painters, and young composers of Latin America,
and perhaps of the entire American hemisphere; and, in mestizo Brazil, the most creative group of medical scientists engaged in the study of the so-called tropical diseases and of
problems peculiar to tropical areas. Brazil is universally known
for the work of scientists such as Oswaldo Cruz, Chagas,
Fontes, Roquette Pinto, the Almeida brothers, Silva Mello,
Vital Brazil. The successful experiments of Brazilian investi-
gators (some of them mestizo) with anti-venom serums to nullify the effects of poisonous snakes save many lives in many
countries every year.

Another fact that seems to refute those who emphatically
generalize on the social and intellectual effects of what they
call "mongrelization" is that for years the Brazilian areas producing the largest number of political leaders and men of literary, scientific, and artistic talent have been the areas notable for
the extension and intensity of ethnic amalgamation and cultural
interpenetration: the northeast (including Bahia and Sergipe),
Rio de Janeiro, Minas Gerais, and São Paulo. During the Empire Bahia was known as the "Brazilian Virginia" because most
of the cabinet presidents came from that province. Some of the
cabinet presidents of the Brazilian Empire, though their formal behavior was like that of members of the British Parliament, were men with Negro blood. And though the qualities
of the Brazilian statesmen during the Empire period were imitative rather than creative, some of them were remarkable for
their political talent as well as for their tact and ability as diplomats.

Brazil as an empire was a country whose stability and peace
contrasted with the turbulent political life of most of the Latin
American republics. Even then it was ruled by an aristocracy
democratic enough to allow men with Negro blood to become

its members, though it remained largely white or quasi-white in its composition. The Republican period, however, has seen the increasing rise to political power and to intellectual, industrial, and ecclesiastical leadership of Brazilians of African origin. As a political system, the Republic established in Brazil in 1889 remained, as the Empire had been, more imitative than creative. Honesty among public men decreased; there was also a decrease in the elegance and dignity that had become characteristic of the Brazilian Parliament in the days of Dom Pedro II. On the other hand, there was an increase in efficiency in practical matters: some of the new political leaders were notable for their ability to deal with economic and sanitary problems, which had been somewhat neglected by the Empire. And a few surrounded themselves with scientists and engineers who began to do really creative work.

It was not until the establishment of the Republic that a series of courageous projects for harbors and wharves, water works, sanitation schemes, city paving, draining, and beautifying began to develop in Brazil, along with plans for a more efficient commercial organization of coffee production. Brazil fell in love with material progress. And in most of these plans one can detect the dynamic impatience of the Brazilians who entered public life with the 1889 Republic: their eagerness to make their country modern, progressive, different from Portugal, different from its colonial or monarchical structure.

Of the new Republican leaders a considerable number were mixed-bloods, men of modest rather than of aristocratic origin. They seem to have made of the Republican regime an expression of their own eagerness for a new and better social status. This may explain the political importance assumed by the army in the new regime. In contrast with the navy, which took special pride in having as officers only Caucasian whites or Indo-Caucasians and sons of aristocratic or wealthy bourgeois families; and in contrast also with the clergy, which during the Empire was chiefly white and aristocratic or bourgeois—the Brazilian army started developing into a socially and ethnically democratic organization, with a number of officers of very modest social origin and some with considerable Indian and Negro blood in their veins. These men assumed an active and dynamic part in the nation's political life. When the Brazilian plantation system began to disintegrate—a disintegration that proceeded rapidly after the abolition of slavery (one year before the founding of the Republic in 1889)—the army and the Church remained the only two organized groups in the country. And of the two the army was the more liberal, progressive, and democratic; the Church, the more conservative, though seldom illiberal or violently opposed to social reform.

Not a few of the younger army officers had come under the influence of the Positivism of Comte, and the most enthusiastic of them were convinced that here they had not *a* solution, but *the* solution, of all Brazilian problems. Members of another group of Republican idealists—a civilian one—were just as convinced, on the basis of what political, juridical, and financial knowledge they had gained from their reading of Anglo-American authors, that a federal and democratic constitution copied from that of the United States would solve all Brazilian troubles.

Between these two groups of extreme ideologues there were Republican leaders whose method was the British one of dealing with each problem as it presented itself rather than according to any rigid philosophical system or logical ideology. Among this third group of new and realistic leaders there were, as in the two others, Negroid Brazilians remarkable for their eagerness to rise to power as well as for their intellectual ability and personal charm—men like Francisco Glicerio and Nilo Peçanha; just as there were descendants of European non-Por-

tuguese immigrants who had arrived in Brazil as peasants or artisans—men like Lauro Müller, son of a German, and Paulo
Frontin, son of a Frenchman. Psychologically and sociologically they were in the same boat: eager to rise socially through
a successful political career as leaders of the new regime in Brazil. And the shrewdest seem to have thought that the most intelligent thing to do was not to commit themselves to a definite philosophical system or political ideology, whose prestige
might rapidly disappear, but to give themselves to a cause that
would remain for a long time dear to almost all Brazilians: the
cause of material progress. Hence the plans for general improvement as the most characteristic expression of Republican
activity in Brazil.

It was at this point that Brazil went into debt on a great
scale, borrowing from European bankers the necessary gold
for building harbors, wharves, water works, sanitation plants,
avenues, railroads, battleships, and so forth. Though much of
this money was spent extravagantly, no one can deny that the
leaders of "the First Republic" gave Brazil public works and
sanitary public conveniences that were essential to social, as
well as economic, development.

Such material works and accomplishments should not be un-
derestimated. They were valuable; they were the first great
contribution of the Republican system of government to Brazilian progress. For now the members of the land- and slaveholding aristocracy were being replaced as Brazil's political
leaders by a new element of the population, an element considerably different from its predecessors in social origin, ethnic
composition, and economic and intellectual interests. Most of
those predecessors had taken the patriarchal, feudal, or aristocratic view of Brazilian social problems; they had regarded
sugar (and, to a certain extent, coffee) as the great Brazilian
problem; they had considered themselves the heads of large

families of sugar- or coffee-producing slaves or semi-slaves—large families whose constellation was Brazil. The new leaders, some of them remote or second- or third-generation descendants of slaves or of peasants or modest immigrants from Europe, had a more democratic experience and outlook on life, though not enough to become effective leaders in the social reconstruction of Brazil. Most of them were too eager for a rise in social status to trouble over any other social or human problem with the exception of sanitary improvements in large towns—a narrowly bourgeois facet of the whole group of social problems confronting the Brazilian people. In regard to economic problems they remained conservative.

Out of the contact of some of the new Republican leaders with the dwindling power of a rapidly disintegrating sugar and coffee aristocracy, there arose a plan for the defense of Brazilian coffee production—a plan that stands as one of the most original contributions of Portuguese America (increasingly mestizo and even Negroid in the composition of its political and intellectual elite) to the science of economics and to the then very vague technique of government control of markets. According to an American specialist in the subject, the Brazilian "valorization" plan for coffee control in 1905 has been followed by Ecuador in regard to cacao, by Mexico for control of its henequen, by British Malaya and Ceylon for rubber, by Cuba for sugar, by Egypt for cotton, and by Italy for citrate of lime. In addition, as the same writer points out, valorization has been applied to numerous commodities in a purely domestic market, a familiar example being the efforts of the Federal Farm Board to raise the price of wheat in the United States. The term "valorization," we are told by Mr. Charles R. Whittlesey in his article on this subject in the *Encyclopedia of the Social Sciences*, "was introduced into English-speaking countries about 1906 from Brazil where it [*valorização*] had been applied to measures regulating the marketing of coffee." [9]

Successful in the valorization of their coffee, the first Republican leaders of Brazil, however, neglected human problems—they developed no plan for the "valorization" of the common people. Keen though they were in regard to financial matters and problems of material progress, they failed in dealing with human problems because they did not get close to human, social, and cultural reality; for example, they neglected the very important problem of directing the transition of a large number of Brazilians from slave work to free work. Apparently the most realistic of them considered that such problems were not for statesmen but for humanitarians, missionaries, lyric poets. Moreover, a few of them—men with slave Negro blood—did not want to appear as champions of a cause whose defense would emphasize a hereditary personal element that they were eager to forget and to have others forget; hence they concentrated on material progress—on borrowing and building, on attracting foreign capital and foreign labor. This latter, the attracting of foreign capital and labor, was typical of the narrowly economic policy pursued for the material Europeanization of Brazil, especially in the coast towns. Little attention was paid to the human, the broadly social and cultural, side of the problem of European colonization.

Early in the nineteenth century, the deliberate importation of European immigrants began, to be increased a few years later when the British took measures against the slave trade so severe that only a few contraband shiploads of Negroes were successfully brought to Brazilian plantations. Statesmen of the last years of the Empire realized that because of the scarcity of slave labor the prospects for Brazilian agriculture were far

[9] "Valorization," *Encyclopedia of the Social Sciences*, XV, 211–12.

from brilliant. But the problem that had to be faced was not merely economic: it was social as well. How could a country dominated by the plantation system, one-crop agriculture, and a feudal organization attract Europeans eager to find in America freer and more comfortable conditions than in their native countries? How could a country almost morbidly devoted to coffee planting and to sugar-cane planting, on immense estates held by a small number of landlords, be changed into a country of peasant coffee planting and diversified agriculture without going through a violent revolution? A great planter of the last years of the Empire, Moreira de Barros, when he held the portfolio of Foreign Affairs, very realistically pointed out that European immigrants to Brazil would "only work for their own hand and on their own lands." What the planters wanted in the way of immigrants was a type content to be merely the passive successors of the plantation slaves; and this the European immigrants were not willing to become.

How generally the human aspect of the problem was neglected in favor of the economic is shown by the attempt of Empire statesmen to bring Chinese coolies to the plantations to take the place of the Negro slaves. This new form of slavery would have been introduced into Portuguese America if in 1883—when the project was so seriously considered that a Mr. Tong King Sing came to Brazil to discuss it—public feeling in Rio and other cities had not risen against the great planters, whose narrow feudalistic habits and economic interests made them blind to broad national problems. This year of 1883 is a historic milestone in the struggle for the economic democratization of Brazil because it was then that the coffee-planting interests lost an important battle to preserve a system that—through originally creative for Brazilian agriculture and society—had, with the developing of new needs and conditions, become wholly parasitic and unhealthy.

The fact that public opinion was so strong against the introduction of Chinese coolies shows that, at least since the last years of the Empire, there has been a public opinion in Brazil. Superficial interpreters of Brazilian life who maintain that the only government for Brazil is a paternalistic dictatorship because "there is no public opinion in the country" forget such episodes as the vigorous popular reaction of 1883. A good and liberal man was then emperor, but he probably would have acted as the great coffee and sugar planters wanted him to act —in favor of their private and feudalistic interests—if public opinion had not manifested itself so emphatically.

For at that time the Brazilians had the right to express their feelings at public meetings and in the press. Indeed, so free was the press that Abolitionists and Republicans sometimes referred to Dom Pedro II as "Pedro Banana," meaning that though an emperor he was too much the weak instrument of powerful private interests—more like a soft banana than like a man. Brazil has had other rulers of the paternalistic type who have been given similar nicknames because, though good, honest, well-meaning men, they have considered powerful private interests above popular interests and national needs: "Tio Pita," or Uncle Pita, for instance—President Epitacio da Silva Pessoa being so called by his political opponents because of his alleged tendencies toward what might be termed avuncular benevolence. Paternalistic government seems not to work well when social conditions cease to favor paternalism and begin to demand strong leadership as directly responsible as possible to the people or to its most vigorous and best-educated elements. It appears to be actually harmful when it does not act as a transition regime interested in incorporating the common people into the civic life of the nation.

But popular reaction was not the only force that served to frustrate the project of importing coolies. Another force appeared, whose motive probably was not so much humanitarianism as it was the hope to compete with coffee- and sugar-producing Brazil. I mean the British Empire. A significant letter on the subject was published (December 1883) in *The Anti-Slavery Reporter* of London—a letter signed by Charles H. Allen and addressed to the Right Hon. the Earl Granville, K. G., *etc.*, Her Majesty's Principal Secretary of State for Foreign Affairs. The writer reported that British abolitionists had made plain to Mr. Tong King Sing the extreme danger that Chinese coolies imported into Brazil under contract would virtually become slaves; and he ended:

> *"I am desired by the Committee to thank your lordship for the prompt measures taken by your lordship's directions, to call the attention of Her Majesty's Representatives at Rio and Pekin to the question of Chinese immigration into Brazil, and to express a hope that your lordship will request those Ministers still to keep this subject before them, as future similar schemes may, at any moment, be introduced in which the planters might have to deal with gentlemen less astute and not so large-hearted as Mr. Tong King Sing."*

More than once, great powers that have outlived slavery or semi-slavery have befriended liberal, democratic reforms in weaker and less-advanced countries; for such countries, in continuing to keep slaves or serfs, may become dangerous competitors of the great powers in agricultural production. This may explain why the Brazilian liberals have at various times had the support even of European politicians notable for realism rather than for humanitarianism in their foreign policy. It may also explain the obverse: why even dictatorial governments in Brazil and other Latin American countries have sometimes had the support of liberal and democratic leaders of great powers interested not so much in democratization as in the rise of the acquisitive capacity of weaker nations.

As soon as the coffee planters of Brazil suspected that the slave business was doomed, the most enterprising among them sought to attract European peasants to the coffee estates through the system known as *parceria*, a system not far removed from serfdom. It is true, as objective critics of the *parceria* system have pointed out, that the colonist had the satisfaction of considering himself an independent worker; but, as he started with a large debt, never owned land, and earned no wages, his lot was a poor one if crops failed or the *fazendeiro* proved to be unfair. The colonist arrived "owing for the passage of himself and family, and was given a house and a quantity of food of the country; he cultivated a certain number of coffee trees, or allotment of sugar cane, took the harvest to the owner's mill and received half the result after milling." [1] Under this system he was entirely dependent upon the planter's fair play; and, as emphasized by some apologists for the *parceria* system, the hard-working Bavarians and Holsteiners in São Paulo often paid off their debts in four years and then had money in hand—a fact that speaks well for the fairness of some coffee planters in their dealings with the European peasant, for they might have kept him indefinitely as a semi-slave, always indebted and always dependent. It may be added that north Italians, not Germans, proved to be the best successors to Negro slaves on the coffee plantations.

Although there was considerable friction between planters and European colonists during the transition phase from slavery to free labor, an adjustment was eventually reached when a government agency known as *Patronato Agricola* instituted a moderate control over the relations between *fazendeiros* and their new white workers, to whom at least medical care had

[1] Elliott: op. cit., p. 61.

now to be given. Although Italian colonization in São Paulo was so successful that about one third of its present population is of Italian blood and people of Italian descent are prominent in business and in society, this was the only old state in which the new adjustment was really a success. For the areas where European colonization has markedly succeeded are those most nearly free from any inheritance of the plantation system: Rio Grande do Sul, Santa Catharina, Paraná, parts of Minas Gerais, Rio de Janeiro, and Espirito Santo. All attempts to establish European colonists in the neighborhood of the old plantation areas, Bahia, Rio de Janeiro, Pernambuco, were failures.

On the other hand, failure was also the lot of most of the Anglo-American colonists who went to nineteenth-century Brazil because it was a slavery country and they were used to being owners of Negroes and their superiors. Dozens of disappointed Southerners went to Brazil after the South was defeated in the Civil War, and very few were successful or happy in their new home. It seems that most of them went there with very little money, and so could not establish themselves as planters and slaveowners and live the life they had been accustomed to in the Old South. To start life as independent farmers in pioneering areas of Brazil—as European peasants did successfully in southern Brazil—was no easy task for men who had grown up having Negroes do all their heavy work for them. Some tried to grow cotton, but under very adverse conditions. These conditions and other factors probably explain the many failures.

Before 1917 an Anglo-American geographer, Mr. L. E. Elliott, inquiring what had become of those fellow countrymen of his who had gone to Brazil after the Civil War, was told a story that he describes as "comedy instead of tragedy." It is told of the group that settled in Santa Barbara to grow watermelons. One year, just as the crop ripened (so the story goes), cholera broke out in São Paulo; the sale of melons was forbidden, and the growers faced ruin. As a new United States consul had just been appointed to Santos by the new President of the United States—Grover Cleveland, a Democrat—the Southerners decided that the new consul must also be a good Democrat. On his arrival, therefore, they wrote him a letter of congratulation and told him of their difficult economic situation. The consul, it seems, replied cordially, suggesting that, as consul, he should visit them; and received posthaste a warm welcome from the Southerners.

> *"The afternoon of his arrival at the colony found the entire population drawn up on the platform, a southern Colonel at the head of the deputation. The train rolls up, a first-class compartment door opens, a gentleman steps out with a suitcase, and walks up to the Colonel with outstretched hand. It was the consul, but a consul as black as the ace of spades. It is said that the Colonel, rising nobly to the occasion . . . shook the hand of the consul, and that he and the other Southerners gave the official the time of his life; but when he departed they vowed that never, never again would they trust a Democratic administration."* [2]

Most of the descendants of the Civil War Southerners in Brazil have learned to forget their prejudice against Negroes and mestizos. Some have had to come into contact with Brazilian senators or prominent business leaders or professional men not purely white: mixed-blood white and Negro, not only white and Amerindian, though the commonest mixture in São Paulo has been the white-Amerindian. This is the dominant mixture at the base of the proud old aristocracy of that state, as well as of other regions of Brazil where it is still a matter of pride for an old family to have among its ancestors an Indian,

[2] Elliott: op. cit., pp. 65–6.

generally idealized as a hero of the wars against the French or the Dutch (who in the sixteenth and seventeenth centuries tried to conquer parts of Brazil), admired as a fighter against the Portuguese, or honored as a princess—the beautiful daughter of some powerful Indian chief. The first cardinal of Latin America, Cardinal Arcoverde, was the descendant of a Pernambuco Indian princess of the sixteenth century, a Brazilian Pocahontas. He was proud of his Amerindian blood. He was also insistent on the need, for Brazil, of a clergy consisting of men born in Brazil or integrated into Brazilian life, instead of one made up entirely of foreign priests and monks. He was not narrowly nationalistic, but he probably saw the danger for Latin American countries of being kept as intellectual and economic colonies of Europe with the indirect assistance of priests who, being European, would usually have a European attitude of autocratic paternalism (if not of absolute superiority) toward Amerindian or Indo-Hispanic or Afro-Hispanic populations.

Such was the extent of Indianism in Brazil, not only in literature, but also in daily life, that when Brazil separated from Portugal and there was widespread feeling against any Portuguese attempt at reconquest, a considerable number of distinguished Brazilian families had their family names changed to Amerindian names. Most of these were poetic—names of rivers or plants; but some were very prosaic, though expressive —names of fish associated with market and kitchen, like Carapeba.

The Indians of Brazil were remarkable, as modern scientists have pointed out, for their knowledge of the flora and fauna of the country; and to the present day many rivers, plants, animals, mountains, towns, and drugs have in Brazil not Portuguese but Amerindian names. According to a European scientist—Professor Konrad Guenther, already quoted—in Brazil, as in Spanish America, not only do many families point with pride to Indian chieftains in their past (a fact that I have already pointed out), but among the descendants of Indians in some regions the Brazilian also seems to be reverting to the Indian type, whereas the Africans are apparently being gradually and peacefully absorbed by the white-Indian population, no fresh recruits from Africa having come in for years.[3]

This German ecologist of pre-Nazi days was sympathetic to race-mixture and Indianism as a means by which the Brazilians could create a homegrown civilization, evolved organically from its environment, with its various departments of activity united at their source, nature. In this connection he found that the many Indian names of natural objects form a connecting link with the Indian source of Brazilian culture, and recommended that more should be done along the same line through popularizing Indian animal stories among Brazilian children of today. Novels like those of José de Alencar—the Brazilian Fenimore Cooper—and the larger utilization of Indian motives in Brazilian modern art might increase the Brazilians' pride in their Amerindian origins and in the natural foundations of their culture.

One should not forget that the Indians of Brazil were a forest people with a forest culture. The remaining Indians and the survivals of indigenous cultures are a very important element to be reckoned with in any cultural policy directed toward a deeper harmony between Brazilians and their natural environment. Such a policy of harmony finds a strong basis in the attitude of the Portuguese colonists in regard to intermarriage with the Amerindian population, an attitude of tolerance and sometimes enthusiasm for Amerindian physical and cultural differences.

The very fact that the Amerindians, nomadic as they were,

[3] Guenther: op. cit., pp. 371-2.

made bad slaves for the first sugar-cane plantations and fought with remarkable vigor against the Portuguese who tried to enslave them created a legend of their "independence," "bravery," and "nobility." This legend is responsible even today for the Brazilian tendency to consider the Amerindian superior to the Negro, though a strictly scientific study of Amerindian contributions to the cultural development of Brazil would probably lead to a different conclusion. However, the enthusiasm of most Brazilians for the Jesuit missionaries of the sixteenth century and the early part of the seventeenth century—priests who did their best to respect the freedom of the Amerindians proclaimed by the pope and the king of Portugal—is based on the same legend.

The work of the Jesuits was continued in recent years by an officer of the Brazilian army whose activity as head of the Brazilian Federal Department for the Protection of the Indians has surpassed that of any missionary. I refer to General Candido Mariano da Silva Rondon, himself a descendant of Indians. Rondon began his work as a lieutenant in 1890, when a government expedition under Major Gomes Carneiro went to the Bororos region in central Brazil to establish telegraphic contact between that part of the then young Republic and the more civilized regions. At that time an intelligent policy of friendly relations with Indian tribes was started by the Brazilian army. This policy has followed the plan for assimilating the Indians sketched at the beginning of the nineteenth century by José Bonifacio, leader of the Independence movement in Brazil and the greatest statesman Portuguese America has had. Bonifacio, a scientist with a European reputation, has been described as essentially a practical idealist. As has been pointed out by the students of his life and ideas, he had as his main concern the development of Brazil into a characteristically American nation free from European race prejudices. A basic idea in his program of social organization was the assimilation of the Indian as well as of the Negro. Nor did he fear the mestizo or mixed-blood. On the contrary, he opposed the segregation policy pursued by the Jesuits in some parts of Brazil. He had little interest in any vague and fictitious equality of Amerindians before the law, but advocated their assimilation by a Brazilian culture that would be enriched by them.

Brazil still has to face the problem of assimilating certain Amerindian tribes as well as those groups of Negroes whose culture remains largely African. Although there are Brazilians with European prejudices who regard as disgraceful any departure from European and Roman Catholic standards of morals, law, and custom, the general tendency among broadminded Brazilians is to maintain, toward such Africans as well as toward Indians, a policy of slow and intelligent assimilation, in which the assimilating group may incorporate into its culture certain values of general interest or artistic importance selected from characteristics preserved by deeply differentiated subgroups or subcultures. A similar policy will probably be followed in regard to the Germans and other European colonists, and also to the Japanese in the areas of southern Brazil where they have lived segregated for more than a generation.

Some students think that Portuguese Brazilian cultural values, regarded as basic to the development of Brazil as a nation and a broadly Christian community (including the Portuguese language and Portuguese freedom from race prejudice), should be emphasized as general values. There should be no subordination, however, of non-Portuguese subgroups or subcultures to a rigidly uniform Luso-Brazilian or Portuguese-Brazilian culture or "race." With a broad democratic policy like this—an ethnically and socially democratic policy—Brazil would become an ideal country for Europeans tired of narrow race and class prejudices and of illiberal nationalism and religious sectarianism. Not only peasants and artisans would have favorable conditions for expressing their creative power, but also the proficient agriculturist, the expert fruit-grower, and the stock-raiser. For, as the Anglo-American geographer Elliott perceived, the hardy and determined pioneer still has a chance in Brazil—though it will not be possible for him to be the individualist that he was a century or half-century ago, when there was no efficient public service for protecting the Amerindians or for conserving the forests and the mineral resources. Such human and natural values are now protected by laws inspired by a real concern for the interests of the Brazilian community rather than by a wish to favor individual exploitation.[4] The program of the present Council of Immigration and Colonization of Brazil includes "controlled colonization" and mixed "colonization nuclei" for both Brazilians (30 per cent) and aliens (70 per cent). This is an old idea of Bonifacio's.

Brazil is famous for its "white," or peaceful, revolutions. Its independence was the result of one of these. Although it remained an empire when all the other Latin American countries were republics, a peaceful revolution transformed it into a republic. A peaceful revolution transformed it from a slaveholding country into one in which everybody is born free. A peaceful revolution separated Church from State, solving a problem that has been the source of much friction in other Latin countries. An almost peaceful revolution, that of 1930, has favored Brazilian town laborers with a social legislation that is, in the-

---

[4] In his *Brazil* (London 1866), p. 389, William Scully wrote that colonists arriving in the Brazilian Empire "enjoyed" special facilities for their settlement." He pointed out that Brazil had then (1866) "a steady monarchical representative government . . . guaranteeing individual liberty by an *Habeas Corpus* law exactly such as exists in England"; there was also "general religious tolerance." Other "political features of the Brazilian nation" of interest to immigrants were "liberty of the press," "trial by jury," "no distinction of castes," "perfect equality before the law," "free right of association and petition."

ory if not always in practice, one of the most advanced of our day. Brazil will therefore probably be able to revolutionize immigration policies without violence either to immigrants or to old residents. Much remains to be done in connection with the colonization of unoccupied land by Brazilians and by immigrants. The "valorization" of the Brazilian native peasant is urgently needed.

Ill-health, especially that caused by malaria, ancylostomiasis, tuberculosis, syphilis, and the Masson-Pirajá disease, seems to be responsible for the laziness of which the Brazilian *caboclo*, or native peasant, has been accused by superficial foreign critics. In everything Brazilian that is unpleasant to their eyes, these critics see evidence of the ill effects of race mixture or tropical climate. More than fifty years ago a Brazilian author who held some of Bonifacio's ideas, Sylvio Romero, wrote that the mixed-bloods formed the mass of the Brazilian population, making the point that both Amerindian and Negro were "inarticulate" in Brazilian society and culture. It was then the fashion for sophisticated Brazilians to cover up everything of Negro origin which they could: blood, food, customs, words, and every other influence or element that could be concealed. A characteristic of the country today is that this almost Freudian censorship of mestizo spontaneity is no longer a strong force in Brazilian psychology or cultural and social life; and the consequence of this sort of psychoanalytic cure for what was a national complex is that Brazilian music, cookery, literature, and art are more and more expressing popular life, needs, and values.

As a whole, the Brazilians have what psychiatrists call a traumatic past. Slavery was their great trauma. For many, color remained for some time the disagreeable reminder of an unhappy social situation or an injurious episode in their past. Certain officers of the traditionally democratic Brazilian army have sought to impede its development into an ethnically and socially democratic institution by trying to introduce into it racial restrictions by which Negroes and obviously Negroid men could not become officers; and this may be considered a neurotic expression of that complex. But it is an almost isolated one. The general tendency in present-day Brazil is to regard slavery as an episode over and done with, having only a social bearing on the history of the total Brazilian personality. Even Brazilians with a family or individual past that has nothing to do with Africa, biologically or ethnically, join Negroid Brazilians in a feeling now general, though not universal, that nothing is honestly or sincerely Brazilian that denies or hides the influence of the Amerindian and the Negro.

[V]

Brazil as a European Civilization in the Tropics

Europeans have been suspicious about tropical America and tropical Brazil since the sixteenth century: they have had visions of the South American or Brazilian tropics as either a paradise or an inferno.

There were men from northern Europe, for instance, who attempted to conquer the Amazon lands and to establish themselves there as colonists. They were not successful. Only the Iberians and their descendants have been able to conquer these lands, where it is said that water and forest run side by side and intermingle in a way that has made human permanent settlement difficult for some and impossible for others.

The man who did most, in the nineteenth century, to destroy some of the European superstitions about the Amazon climate was H. W. Bates, who lived for eleven years in the Amazon jungle and in the rustic Portuguese or Brazilian pioneer settlements around it. When about to return to England, he hesitated over leaving the tropics. He wrote that as he thought of living again in a cold European country, "pictures of startling clearness rose up of the gloomy winters, the long grey twilights, elongated shadows, chilly springs, and sloppy summers; of factory chimneys . . . confined rooms, artificial cares . . ." while, in leaving tropical Brazil, "I was quitting a country of perpetual summer. . . ." But it is true that three years after his return he wrote: "after three years' renewed experience of England, I find how incomparably superior is civilized life. . . ." [1] Bates's change of mind poses the question: is it, or is it not, possible to combine the advantages of civilized life with the advantages of tropical climate? The Brazilian experience—or experiment—seems to be an answer to this question. And this answer seems to be "Yes." Brazil is one of the largest national spaces in the world. It is like an American Russia or a tropical China. In this vast tropical, national space swells a people whose European culture is mainly Iberian and Catholic, and whose ethnic composition is also Iberian to a considerable extent. And today its civilization is perhaps the greatest, or at least the most advanced, modern civilization so far developed in a tropical region.

It is true that the vast Amazon area of Brazil remains a challenge to Brazilian capacity to deal with tropical difficulties, which are numerous there. But there are encouraging aspects of the Brazilian effort to overcome them, creating there the same civilization that the Portuguese pioneers and their Brazilian descendants, generally men of mixed blood, white and Amerindian, and known as *bandeirantes*, were able to create

[1] Henry Walter Bates: *A Naturalist on the River Amazon* (London, 1915 edition), p. 388.

in other parts of Brazil. The accomplishments of these *bandeirantes* were remarkable, sufficient to make one accept the mixture of whites and Amerindians as a desirable ethnic combination. They met, with a rare energy, all kinds of human opposition—from wild Amerindian tribes, from Spaniards, from
Jesuits. And there were the hazards of insects, animals, high
mountains, deserts, swamps, and tropical rains. A historian has
written that they not only did make possible the vast Brazil of
today, but also they poured millions of pounds of gold into
world economy in the crucial years when England was becoming a banking and industrial power. This historian, Professor Paul Shaw, goes on, in his appraisal of the Brazilian *bandeiras*,[2] to remind us of the words of Werner Sombart, the well-
known German sociologist: "Without Brazil's gold we would
not have modern economic man," and the equally significant
statement of an English historian, Wingfield Stratford, that the
influx of Brazilian gold into seventeenth-century England contributed to the basis of modern economy. If this is true, we
have to come to the conclusion that a mixed group of whites
and Amerindians—vigorous racially and culturally—not only
laid the basis for a new type of civilization in tropical America,
modern Brazil, but also contributed to the basis of modern
economy in Europe.

In this the African Negro and the descendant of the Negro
(the African was imported to Brazil as a slave) also played
their part. This fact—that Amerindians and Africans, as well
as Europeans, and their mixed descendants have made an active
contribution to the development of Brazil—seems to explain
why Portuguese America has now a civilization with such
vivid characteristics of its own, and why one of these characteristics is what has been described by some authors as Bra-

[2] Unpublished essay written when Professor Shaw taught History of the
Americas at the University of São Paulo.

zilian ethnic democracy. Many characteristics of modern Brazilian civilization originate in the fact that the Negro, because of the comparatively liberal treatment given to him in Brazil, has been able to express himself as a Brazilian and has not been forced to behave as an ethnic and cultural intruder. He behaves as a Brazilian of African origin and not as a "Brazilian Negro" —differing thereby from the "American Negro" of the United States. And of course the same thing has been true in an even more vivid way of the Amerindian; just as the same thing is becoming true of the Japanese, as well as of the German, the Italian, and the Polish immigrant. Some of these are becoming, in the second generation, prominent in Brazilian political life, not as German-Brazilians, or Italian-Brazilians or Polish-Brazilians, but as Brazilians; and they are also taking their place in Brazilian art and in Brazilian literature (written, of course, in Portuguese), which has been enriched with words from other languages without losing its Portuguese structure. The new literature of Brazil is beginning to attract as much attention from Europeans and North Americans as the modern architecture, the music, and the cuisine of the Brazilians.

It may be said that the civilization Brazil is developing in the tropics is not a purely Western or European civilization. This view, or a similar one, has been duly considered by an Anglo-American scientist, Dr. Marston Bates. He once wrote that "Latin America might possibly be used to support the thesis that Western civilization, in its pure form, is not readily adaptable to tropical conditions." But he added: "This is hardly damning except to those who consider the Western variety to be the only possible form of civilization in general." [3] He points out, concerning Mexican art—one of the greatest expressions of modern culture in the tropics—that its interest is in its not

[3] Marston Bates: *Where Winter Never Comes* (New York, 1952), p. 83.

being typically Western, in its enrichment by elements drawn from the local environment or from the tropics.

The same thing can be said of the civilization that the Brazilians are developing in tropical America. It is not a mere sub-European civilization. It is predominantly European, but not entirely European. In some respects it is extra-European: it seeks to adapt itself to conditions and possibilities that are not European but tropical: tropical climate, tropical vegetation, tropical landscape, tropical light, tropical colors. So it is that São Paulo has become what is generally described as the greatest industrial center of Latin America; and this is certainly an anticipation of a technical or technological development that seems to be either following or preceding other cultural developments in other areas of Brazil, including the northeast and the extreme northern part of the country, the equatorial part.

What is happening to industry, cattle raising, and agriculture in Brazil is also happening in other human activities that form part of a civilization or a culture. The art of gardening, for instance. Through the use of the same methods or techniques of combining tropical experience with European science, Brazil is developing its own styles of ornamental gardens complementary to its own styles of architecture. Here, as in other matters, Brazilians agree with G. V. Jacks and R. O. Whyte, when the authors of *The Rape of Earth* maintain, with the approval of R. J. Harrison Church, in his book *Modern Colonization* (London, 1951), that European men, despite their skill and power over nature, have learned only how to cultivate European soils in a European climate.

This is why some modern students of these and other problems concerned with the expansion of civilization think that a new science has to be developed to deal with these complex problems from a tropical point of view or angle complementary to, if not in place of, the European or boreal one, so far overdominant in science and technology. Why not a special science—a Tropicology—to deal with the adaptation of European science and technology to tropical situations, even with the invention of new techniques designed to solve problems peculiar to the tropics? Problems not only of cattle raising, agriculture, architecture, urbanization, and regional planning, but also of psychology, problems relating to education, to political organization, to mental hygiene. For the behavior of man in the tropics has to be considered, in some of its aspects, in relation to situations and conditions peculiar to tropical environment; to the fact, for instance, that a tropical climate is favorable to an easy, informal contact between crowds and political leaders in public squares, without the need of indoor party meetings that create a distinctly party atmosphere. Music, the drama, theatrical performance, religious rites may be similarly affected by tropical weather or climatic conditions, so that they develop new forms through a new psychological and social relationship between artists or religious leaders and large crowds as crowds, a relationship not to be achieved through the radio and the television, whose importance is probably greater in boreal than in tropical countries.

One thing at least is true: the development of a modern civilization in Brazil is becoming more and more the development of a new type of civilization, which makes the Brazilians, already considerable pioneers in their history, pioneers of a new and even more exciting future. More than any other people, they are developing a modern civilization in the tropics whose predominant traits are European, but whose perspectives—I should insist on this point—are extra-European.

The Portuguese found in tropical America an ideal space for the expansion and development of their ethnically democratic, though, in some other aspects, aristocratic and even feudal civilization, which had begun to flourish in the African and Asiatic tropics. Following assimilative methods that they seem to have learned from the Moors, the Portuguese have been successful, as no other European seems to have been, in assimilating into the institutions of social forms of Portugal, or of Christian or Latin Europe, local populations that even to-day, though predominantly yellow as in Macao, or predominantly brown as in Portuguese East India, or black as among the assimilated Negroes of Portuguese Africa, consider themselves Portuguese. Professor H. Morse Stephens of Cambridge, who through his books on Portugal in the East became an authority on the subject, has referred to this policy as "unique in the history of Europeans in India" and as "far-reaching in its results. . . ." In fact it has been unique in the history of European expansion in the tropics and far-reaching in its results and influence upon the present conditions of Europeans in tropical regions everywhere, though one must admit that in some of these regions the Spaniards have shown a tendency to act like Portuguese.

Brazil is a much vaster tropical space than Portuguese India, and here the Portuguese, in 450 years of ethnic and especially cultural presence, have succeeded in assimilating not only the Amerindians found in the part of America that is now Brazil, but also the African slaves imported from eastern and western Africa to work on plantations, and, more recently, Spanish, Italian, German, Polish, Syrian, Japanese, and other immigrants. Brazil is today remarkable for its unity, though recently arrived immigrant groups, still in the first stage of the process of being assimilated, seem sometimes to contradict this. But they probably will follow older groups and become Brazilian through the Portuguese or Luso-Brazilian pattern or way, though retaining some of their non-Portuguese characteristics. Brazil has been—and seems to continue to be—an example of ethnic and cultural pluralism, though diversity is possibly becoming less evident than unity.[4]

Within this process of assimilation, do national and ethnic groups of non-Portuguese origin play each a characteristic or particular role in modern Brazilian society and politics? In Brazilian society—in its development into a complex national society—yes: these groups have made and are making distinct contributions to such a development as a total, comprehensive pan-human and not narrowly Portuguese or Luso-Brazilian development. In politics this has hardly been true, for there has not been in Brazil a "German vote" or an "Italian vote,"

[4] Commenting on the city of São Paulo, as he knew it during the first decade of the present century, Charles Domville-Fife, a British observer, wrote: "The cosmopolitan element, such as the Italians, who number half the population of the city, the Portuguese and the Spaniards, although in many cases born under European skies, and owing allegiance to their Majesties the kings of Italy, Spain, and Portugal, soon forget their Fatherland, and become Brazilians at heart" (*The United States of Brazil*, London 1910, p. 209). According to the same observer, in the city of São Paulo, "the throng of varying nationalities" was "confused," though happiness seemed to prevail "in most quarters," with "work and air-space for all." He did not find, however, that the laborer in a place like São Paulo enjoyed "more freedom or security, or even as much, as he does under the limited monarchy of Great and Greater Britain."

It is interesting to note that half a century before Domville-Fife another Britisher, William Hadfield, had not been very optimistic about the possibilities of European immigration into Brazil. Hadfield wrote, in his *Brazil and the River Plate* (London, 1869), that slave labor was then "an impediment to the more general influx of Europeans . . ." (p. 154). He thought that "large landowners, whose estates are now only partially worked, might devote a portion of them to newcomers . . ." (p. 155). As to the northern provinces of the Empire, it was his impression that "nature" of their "climate" was "more adapted to a people like the Chinese than to Europeans." He even thought that "a further introduction of the African race as free laborers could be very advantageous" (p. 156). More optimistic was Hastings Charles Dent in 1886. In his book *A Year in Brazil* (London, 1886) Dent, describing what he had seen in the valley of the "Rio Camapuão," remarked that there was room there for "immigration on a gigantic scale to one of the healthiest climates that exist, as is shown by the success of the German colony at Petropolis" (p. 134). In this optimism, Dent was preceded by Scully.

much less a "Negro vote," as has been the case in United States politics.

The absence of such solid expressions of national or, rather, sub-national exclusiveness in Brazilian politics seems to indicate that in Brazil the tendency of national or sub-national or ethnic groups to remain apart as monolithic groups in the national culture, or even in the national society, has been much less vigorous than in the United States. The tendency to fusionism, ethnic and cultural, in Brazil has been much more decisive as a basis for attitudes toward national issues of a political or even a social or cultural order than in the United States, or—if one takes the case of the Indian or the Amerindian in particular—in some of the other American republics, in which the so-called "Indian problem" has taken the configuration of an ethnic or at least a culturally or socially ethnocentric revolt against the white or quasi-white groups in power, described by some observers as "oligarchical" in character or as equivalents of "castes" in their composition and behavior.

This is not to suggest that Brazil is, or has been, a paradise compared with its sister republics of the continent or with non-American nations with a national structure similar to its own (that is, made up of ethnically and culturally heterogeneous elements of which one is predominant, if not ethnically, then culturally or politically). What happens, or has happened, is that its most important maladjustments and sharpest crises as a nation have been caused much less by conflicts between sub-national or ethnic groups—eager for control of the national situation or impatient or disgusted at being treated as "inferior" on account of color, race, or ethnic prejudice—than by conflicts between regional cultures or regional groups, owing to the isolation, economic disorganization, and consequent regional differentiation of a few of these groups in relation to the technically and intellectually dominant ones. Even class antagonisms (more powerful in Brazil than race conflicts) have been so interrelated with that other type of maladjustment—interregional maladjustment caused by the isolation that has made some groups tragically archaic in relation to the progressive ones—that sociologists have come to admit that such interregional maladjustments have been, and are still, the most critical and the most dramatic ones in modern Brazilian social, cultural, economic, and political organization or, rather, disorganization. For Brazil, geographically immense as it is, and surprisingly firm as it has been in its cultural and political unity, lacks a dynamic interregional balance based on an economic planning in which industry and agriculture become better interrelated.

The fact is that the nearest approaches to civil war that Brazil has known—for Brazil has never gone through a large-scale civil war like that of the United States or like the so-called Mexican Revolution, both strongly colored by conflicts between races or fought to maintain or alter the status of a particular ethnic group or modify the treatment it should receive from "the Nation" or "the Republic" as a national whole—have been conflicts rather between sub-groups, regionally differentiated in their culture or economic activity, than between "national" or "ethnic" sub-groups badly adjusted to the national community. A characteristic example of this is the so-called Canudos War, subject of Euclides da Cunha's famous book *Os Sertões*, which Samuel Putnam translated into English (*Rebellion in the Backlands*).

The *sertanejos*, a virile and energetic sub-group led by Antonio Conselheiro, a mystic, were not a clearly differentiated ethnic group. They were ethnically a very heterogeneous population. Their unity of purpose was based on regional status and historical backwardness as a population isolated from the

politically and culturally dominant populations by physical location in a distant interior region of Brazil and by the fact that,
thus isolated, they retained in the nineteenth century customs
and cultural patterns that had prevailed in the sixteenth and
seventeenth centuries.

Previous conflicts that had agitated Brazilian life as a colony,
later as an empire, and finally as a republic were of the same
character with one or two insignificant exceptions. One of
these exceptions, the so-called Malê Revolt in Bahia, was a local
slave revolt against the politically, economically, and culturally dominant group by a sub-group that may be considered a
vague "national minority" fighting for its minority rights. It
was largely made of African slaves (an ethnic category) who
followed the Mohammedan faith (a cultural rather than a
national category), and as an African Mohammedan sub-group
felt that they were being oppressed by Catholic whites or
quasi-whites. But even in cases like this, it may be stated that
the ethnic or national category was secondary, though present,
and that the real basis for violent action against the dominant
groups was a revolt against an economic and social status that
the Malês, as a sub-group conscious of its cultural superiority
to other African sub-groups of slaves, felt to be unjust to them.
But it would be going too far to state that Malês or other
African sub-groups in Brazil have acted in a systematic and
continuous way as ethnic groups or sub-groups conscious of
"national" or Pan African rights in the face of a population,
like the Brazilian one since the colonial days, which has been
predominantly European and Christian in the decisive and
characteristic aspects of its pre-national and national culture
and in the decisive and characteristic expressions of its political behavior.

The lack of such an attitude of systematic and continuous
African opposition to European dominance in Brazil seems to

be owing to the fact that European dominance in Portuguese America never became sharply exclusive, as in areas of Anglo-Saxon colonization or even in some parts of Spanish America. That this dominance nonetheless existed in Portuguese America explains why Brazil, in spite of its large non-European population, remains an area characterized by the presence of a European and Christian civilization, preserved, carried on, and developed—with inevitable and desirable changes—not only by pure descendants of Europeans, but also by pure descendants of non-Europeans and by a large number of intermediates, partly European, partly non-European in their ethnic composition and cultural origins.

Professor Eric Fischer seems to be right when in his *The Passing of the European Age—a Study of the Transfer of Western Civilization and Its Renewal in Other Continents*,[5] he claims that in addition to the shift of political power from Europe to non-European areas, there has been a gradual transfer of predominantly European cultural centers from Europe to non-European and especially American countries. Brazil has been one of these American countries (the center of Portuguese literature, for instance, is now Brazil, not Portugal), and the Brazilian case seems to be a positive denial of the theory—held by many white South Africans—that where a population has become ethnically mixed there is no possibility for the survival of a civilization such as the one developed by Christian Europe. Brazil is an area where a national civilization has developed whose main or decisive characteristics are European and Christian—culturally European and sociologically Christian—though non-Europeans have been numerous since the sixteenth century in relation to Europeans, and where non-Christians have been admitted in considerable numbers in

[5] Cambridge, Massachusetts, 1948. This is the thesis maintained throughout the book.

recent decades, through a policy of religious toleration which has put on trial Christian cultural vitality in face of Mohammedan, Japanese, and especially Jewish immigrants.

This does not imply that Brazilians, by being carriers, in a sociological sense, of a civilization that must be considered, in its decisive traits, a renewal of a Christian European civilization, are only and passively an expression of a sub-European civilization. They are increasingly becoming ultra-European. They have been developing more and more as a renewal of Western civilization in the American hemisphere and as an artificial preservation of European values and cultural styles in a tropical area of America in which physical conditions have been and are the first to call for adaptation of the same values and styles to new surroundings. The very fact that the largest part of Brazil is tropical and quasi-tropical has been a stimulus for Brazilian social and cultural differentiation in relation to Europe and for the adaptation by Brazilians of various ethnic and cultural origins—Italian, German, Polish, Japanese, *etc.* —and ways of living and dressing, cookery and architectural styles, recreation and musical tendencies, which represent a pre-American Portuguese adaptation that goes back to Portuguese experience in tropical Africa and in the tropical East, previous to the Lusitanian colonization of Brazil.

Perhaps this explains why immigrants, though able and free to introduce, as they have introduced, into the Brazilian variant of European and Christian civilization, a considerable number of Italian, German, Polish, Japanese, English, and Gallic culturalisms, have shown a general tendency to conform to a Luso-Brazilian structure of that variant. Therefore, this Luso-structure is a national and not a regional phenomenon in Brazil, regional phenomena here being the predominance of diverse ethnic and cultural additions to the same structure: German, in Santa Catharina and part of Rio Grande do Sul; Italian, in

Rio Grande do Sul and São Paulo; Polish, in Paranà; Japanese, in São Paulo and now in part of the Amazonian region; Syrian, also in São Paulo. There were attempts in some parts of southern temperate Brazil, by some of these non-Portuguese ethnic-cultural groups, to keep apart from the Luso-Brazilian or Luso-Afro-Amerindian community or from the Luso-tropical larger community or civilization.

"Luso-tropical civilization" is an expression I have suggested to characterize what seems to me a particular form of behavior and a particular form of accomplishment of the Portuguese in the world: his tendency to prefer the tropics for his extra-European expansion and his ability to remain successfully in the tropics—successfully from a cultural as well as from an ecological point of view—an intermediary between European culture and such tropical cultures as the one found by him in Africa, India, Malaya, and the part of America that became Brazil. This suggestion is not extravagant, for it harmonizes with the tendency among some modern historians and sociologists to give "intercontinental names"—as Mr. Oscar Halecki writes in a recent article, "The Place of Christendom in the History of Mankind," published in the *Journal of World History*,[6] to large intermediate regions of the Eurasian type. As in the case of a Eurasian conception of regional history, the Luso-tropical conception of regional history and regional sociology "seems to open an entirely new field of study," based, as it is, on what Professor Arnold Toynbee calls "intelligible fields of study," made not by individual nations, but by larger transnational communities.

When one sees Brazil as the leading member of that larger community—the Luso-tropical community—one understands better its cultural vitality and the ability or capacity it has shown to resist attempts of such sub-national ethnic groups as

[6] Vol. I, n. 4, Paris, April 1954, 927–50.

the German in Santa Catharina to remain apart from the Brazilian national society and culture, as in a plural or heterogeneous society where groups not only speak different languages, eat different food, wear different clothing, live in different types of dwellings, and worship different gods but also— what makes them unhealthy from a national point of view— have little or no common "will," and, as Professor Eric Walker points out in his *Colonies*, "can therefore have little common political or social life." [7] Such attempts by German or Japanese or Polish sub-groups to lead in Brazil a separate life as super-groups—based on a *mystique* of being not only *different*, but also superior, to the Luso-Brazilian community—have failed. It would be difficult for a sociologist to find in America a national society that in spite of the vast territory it occupies—a sub-continent, indeed—is so psychologically and culturally unified as Portuguese-speaking Brazil, in regard not only to all feelings and cultural styles, but also to the decisive forms that characterize a national society or culture as a unit that may serve as "a clearly understandable field" of historical, sociopsychological, and sociological study.

This seems to be supported by the fact that Brazil does not stand alone as a social-historical and ecological complex, but is part, and a vital part, of that larger Luso-tropical community and, as such, a very satisfactory example of Mr. Oscar Halecki's application of Professor Toynbee's theory to a concrete historical and sociological analysis of regional situations. To Mr. Halecki, as modern historians are looking for units smaller than continents, or at least independent of their physical limits, which could serve as clearly understandable fields of study and thus as preparatory approaches to the tremendous task of a world-wide synthesis, students of civilizations should consider regions rather than nations or continents, in order to grasp "the

[7] Cambridge (England), 1944, p. 73.

concrete relationship between land and man." This recent statement perfectly harmonizes with my early suggestion that in order to understand Brazilian civilization one should consider it as a regional civilization in the tropics, intimately related to other civilizations established and maintained by the Portuguese in tropical lands as dynamically homogeneous societies and not as colonial dependencies under the form of stratified plural societies, as has been the Dutch and the English method in tropical areas.

We cannot understand the present status of non-Portuguese sub-groups in the Brazilian community—structurally a Luso-Brazilian community and part of a Luso-tropical totality—except against a background of the whole; and this whole is a Luso-tropical reality that for more than five centuries has developed through a gradual process into a new type of civilization in the tropics: one that, decisively European and Christian in its main characteristics, has not attempted to be or become exclusively European or Christian in its styles. On the other hand, this lack of exclusiveness has never meant the social plurality or cultural pluralism that, based on European economic, strategic, or narrowly political or superficially ethical motives or aims in a tropical area, allows what an English analyst of colonial problems in the Asiatic tropics, Mr. J. S. Furnivall, has described as a plural society in which different communities live side by side but separately, and have no common interest except in making money.[8]

Tendencies to this sort of pluralism were not entirely absent from the early efforts of Portuguese colonization in the tropics. Even today they are noticeable in some sub-areas of the Luso-tropical area, which includes tropical lands in different parts of the world. But the fact is that such tendencies never became

[8] J. S. Furnivall: *Colonial Policy and Practice: A Comparative Study of Burma and Netherlands India* (Cambridge [England], 1948).

so strong as to overshadow, in any of these sub-areas, a characteristic trend common to all of them: the tendency toward a common pattern and fundamental unity—both social and psychological—in spite of what ethnologists and ethnographers may consider, by comparing differences in ethnic composition and even cultural configurations in these various Luso-tropical sub-areas, as "a many-colored patchwork of diversity."

This common pattern comes from the fact that Luso-tropical societies (and Brazil is one of them: the most advanced of all, economically and culturally, and the most politically mature also) roughly correspond to that almost ideal condition for human and social development in the tropics—development admittedly from a European point of view and based on a European conception of progress—outlined by Professor Eric A. Walker, in his excellent essay on *Colonies* already referred to. This almost ideal condition is made possible by the existence—as he admits, and as the Luso-tropical civilization confirms to be a present-day reality—of "mixed societies" that "are homogeneous enough because their various racial groups belong to the same civilization and have the same fundamental ideas, regardless of pigmentation or the shape of the nose." This "happy situation," he adds, "is still rare," the rule being for societies in the tropics under European influence to consist of "a number of more or less self-conscious groups, often marked off from one another by distinctive colors, which try to live their separate lives within a single political framework." Professor Walker seems to me to be right when he generalizes that "color is the world problem of minorities translated into tropical terms with this difference, that in many colonies the depressed class constitutes the majority." [9]

The position of ethnic minorities in terms of color or race has never been a major problem for Brazil, either in its pre-

[9] Ibid., p. 72.

national or national days. It has been always a minor problem
for Brazilians, socially and politically insignificant for most of
them. In the afore-mentioned societies established by Europeans in the tropics and in sister-republics of Brazil where the
"Indian problem"—the problem of the Amerindian in face of
such national developments as those of Peru, Bolivia, Ecuador
—has taken the most dramatic forms, the relations between
ethnic groups have even become the real motives for civil wars
and revolutions. But in Brazil the assimilation not only of
Amerindians, but also of African Negroes into a national society whose decisive traits have been culturally and psychologically Portuguese and Christian, has been a relatively peaceful and smooth process, with only a few instances of cultural
and class conflict in which race antagonism has been also present. In Brazilian politics there was no time when a predominantly ethnic problem presented itself as an important issue, as
has been the case with the "Indian problem" in Peru, Mexico,
Bolivia, and other Latin American republics. The very peaceful way by which the abolition of slavery was accomplished in
Brazil is well known to all students of Latin American social
history.

As to the problem of the German, Polish, and Japanese
"minorities" during the Second World War, it was rather a
deliberate attempt of Nazi and para-Nazi powers to apply to
Brazil a Nazi thesis, politically valid in other areas where ethnic
minorities have really developed as separate groups, than a
problem created by Brazilian conditions. It is true that in some
sub-regions of southern Brazil, political parties before 1930
found it convenient to treat Brazilian voters of German or of
Italian origin as "German voters" or "Italian voters." Through
intermediaries of the same origin, these voters usually voted for
the government, not without claiming for their particular cultural rather than ethnic groups certain privileges that normally

and according to the already well-established Brazilian traditions should not be given them: the right to have their own
schools, where the entire teaching should be in their national
language, for instance.

When a regime, if not para-Fascist as claimed by some critics,
at least authoritarian, was established in 1937, with Getulio
Vargas as its chief, and not having to depend upon voters of
any kind, carried out in southern Brazil (sometimes with the
collaboration of the Brazilian Army) a nationalistic policy that
may have had its excesses, but was beneficial to the development of the country as a single community, it was inspired by
the old Luso-tropical tendency toward predominantly but not
exclusively Portuguese populations or cultures established in
the tropics, toward the growth of national or pre-national
communities and not of plural societies of the heterogeneous
type established by the Dutch or the English in tropical places.

That nationalistic policy prevented Germans, Poles, Japanese, and Italians from having schools with all teaching in their
national languages, as if they were not in Brazil, but in some
un-Brazilian territory. Other measures were adopted, some
of them too severe for rigid enforcement. They implied an attempt to uproot Brazilians of non-Portuguese origin violently
and rapidly from their maternal cultures, so capable of contributing, within reasonable limits of cultural pluralism, to the
enrichment, through regional sub-cultures colored by this or
that non-Portuguese culture, of the general national culture of
Brazil. Analysts and interpreters of this general culture who
consider it a particularly happy adaptation of a plastic type of
European and Christian civilization to the tropics and to
tropical cultures, without claiming that it should be exclusively
or almost exclusively Portuguese and Christian, do not fail to
recognize how the Brazilian nation may benefit from a freer
participation and expression by even non-Christian Brazilians.

The only restriction would be against non-Portuguese and non-Christian Brazilians claiming the right to live apart from the Luso-tropical community that Brazil has been for more than four centuries, with a language and basic processes of adaptation of Europeans to the tropics which time has proved to be sociologically valid and sound processes.

Broadly speaking, this accommodation has been reached in a fairly satisfactory way and since the first non-Portuguese European groups established themselves in Brazil, their normal tendency or attitude—exceptions do not invalidate the general rule—has been to adopt Luso-tropical values as well as methods of living in the tropics and of dealing with tropical nature, tropical populations, and tropical human cultures. By doing so, some of them have been able to introduce Italianisms, Germanisms, Anglicisms, Gallicisms, *etc.*, into Brazilian culture in a way that has proved valuable to this culture without taking Brazilian society to the dangerous excesses of pluralism or introducing in Brazilian politics the equally dangerous habit of groups voting solidly one way or another as narrowly ethnic or national groups.

It is also interesting to note that Brazilians of Italian origin, for instance, who are so numerous in the state of São Paulo and in parts of the state of Rio Grande do Sul, instead of concentrating in a political party or voting as a monolithic group, spread themselves in so many parties that it seems impossible to link "Italian vote" in modern Brazil to any particular political ideology or tendency. Some of them are conservative, and have as their representative Senhor Cyril Junior, a brilliant lawyer and an eloquent orator, who presided for some time over the Brazilian Chamber of Deputies with the tact and the finesse of an Italian cardinal intimately acquainted with the most characteristically Luso-tropical linguistic subtleties as well as with psychological variants of behavior of Brazilians from the various regions of Brazil. In this he had a predecessor, in the early days of the Republican regime, in Lauro Müller, the Brazilian son of German colonists, born in Santa Catharina, who rapidly became as astute a politician as a Bahia-born Brazilian. He was for years a presidential possibility, just as David Campista—the Brazilian son of a German Jew, and a very capable member of the National Parliament who also revealed his political talent as a Minister of Finance—came very near being chosen and elected President of the Republic. Neither in his case nor in the case of Müller had the fact that they were the sons of non-Portuguese colonists anything to do with their failure to become President.

It is true that Brazilian sons of non-Portuguese colonists who are active in politics or even in the industrial and commercial life of the nation have, in many cases, shown a lack of finer moral scruples which has given them the reputation of being always morally or ethically inferior. This is true of some of the most prominent leaders of political groups today: Brazilians with non-Portuguese surnames who are considered to display the reverse of public spirit or of elementary ethics in political activity, and are given as examples of the fact that the sons of "immigrants" are morally inferior to the sons of old Brazilian families as political leaders, businessmen, and industrial pioneers. Of course, sons of immigrants who follow such careers are freer than the members of old and well-known families from certain moral controls that act upon men deeply rooted in their towns or countries or regions. Some of them, having ceased to be influenced by the moral standards of their parents' national group, have not acquired a new national morality: they are, therefore, transition men who easily succumb to the temptations that surround political, industrial, and commercial leaders in such a phase—also a transition phase—of rapid industrialization as the one that Brazil has been going through in the last few decades.

It would be, however, unfair to accept as valid the generalization that the sons of immigrants, when engaged in those activities, act always as morally or ethically inferior citizens. There are too many examples to the contrary. Men such as Dr. Raul Pilla—the son of an Italian colonist who has been for years a political leader and is a distinguished Brazilian known for his moral integrity both as a private citizen and a politician and member of the National Parliament—are not rare, but almost as numerous as the men of the "transition type" who are willing to do anything to make a fortune in business or in industry or in politics. One should not forget, in this connection, that men of the pathological "transition type" are as numerous among Brazilians of old Portuguese origin who come from agrarian or pastoral provinces of northern or central Brazil to the industrial centers of southern Brazil as they are among the sons of immigrants. They are the victims of the same adverse environment, the same absence of moral controls, so much more powerful in one's ancestral environment than in a comparatively new one.

Here one faces a problem not peculiar to Brazil, but common to all communities in which most of the sons of immigrants go through a period of transition that is also one of incomplete assimilation. Therefore, instead of being positive in the part they play in society and politics, some of them become noted for a negative activity: negative from an ethical point of view.

In dealing with almost the same problem—that of immigrants who have been incompletely assimilated—as it presents itself in the United States, Professor Max Ascoli pointed out a few years ago that some of them "have become Americans before they were ever Italians, largely unaware as they were, as rustic Italian peasants, of the Italian civilization." "To a peasant of Sicily," he suggested, "Milan would have been as much of an alien city as New York." And as to the "second generation"—that is, the first generation of Americans born in the United States of Italian parents—it has been remarked by students of the subject that a regular political career has been difficult for them, on account of having to work "within the framework of Jewish or Irish machines." Hence their attempts to attain success through other methods. In Brazil there are fortunately no Jewish or Irish "machines" in politics; and sons of non-Portuguese immigrants have at present wide opportunities to rise to positions of authority and leadership, not only in regular political careers, but also through ecclesiastical, military, technical, and commercial careers equally regular or normal.

This explains the increasing number of non-Portuguese family names in the "society" columns of newspapers; the increasing number, also, of such names among the members of the National Parliament and the Brazilian diplomatic service; and even in the army, the air force, and the navy—in which, for some time, only such aristocratic foreign names as Hoonholtz appeared beside old Portuguese names among the officers. This explains also a number of bishops of the Roman Catholic Church in Brazil who are equally the sons or grandsons of non-Portuguese immigrants, of peasant or humble origin, and who have outnumbered in these and other positions of authority and leadership the descendants of the old agrarian or urban aristocracy of Iberian origin, sometimes—as in the case of the first cardinal of Latin America, who was a Brazilian from an old Pernambuco family—with an Indian, that is, Amerindian princess or cacique or captain, among their ancestors.

Sons and grandsons of modest immigrants are rapidly rising in Brazil to leadership in business, industry,[1] politics, religion, the press; in medicine, men like Mario Pinotti; in science, like Cesar Lattes; in art, like Candido Portinari; in architecture, like Henrique Mindlin; in music, like Mignone. And also to prominence in literature, an activity in which some of them are surpassing the descendants of old Portuguese families as masters of the subtleties of the Portuguese language, some as philologists, others as literary artists. Almost on a level, in some respects, with Machado de Assis—the greatest writer of fiction Brazil has ever produced, who was of Portuguese ancestry, but was also African in his ethnic condition and plebeian in his social origin—there are now in Brazilian literature a number of authors of non-Portuguese origin who are greatly contributing toward developing the Portuguese language of Brazil into one of the great modern literary languages of the world: men like Augusto Meyer, the scholarly and enthusiastic analyst of Portuguese classics; Vianna Moog, the novelist and essayist; Menotti del Pichia, the nationalistic poet; Augusto Frederico Schmidt, another poet with nationalistic as well as universal-

[1] In his chapter on "Industry, Commerce, and Finance," in *Brazil* (edited by Lawrence F. Hill, Berkeley and Los Angeles, 1947), Professor Frederic William Ganzert has this to say about the relation between immigration and industrialization in modern Brazil: "The impetus to industrialization in the twentieth century came as a result of the overproduction of coffee, attended by the release of a large number of workers to industry. . . . As the tide of immigration from Europe brought in new workers, as railroads and highways were built and abundant sources of cheap electric power were utilized, industrial plants multiplied and new and important markets were developed" (pp. 254-5). Visiting Brazil in the last decade of the nineteenth century, Maturin M. Ballou had the impression that Italian immigrants were not of the most desirable type, most of them "giving the police force a great deal of trouble" (*Equatorial America*, Boston and New York, 1892, p. 163). A rather sweeping generalization, but characteristic of the attitude of some Anglo-Saxons at that time toward Italian immigrants. The fact is that Italians have been a valuable element in Brazilian life, showing a plasticity in adapting themselves to tropical conditions second only to that of the Portuguese.

istic learnings; Sergio Milliet, the literary critic; Marcos Konder, the young poet; Castão Cruls, a novelist who has specialized in the description both of the Amazonian region and of the Rio bourgeois society; Raul Bopp, another specialist in the Amazonian region, which he has extolled in good modernistic verse. When assimilation goes as far as to include literature of the most lyrical and intimately introspective kind, this means that Brazilians of European non-Portuguese origin are really becoming a new force in Brazilian life and culture, by the side of descendants of Portuguese, Amerindian, and Negro, through old instruments of expression such as the Portuguese language and the Portuguese lyrical tradition.

[VI]

Brazilian Foreign Policy as Conditioned by Brazil's Ethnic, Cultural, and Geographical Situation

B razil's national status is not an expression of race-consciousness, for no single pure or nearly pure race made the country. No European people engaged in colonizing America was less animated by a race-superiority or race-purity complex than the Portuguese, an almost non-European nation. Its unity or purity *mystique* was of religion or religious status, not one of race.

Brazil's national status is an ethnically negative one. Few modern nations are so heterogeneous from an ethnic point of view as the only Portuguese-speaking republic of the American continent. In Brazil no ethnic minority or majority really exercises an absolute, systematic, and permanent cultural and social domination over politically or economically less active elements of the population. Among a few whites there may be a desire to dominate the many colored members of the Brazilian community, but these few are too inarticulate as an ethnic or cultural aristocracy to be considered seriously as a decided imperial influence on domestic cultural policy or as a significant factor in determining, in whatever way a culture or race-superiority complex might affect it, the foreign policy of Brazil.

As a national community, Brazil, it seems to me, has to be interpreted as a community increasingly conscious of its status or destiny as a social and ethnic democracy and aware of its pioneering in this field. As such, it is second only to the Soviet Union as a community quasi-officially, if not officially, committed to a frankly equalitarian racial policy. Even Mexico seems to be less tolerant of Negroes than Brazil is. From my drawing such comparisons, however, no one should understand me as implying that Brazil is a perfect ethnic democracy. It is not.

Brazil has become prominent as a community inclined toward ethnic democracy because of the contrast between its racial policy and that followed by most other modern nations. In many countries even organized Christianity has been affected in such a way by racial interests or by the national or class element in race discrimination that one is led to regard the attitude of some Roman Catholic orders that refuse to admit Negroes or mulattoes as distinctly less Christian than the attitude of secular or semi-religious organizations in Brazil which admit colored persons freely. When C. S. Stewart, an officer in the United States Navy, visited Brazil during the middle of the nineteenth century, he was impressed by "the fearfully mongrel aspect" of most of the population; but at the same time a Portuguese institution that has flourished in America since the early days of the colonization of Brazil, the *Misericordia*, made him an admirer of race tolerance as he saw it practiced in the Brazilian Empire. Stewart pointed out the fact that the doors of the *Misericordia* hospitals in Rio were open at all hours, night and day, to the sick of both sexes, of all religions, and of every country and color, without any form or condition of admittance.[1] In qualification of Stewart's praise of Brazilian tolerance one must admit that until a comparatively recent date Brazilians were famous for their intolerance in regard to burial places: not only pagan or unbaptized Negroes, but also Protestant Europeans and Americans were denied the right to be buried in the so-called sacred or holy cemeteries, the official ones. But this particular intolerance affected only the dead.

Some modern students of race policies think that the Soviet theory of equal opportunity for men of all races goes farther than most Christian agencies in removing not only the psychological and emotional causes of race conflicts, but also their economic roots. This is the view of Professor Hans Kohn, who writes also that the Soviet Union is now the only large area inhabited by many races which is free, as far as governmental agencies are concerned, of any form of race prejudice; the only one where "the rational belief in the complete equality of all races has become the official creed, and energetic educational efforts are being made to raise the social and economic

[1] *Brazil and La Plata: The Personal Record of a Cruise* (New York, 1856), pp. 228–9.

conditions of the underprivileged races." [2] I have not visited the Soviet Union, and cannot confirm Professor Kohn's statements. But I do know that Brazil, though far from being entirely free of race prejudice, has a number of official, semi-official, and private institutions more advanced than some Christian organizations in dealing with problems of racial relations in a democratic and Christian way.

So general is this liberal attitude in Brazil that international policy is bound to be conditioned by it: if not always through the initiative of official leaders and conventional diplomats, at least under the pressure of its non-official but effective intellectual leaders, whose influence is growing every day, both among the popular elements that form basic Brazilian public opinion and among the intellectual youth and the intelligentsia. In the matter of attitudes toward race-relations problems, no more natural ally of the Soviet Union is to be found among the most powerful nations of America than Brazil. And considering, as we should consider, the increasing importance of such problems in international life and in the field of interhuman relations, we may readily anticipate that such solidarity will be more than a vaguely humanitarian one; it will probably be the basis for common action or common initiative in the field of international law, in which Russia and Brazil will have a right to suggest important changes of attitude and practice. Their suggestions will be based, not on vague or purely sentimental theories, but on the concrete experience of each of the two communities as areas almost free, or increasingly free, of race prejudice, race conflict, and race discrimination.

The Soviet Union and Brazil, though fundamentally different in their conceptions of social and economic organization,

[2] "Race Conflict," *Encyclopedia of the Social Sciences*, XIII, 40. See also Hans Kohn's *Orient and Occident* (New York, 1934) and Paul Lewinson's *Race, Class, and Party* (London, 1932).

will probably join in the near future as leaders of a movement toward making racial equality an international issue similar to the one that united such different communities as China and Japan in 1919. As we are reminded by a historian of international relations: "On only one issue debated at Paris [in 1919] were the Chinese and Japanese of one mind and that was on the proposal to amend the League of Nations Covenant so as to recognize racial equality. France and Italy acted in favor of the measure, but Britain, Australia, and New Zealand were bitterly opposed. The proposal was adopted by a vote of eleven to six with Wilson and Colonel House not voting; but Wilson, who was presiding, ruled that it was not effective because the vote was not unanimous." [3] Whatever Wilson's motives, Japan blamed him and grew bitter against the United States. In Brazil the decision had little repercussion at the time and hardly affected Wilson's enormous popularity. But Brazil is becoming increasingly conscious of the fact that its mixed population gives its people a feeling of unusual solidarity with Asiatic, African, and Indo-Hispanic nations.

At present Brazil occupies a more important place on the international scene than it did in 1919. Since that year its intellectual and economic development has been considerable: its writers, artists, and scientists are now freer to express—sometimes to glorify—the non-European or non-white aspects of Brazilian culture. This change means that Brazil will probably take a leading role in promulgating the racial-equality principle.

There is one request already anticipated from China: that the future world-security organization acknowledge the doctrine of racial equality. And Russia is constantly agitating the racial-equality issue. Speaking to Mexicans, the late Soviet Ambassador to Mexico, Constantin A. Oumansky, said that in

[3] Hallett Abend: *Treaty Ports* (New York, 1944), p. 242.

war and peace Stalin had put foremost "the abolition of racial discrimination"; and also that, at the Moscow Conference of the three powers, Stalin projected into Russian foreign policy a principle already established in the Russian constitution: the abolition of racial discrimination.

At the time of Ambassador Oumansky's remarks Mr. Carleton Beals, well-known American student of Latin American affairs, was told by a high Mexican foreign-affairs official—a fervent admirer of the United States—that because of American racial discrimination, "so greatly feared in Latin America, and because of our [United States] support of dictatorships, we were on the way to losing our moral and political leadership in the countries to the south of us; that the people and governments would turn more and more to the Soviet Union." [4] This is precisely what is happening. Disappointed liberals of Latin America—in the face of a United States foreign policy that they believe to be as definite in its support of Franco's Spain as that of the most conservative Tories of Great Britain, and equally undemocratic in its attitude on the racial-equality issue—are leaning toward the British Socialists and particularly toward Russia, now considered by them (perhaps with some naïveté) the same messianic nation as the France of the French Revolution was for their eighteenth-century ancestors and as the United States of Washington, Jefferson, and Woodrow Wilson was to Latin American idealists of the early nineteenth century and of twenty-five years ago.

An American expert on international affairs wrote some years ago [5] that there was scarcely a country in the world where Russia's influence was not on the march. According to him there was only one way in which the Western nations, for

---

[4] See Carleton Beals: "The Soviet Wooing of Latin America," *Harper's Magazine*, August 1944, p. 212.
[5] *Time*, November 13, 1944.

whom even an economically secure life without political liberty is not worth living, could meet this challenge: by freeing themselves from want, fear, and suffering while remaining free politically. This would be the ideal solution for Latin Americans, who are still fundamentally Hispanic in their love of personal dignity and freedom and in their distaste for rigid regimentation. But their disappointment with Anglo-Saxon liberalism is increasingly bitter. This explains why, with France reduced to a second-rate nation and Spain paralyzed by what not a few Latin Americans consider a semi-Fascist regime, some of them still look to Russia as to a messianic nation. Even Catholic priests have taken this attitude; the Bishop of Maura was one of them. He went so far that he left the Church and founded a sect of his own which has become something of a burlesque.

Brazilians have a way of expressing their political or ideological leanings in the names they give their children. There was a time when children were named for saints of the Catholic calendar and from sacred history. Then came the independence movement, and children were given Amerindian names. Still later, they were called after French, Spanish, and Spanish American revolutionary or romantic heroes: Ubirajara, Danton, Lamartine, Lafayette, Benjamin Constant, Chateaubriand, Cid, Bolívar. (I had a great-great-uncle whose name, instead of being that of a Portuguese saint, was Voltaire.) Then came another phase: names were taken from Greek literature and Roman history—a phase that corresponded to the reign of Dom Pedro II, a good man, but a somewhat pedantic student of the classics. With the Republican movement, anti-monarchical and extremely liberal parents began to give their children names taken from British and United States history: Milton, Newton, Washington, Jefferson, Lincoln, Gladstone, Franklin. Some anti-clerical parents went so far as to name their children after Luther and Calvin. Juárez was a name given to many. And soon after the First World War, numerous Brazilian children were given the name of Wilson. It is significant that at present there is a tendency among some Brazilian parents to choose names from Russian novels and Russian history.

There seems to be no doubt that Russia's standing on the race issue is fascinating to liberal and perhaps naïve Brazilians, while the United States prejudice against the half-breed continues to be an obstacle to the development of really friendly relations between the two peoples. Some years ago a Yale professor, Hiram Bingham, wrote that the fundamental difference in racial attitude between the average Anglo-Saxon American and the average Latin American made it difficult for the Anglo-Saxon Americans "to treat fairly" with their southern neighbors.[6] This difficulty has not entirely disappeared with the "Good Neighbor" policy, and it will be probably used against the United States by clever Russian diplomats and even by shrewd Britons if power politics continues to dominate international relations, with Latin America as one of the best markets for imperial, if not imperialistic, nations during the next decades.

Some students of international affairs think that instead of sending to countries like Brazil diplomats of the conventional type, who associate only with men in power, church authorities, and elegant society lions, the United States government would be wise to appoint men who could acquaint Brazilians with the work done in the United States for more democratic racial relations—men familiar with the activities of the Council against Intolerance in America, the Council on Intercultural Relations, the Bureau of Intercultural Education, the National Association for the Advancement of Colored People, the Fed-

[6] *The Monroe Doctrine* (New Haven, 1915), p. 24.

eral Council of Churches of Christ in America, the National
Conference of Christians and Jews, several large labor unions,
the Fair Employment Practices Committee, and the Bureau
of Indian Affairs. Very few Brazilians know anything about
the splendid work being done by liberal and Christian leaders
in this country for more democratic relations between whites
and Indians, whites and Orientals, whites and Negroes; they
hear more about ethnic democracy in Russia. Even now, with
desegregation in the schools of the United States—a courageous measure, to be applied to southern states—little is
known by Latin Americans of these new attitudes of Anglo-
Americans in regard to Negroes or "colored."

The results of a policy of race equality such as is officially
followed in modern Russia—though it seems that anti-Semitism has made itself felt in recent Soviet affairs—or of approxi-
mate race equality such as has long been practiced in Brazil do
not seem to confirm the fears of those who speak or write of
mongrelization as a biological catastrophe. On the contrary,
the evidence appears to favor those who describe the results of
miscegenation as attractive even aesthetically. The theorists of
"racial integrity" need to revamp their arguments against race
mixture or to invent new ones. The Russians, a large number
of whom are mixed-bloods, are certainly far from being de-
based or decadent peoples, or "passive," "feminine" races, as
some prejudiced anthropologists and sociologists of the nineteenth century and early twentieth century called them. Look
at statements like these: "The Russians, with their strong infusion of Mongoloid blood, excel rather in suffering and endurance than in action that brings freedom" (Fritz Lentz); or
"The Russian folk . . . is by temperament passive, rather
gentle, ready to obey, feminine rather than masculine in character" (F. R. Radosavlevich); or "The European stocks with
a strong infusion of mongoloid blood have a rather heavy

mentality; they cling to the traditional," and "advanced technical methods are much weaker there than in the regions where the nordic race predominates" (Lentz). In recent years such statements have been applied oftener to countries like Brazil than to Russia. But Brazil's development has already begun to refute those generalizations. Nor are the Mexican people, likewise mixed-bloods, regarded by modern anthropologists as "passive," as they were by critics in the days of the Díaz dictatorship.

Not all German, English, and American scientists who have been to Brazil have been so pessimistic over "the fearfully mongrel aspect of most of the population" as was the French diplomat and littérateur Gobineau or the American Navy officer C. S. Stewart. The most authoritative ones, in point of scientific training and sociological vision—men like Martius in the early nineteenth century, Alfred Russel Wallace, Bates, and Professor Konrad Guenther, not to mention specialists on race mixture like Professors Rüdiger Bilden and Donald Pierson—have written almost enthusiastically about the social and aesthetic results of race amalgamation in Brazil. "Mongoloid" or "Negroid" Brazil is credited with creativeness in more than one field of artistic and technical activity; it is being praised also for its traditional race tolerance.

One of the most intelligent travelers who visited Brazil during the first half of the nineteenth century was an American, the Reverend Walter Colton, U.S.N. He noticed in relation to the African slaves that "their freedom in many cases lies within their reach and may be obtained, as it often is, by industry and frugality." He also observed:

"When free, he [the slave] goes to the ballot-box, and is eligible to a seat in the national legislature. Nor would anybody here go into hysterics should he marry a woman

whose skin should be a shade whiter than his own. It is for us Americans to preach up humanity, freedom and equality and then turn up our blessed noses if an African takes a seat at the same table on board a steamboat. The misery is that they who preach equality the loudest are generally the last to practice it." [7]

Two other American divines who visited Brazil during the reign of Dom Pedro II reacted in the same way to the ethnically democratic situation they found there; I refer to J. C. Fletcher and D. P. Kidder, authors of *Brazil and the Brazilians*. The Reverend Mr. Fletcher wrote:

"Some of the most intelligent men that I have met with in Brazil—men educated at Paris and Coimbra—were of African descent, whose ancestors were slaves. Thus, if a man has freedom, money and merit, no matter how black may be his skin, no place in society is refused him. It is surprising also to observe the ambition and the advancement of some of these men with negro blood in their veins."

Though he admitted a certain, though by no means strong, prejudice in favor of men of pure white descent, he pointed out that in the colleges, and in the medical, law, and theological schools, there was no distinction of color. [8]

I have already mentioned the book published in 1926 by a scientifically trained American, Mr. Roy Nash, as one of the best ever published about Brazil. Referring to the miscegenation process, he says that it "has not gone so far in Brazil that there are not still large numbers of unmixed Portuguese, Indians, and Negroes, still some consciousness of color and even more of caste; but it has gone so far that one may expect its completion perhaps within five or six generations." [9] The

[7] *Deck and Port* (New York, 1850), pp. 112–13.
[8] *Brazil and the Brazilians* (Boston, 1879), p. 133.
[9] Nash: op. cit., p. 60.

question: "Does Brazil's four hundred years of history prove that the admixture of widely different stocks spells degeneration?" is emphatically answered by the American author: "By no manner of means. The indictment of a ruling class, of an economic system, of a false philosophy is not the indictment of a people. . . . Many are the Brazilians who know better than I that . . . of the hardburnt bricks of freely cooperating labor, public health and popular education must be built the Brazil of the Future." [1]

This is also the view of able and conscientious Brazilian students of the social history and the ethnic and social conditions of their country like Roquette Pinto. They have pointed out, in sociological essays and anthropological works, the pressing need for Brazil's pursuing a policy of social recuperation. Regions where slavery has been for centuries the dominant system of social organization are similar to areas that have suffered devastation in long or successive wars: they need social recuperation, not the replacement of the mestizo population by an "Aryan" one.

Brazil's foreign policy is bound to be increasingly affected by the progressive change in the economic basis of its social structure from slavery and a semi-feudal regime of one-crop agriculture and latifundium to an economically and socially democratic regime marked by diversification of crops and fragmentation of large estates. This change is enabling Brazil to attract the best type of immigrants instead of being forced to look to Chinese coolies as substitutes for slave labor. It also makes it possible for Brazilians to raise the standards of living of those descendants of Indians, Negroes, and Europeans who have remained ill-fed and almost orientally poor, as well as landless, in a country famous for its immensely large and undeveloped estates and extensive unoccupied land. It seems to

[1] Ibid., pp. 356–7.

anthropologists and sociologists who know Brazil well that the poor or miserable part of the Brazilian population, whether wholly white or mestizo, needs only to be given better opportunities to reveal its capacity and strength. After his contact with the Brazilians of central Brazil, Theodore Roosevelt wrote that the "endurance and the bull-like strength" of the men of the Brazilian common people whom he knew, as well as the "intelligence" of the officers of the Brazilian army with whom he traveled—most of them men of mixed blood—made him "wonder at the ignorance of those who do not realize the energy and power that are so often possessed by, and that may be so readily developed in the men of the tropics." [2]

Few responsible Brazilians, particularly of the younger generation, have any doubts concerning the energy and capacity of their landless and diseased fellow countrymen who have not been given a real opportunity to develop their qualities and to become efficient contributors to the growth of Brazil. Actually many consider the integration of these men into the community as a creative element as more important than the attracting of immigrants to Brazil. Both problems—that of developing native man power through education, sanitation, and the democratizing of land ownership and of attracting immigrants—make it imperative that Brazil adopt an increasingly democratic attitude in regard to human relations at home and relations with foreign countries.

Brazilian foreign policy is conditioned by the fact that Brazil, now in a phase of industrialization, mechanizing of agriculture, and scientific colonizing of such areas as the Amazon, needs immigrants. But not only is the foreign policy affected by such a need; domestic policy also is concerned, for no colonization of Brazil by free men is possible without a more democratic disposition of public lands.

[2] *Through the Brazilian Wilderness* (New York, 1914), p. 254.

Lord Bryce regretted the absence from Brazil, as well as from the other South American countries he visited, of small landowners whose interest in good administration would be intelligent and strong enough to rouse them to their civic duty.[3] Only in certain areas of southern Brazil is a development of this sort taking place. In this connection, one aspect of the problem should again be pointed out; in the colonization of most areas of northern and central Brazil it will be impossible for the pioneering immigrants really to succeed as individuals. Enlarging the tradition of the *bandeiras*, they will have to be organized in co-operative groups and protected by the Brazilian government or by special organizations.

As individuals the Brazilians from the northeast who have gone to the Amazon area have been heroic. Some of them have done wonders for the colonization of that area. But little can be accomplished in this way. The Brazilian colonization of the Amazon will probably have to be a co-operative task in which the army will find an opportunity to do an even greater work in promoting large-scale sanitation of a tropical region than the one the United States Army did in Panama.

Some Brazilians have been insisting on the employment of the army, when it is not engaged in national defense, in contributing to public works; for instance, in the construction of railways, which serve both a strategic and an economic and cultural purpose. This is an old French idea not very well received by French orthodox advocates of an army for strictly military purposes only; nevertheless, a Frenchman was bold enough to suggest, years ago, that if the nation co-operates with the army in time of war, it is but just that the army should assist the nation in time of peace. To a certain extent this has been done in Brazil. Many Americans have heard of the remarkable work of General Rondon and other officers of the

[3] Bryce: op. cit., p. 537.

Brazilian army among the savage tribes of central Brazil and in the construction of railroads and telegraph lines in that part of the country. Work of this sort may be accomplished on a larger scale by the Brazilian army in the Amazon area, colonization of which is too tremendous a task to be accomplished by individuals.

The idea of the semi-military development of a region is not original with the suggestion that the Amazon be thus colonized. More than half a century ago a Brazilian, Henrique Velloso de Oliveira, presented a plan for the colonization by "industrial armies" both of old areas dominated for centuries by feudal landowners and of virgin lands. The members of the so-called "industrial armies," instead of acting like individual pioneers, would act under a plan. Co-operation would be their method; diversification of agriculture would be developed; and pioneering activities would be stimulated.

The basic element of such "industrial armies" would be Brazilian young men. But to them would be added, as soon as prosperity came to them, European colonists. A number of European girls would be imported to be the wives of the successful or prosperous Brazilian members of the "industrial armies" who would prefer to marry blondes. Among the Brazilians there would be white descendants of Europeans, but also a large number of mixed-bloods. Portuguese, Spanish, Italian, and even German immigrants, male and female, have not hesitated to marry Brazilians of Indian and Negro origin; and in view of this fact it would be easy to develop ethnic democracy among the "industrial armies."

It seems to me unfortunate that Oliveira's plan was never put into practice. Probably it would have solved some of the problems connected with the European colonization of Brazil, especially that of the democratic disposition or redistribution of public and feudal lands. As I said before, this problem remains a serious one to be faced by Brazil before good European peasants and agriculturists come there to establish themselves as farmers free from strict control of agencies of their own governments such as the Japanese and also some European groups have had. Control of immigrants is the Brazilian government's business, though agreements may be reached through which European or other governments may be allowed the right to have their representatives act, not as supervisors, but as advisers to and collaborators with the Brazilian government concerning migration problems of common interest.

Brazilian foreign policy will be influenced for a long time by Brazil's relations with countries likely to continue to enrich Portuguese America with their blood, their human values, and the work of their peasants, laborers, and artisans, for Brazil needs immigrants. To meet this need, it is the hope of Brazil to receive from the various countries of Europe a large number of agricultural and industrial workers. Some students of the subject think that the Italian farmer fits into the Brazilian way of life especially well. But it is to the political as well as to the economic and cultural interest of Brazil to receive as many agricultural immigrants from Portugal as possible; they and the Spaniards are of the type basically needed.

Brazil's foreign policy will be greatly affected—is being affected already—by the rapid industrial development of the country. Portuguese America is said to be ready to produce all the steel that she needs for her own use, and eventually some to be exported. This portends an important change in the country's economic as well as political life and relations. From the point of view of an international policy, diversification of production and industrialization means that the Brazilian economy is ceasing to be passive or semi-colonial. As Mr. Normano points out so well in his *Brazil: A Study of Economic Types:* "the monoproductive character of Brazilian economy has made the country a captive of world prices" and "the change in the leading products influences not only national but international politics too. . . . The chief market for sugar, gold, and cotton was Europe. Rubber and coffee were the bridge to the United States." [4] But with the development of industries, Brazilian economy is becoming an active one. Oil may become an important factor in this development. This means a greater independence in political attitudes, and the end, or the beginning of the end, of semi-colonialism.

Through the expansion of its textile industry, Brazil is also becoming an exporter of cotton cloth to other Latin American nations. Some of it is made in response to the need for adapting wearing apparel to a tropical climate and according to the standards of taste prevailing in a large part of the Brazilian population and an equally large part of the Spanish American —especially Spanish-Indo-American—population. But some of the Brazilian cotton and silk products have been sold in the Latin American republics lying in the temperate zone. This fact means another transformation in Brazilian economic life and economic relations, for this widening of trade is stimulating the development in Latin America of what someone has called "a mutual discovery phase."

Closer relations between Brazil and the other American republics and between Brazil and Portuguese Africa, Portuguese Asia, the Cape Verde Islands, the Azores, Madeira, and Portugal will probably result from the development of air transportation. Brazil already has a factory for airplane motors. Because of the development of industrial areas, its many and valuable resources, and its technical and intellectual progress, Brazil is in many important respects becoming the American leader of the entire Portuguese-speaking world: of a Luso-tropical system of civilization led in Europe by Portugal. This

[4] Pp. 55–6.

world may soon become a federation with a common citizenship and a number of other common rights and responsibilities. Reciprocal duties will then be involved. It is interesting to note the growing tendency of the new generations in Portuguese India,[5] Portuguese Africa, in the Cape Verde Islands, and, to a lesser extent, in the Azores, to follow inspirations and suggestions from Brazil.

The new Brazilian literature and art, and recent advances in social and scientific studies in Brazil under intellectual leaders and through the use of methods more daring, aggressive, and modern than those known in Portugal seem to be affecting the traditional system of interrelations in the Portuguese-speaking world in such a way that Brazil is becoming its intellectual, artistic, and scientific center. Julio Dantas, a distinguished Portuguese intellectual, has said that the best writers of the Portuguese language are now in Brazil; this is also the opinion of other Portuguese critics. And some of the most prominent Portuguese scholars are now established in Brazil, where they teach, or write, or have their books published. Nevertheless, Portugal remains the reservoir of many ancestral or traditional values that none of its former colonies is able to produce, not even mature Brazil.

Brazilian foreign policy is conditioned also by the geographical situation of Brazil as an American nation. We may be in the first phase of development of another federation of which Brazil is as natural a member as of a Portuguese-speaking one —a Pan American federation. The two federations, if they develop, may become sub-federations in regard to a larger one: an Atlantic Federation, in which the place to be occupied by Brazil will be determined by its geography and history.

[5] See on this my two books on my 1951–2 travels in Asia and Africa, specially the Portuguese Provinces, entitled: *Um Brasileiro em Terras Portuguesas* and *Aventura e Rotina* (Rio, 1953).

From the point of view of plant or animal ecology, South America may be one continent, North America another. From the point of view of human ecology, Latin America may be one continent, Anglo-Saxon America another. But from a broader point of view that takes into consideration all aspects of interdependence among the American nations—interdependence in both physical and social space and relations—the American hemisphere is increasingly one continent. As such it needs a combined continental policy in which variety is not disregarded for the sake of an excessive uniformity. The American nations seem to have common enemies. All the evidence leads us to believe that a Japanese or German feudal imperialism would be far less tolerant of an ethnically and culturally free and democratic development in Latin America than British or Anglo-American bourgeois imperialism is or has been. With all their imperfections, Britain and the United States are constantly improving or seeking to improve their politically democratic systems or, rather, their methods of dealing with interhuman relations and human differences.

Latin American nations came into existence through a widespread revolt against European autocratic systems of repressing human and cultural differences and of exploiting human labor. Their political independence sprang from a revolt whose cause was similar to that of the American Revolution: taxation without representation. They separated from Spain and Portugal because they were being exploited and at the same time repressed—intellectually, economically, and politically repressed by narrow Portuguese and Spanish politicians.

Since its first attempts to become an independent nation, Brazil has looked for a defensive and offensive alliance with the United States, against Portuguese threats of reconquest. The first Brazilian *chargé d'affaires* in the United States went so far as to propose an alliance between Brazil and the United

States "in order to resist European interference in case Portugal called a partner to her assistance." [6] Even before that, during Brazil's attempt in 1817 to separate from Portugal through a romantic and unsuccessful republican revolution, the rebels of Pernambuco tried to secure the aid of the United States for their cause. And as far back as the eighteenth century, the rebels of Minas Gerais tried unsuccessfully, through a Brazilian student in France named Maia, to interest Thomas Jefferson in that first effort toward Brazilian independence. According to Oliveira Lima, the appeal addressed from Philadelphia to the President of the United States by that plenipotentiary *in partibus* of the Brazilian Republicans of 1817 contained the essential principles of Pan Americanism in an empirical form, just as Bolívar's plan for an American union was its "scientific conception." Perhaps the failure of the Brazilian Republicans of 1817 to obtain the help of the United States was in part caused by the fact that they sent a colored man as their emissary.

It was not until 1857 that the idea of an alliance of the United States with Brazil was officially considered from a United States point of view. The American minister in Rio, Richard Kidder Meade, in a speech presenting his credentials to the Emperor Dom Pedro II, said then that "such an alliance will ensure for mutual defense a unity of action and feeling that will prove invincible in the future." Since that year, however, the idea of a political alliance has disappeared under a broader conception of inter-American relations: the so-called "scientific conception" of Pan Americanism first outlined by Bolívar. But the fact remains that both similarities and differences attract Brazil to the United States in a special way and make the two countries particularly complementary.

[6] Oliveira Lima: "Brazil's Foreign Policy" (a lecture given at Williamstown in August 1922, *ms.*).

From a purely social point of view, such have been the changes for the better in the relations between the two countries that today even a colored man, if sent as emissary from Brazil to the United States, would probably find a decent (if not warm) reception, at least among the best-educated Americans. The point is important: a changed attitude toward men of colored races seems to some students of inter-American relations essential to the development of Pan Americanism if the latter is to mean real reciprocity and effective mutual respect. One should not forget that the commercial success of the Germans in Brazil before 1914 was largely owing to the fact that, more than the Anglo-Saxons, they were then socially democratic in Latin America. For, though some Germans in Brazil have married into old white or white-Indian families, a number of them—like a number of Portuguese, Italian, Spanish, and French—have married beautiful mulatto, quadroon, or octoroon girls. I do not mean that racial intermarriage is a necessary prerequisite to a vital or honest Pan Americanism. I do not mean that every American, North and South, should marry outside his racial class in order to be a good Pan American. Far from it. International and interracial marriages are always adventures, just as it is an adventure, in the present social organization of our Western civilization, for a man to marry a woman palpably below his own rank. One disagreeable consequence may be a domestic conflict of cultures, with the mother-in-law playing an important role. But in democratic America, color or race should not in itself taboo such adventures—too many individuals have made a success of it. No man ever had a more devoted and understanding wife than the Brazilian psychiatrist Juliano Moreira, who was a very dark Negro; she was a German. And other such cases might be mentioned.

Reciprocity and mutual respect seem to me an essential basis for developing really friendly inter-American relations. This mutual respect should take into consideration the fact that a democratic tradition is common to all Americans, Latin and Anglo-Saxon. The Latins have developed the ethnic aspect of democracy more than the political, and the Anglo-Saxons the purely political aspect more than the ethnic. If they are to become really good neighbors and increasingly democratic in their organization and culture, Latin and Anglo-Saxon Americans will probably enrich each other with the best results of their special cultural developments. But it would be a sociological error to work for uniformity in the American hemisphere instead of for unity combined with variety—though the respect for variety should not go so far as to include tolerance of such undemocratic institutions as *caudillismo* or lynching, anti-Semitism, and the Ku Klux Klan.

Though the static part of the Brazilian masses, still influenced by four long centuries of life and work under slavery, tends to tolerate the despotic paternalism of *caudillos*, there is a dynamic part of the same masses whose eagerness to rise socially and culturally and to improve its material and intellectual conditions of living manifests itself in the opposite direction: as a constant revolt against autocratic or despotic paternalism. This is also the attitude of most Brazilians who are the descendants of the old master class; they, too, are opposed to *caudillismo*. Some of them may be inclined—this is another story—to forms of government more like the British than any other, in their combination of aristocratic control of public affairs with democratic opportunity open to all capable of participating in that control.

Foreign observers who generalize about Brazil, taking into consideration only the politically dead or inarticulate part of its people, seem too hasty in their conclusions in favor of strongly paternalistic regimes for Portuguese America, as well as for other parts. Centuries before Fascism and Nazism rose in Europe, Brazil tasted the good as well as the evil of a quasi-Fascist or quasi-Nazi regime. I mean the Jesuit missions. It is well known that the Jesuits exercised a benevolent paternalistic control over large groups of Indians of Brazil and Paraguay. How nearly perfect this technique was is illustrated by their way of setting up a large wooden image of some terrible-looking saint, inside of which a man (a Jesuit) was introduced, to tell the Indians what they must do. I have seen some of these old images in Rio Grande do Sul; a child should not see them, lest he develop deep neurotic fears. But nobody can deny that in Brazil, as in Paraguay, the Jesuits were efficient administrators who developed agriculture and industry in their missions, introduced new plants, and had every detail in the daily life of every mission Indian under their paternalistic discipline. Professor Walter Goetz writes of the Jesuit "state" of Paraguay—which had an extension in southern Brazil—that "it was a virtual autocracy, controlling the native population by communistic economic and social regulations." [7] He adds: "That the natives received good treatment from the Jesuits is beyond doubt." But it was the sort of "good treatment" that tends to keep a human group mere children. The same efficiency, as far as material prosperity is concerned, is recognized by another authoritative student of the subject, José Ots y Capdequi. But he thinks that "the mission regime made impossible the development of a self-reliant personality." [8] The mission regime was also imperialistic in its lack of faith in the native; its organizers seem to have had little confidence in the capacity of the natives and of the descendants of the Spanish and Portuguese settlers of America, both creole and mixed-blood, to develop cultural autonomy and political self-government.

[7] "Jesuits," *Encyclopedia of the Social Sciences*, VIII, 388.
[8] "Native Policy," *Encyclopedia of the Social Sciences*, XI, 259.

If one goes today to the part of Brazil that came under the most direct control of the Jesuits, one finds among the descendants of the mission Indians, not pleasant recollections of that paternalistic regime, but hatred toward the well-meaning but autocratic missionaries. I do not know of any Brazilian from that area who has the slightest enthusiasm for the once theocratic lords of the Rio Grande do Sul missions. There is nothing like the tolerant feeling toward benevolent paternalism which one finds among a large number of descendants of plantation slaves in the northern provinces of Brazil. On the contrary, it seems that the war cry of seventeenth-century Indians against the Jesuits of the *reduçoes* expressed what is still the core idea in the revolt of their descendants against autocratic control of their lives: "*Me mata mas não me reduz*" (You kill me, but you will not "reduce" me).

With such traditions alive in Brazil—alive among the most dynamic groups of its population, both educated and illiterate —it is possible to conclude that this country is among the modern communities inclined to democracy; inclined to democracy, not only through the socially and ethnically democratic process of race amalgamation and cultural interpenetration which has been active among its people, but also through the eagerness of many Brazilians for forms of government in which the development of human personality is not neglected. It appears that the Brazilian ideal of human happiness (an ideal affected by many traditions and tendencies of its intelligentsia and its common people alike) does not stop at material gains or conveniences; it includes the development of human personality in ways that seem to have been accentuated through the wide exchange of intellectual and moral values made possible by democratic contact among various races and cultures.

It seems that Brazil has a distinct contribution to make to the development of human personality in the modern world. The contribution will probably come from the extra-European type of civilization that the most dynamic and creative groups of the Brazilian population are developing in spite of immense difficulties. It will manifest itself through the inter-American and foreign policy of Brazil as well as through all authentically Brazilian art and literature. But the policy, the art, and the literature will be hypocritical whenever Brazil seeks to express herself intellectually and politically as an altogether white nation; whenever she acts as if her interests, her problems, and her ideals were those of a European or sub-European nation and not those of a really new and dynamic American community, not ashamed of its Amerindian, Jewish, and African basic elements, but proud of them.

A few years ago I visited Argentina, Uruguay, and Paraguay, and in each of these countries—especially in the first—I found that, in spite of the fact that the majority of the people and the best elements in the press were and are friendly toward us, there was a well-prepared movement against Brazil that reminded me of similar agitations cleverly prepared by Nazi secret agents against Great Britain and France in the Balkans before the Second World War, movements characterized by the same technique of psychological war. The agitation in Argentina against Brazil in the late thirties and the early forties (possibly by Nazi agents) took the color of a nationalistic movement in favor of a great Argentine figure of the past— the dictator Rosas—presented to the popular mind as a powerful and brave enemy of "Jews" and "Brazilian mulattoes." According to the legend, "Brazilian mulatto diplomats," through shrewd diplomacy, had robbed Argentina of lands that rightly belonged to the Argentine "white people." The note of race hatred is present in a most characteristic way in the pro-Rosas, pro-Fascist, anti-democratic, and anti-Brazilian movement in Argentina, a movement whose main purpose is evidently to divide the people of Argentina from the people of Brazil.

Such general remarks about there being mulattoes in Brazil, as well as specific statements about specific Brazilian mulattoes who in the Empire and the Republic have been responsible for Brazilian national and international policy, still trouble some sensitive Brazilians—fifty- , sixty- , and seventy-year-old Brazilians. But they do not disturb the majority of the young generation, who are practically free from morbid sensitiveness about the fact that Brazil has a mixed-blood population. So strong are the evidences of a capacity to build a new and original civilization in America already given by Brazilians of the most diverse ethnic origins that young Brazilians, facing truth as it is being revealed to them by historians, anthropologists, and sociologists who have ceased to be sub-European in their outlook and have become American in the best sense of the word, are proud of their mestizo heroes, their mestizo composers, their mestizo statesmen, their mestizo writers, artists, industrial leaders, inventors, scientists, and administrators. And they could remind the Argentine race purists that a great statesman of nineteenth-century Argentina was a mulatto, and that Manuel Ugarte, the famous writer, was also a mulatto.

As I pointed out before, under the monarchical regime of the nineteenth century, any Brazilian, no matter what his origin, race, or color, could become prime minister and lead the country if he was a man of exceptional talent or personality. During the Republic it has been perfectly natural to see a man like Nilo Peçanha, a mulatto of very humble origin, succeed, as Minister of Foreign Affairs, Lauro Müller, the blue-eyed and purely "Aryan" son of a German colonist from Santa Catharina. Brazilian race purists are today a very small and almost ridiculous group.

Young Brazilians consider it more and more their duty to

oppose all forms of race snobbery which might prevent Brazil and the population of Portuguese-speaking areas culturally led today by Brazil from carrying on their vast experiment in ethnical and social democratization. In this connection it is instructive to note that even the Brazilian quasi-Nazi or quasi-Fascist organization—the so-called "Integralismo"—did not lift its voice officially against those who favor the incorporation of all racial elements into the Brazilian community—a fact that suggests the strength of that tendency. Hence the remark of Professor Lewis Hanke that Nazi racial ideas can expect only opposition from the Latin American cultural fusionists, and what is more important, that "this group—the fusionist—is more nobly nationalistic than any other in Latin America."

Fusionism being the dominant policy in Brazil, that nation is out of harmony with European or sub-European white nations every time they speak or act as European or sub-European powers and look down upon non-European nations. But she is also out of place among predominantly colored communities whose race consciousness is stronger than their national consciousness. Owing to the possibilities for social improvement and cultural expression, there never was any chance for the Brazilian descendants of Africans to develop that consciousness of being Negro which exists in the United States even in individuals of distant or remote African blood and of physical characteristics clearly acceptable according to Greco-Roman and Nordic aesthetic standards.

[VII]

Slavery, Monarchy, and Modern Brazil

Twenty-five years ago I published in Portuguese an essay in which I claimed that slavery—slavery of a patriarchal type—more than any other social institution or social process, had left a mark on Brazilian social development and on the character and the culture of the Brazilian people. In 1941 a similar book appeared in the United States. I refer to W. J. Cash's *The Mind of the South*, in which one finds a very penetrating analysis of the effect of slavery on the mind of the South of the United States. On a number of points this analysis confirms what the Brazilian analysis brought up as to the general psychological effects of an institution like slave labor—with the inevitable master-and-slave relationship—upon descendants both of masters and of slaves. Although sociological effects have been somewhat different in the two areas because of a number of historical and ecological factors, the psychological effects have been almost the same. One of the factors of sociological differentiation has been the presence in Brazil of an institution that was at once complementary and corrective to patriarchal slavery: patriarchal monarchy of a type more classic than romantic.

Romanticism was one of the general psychological effects of the plantation and slavery system upon Brazil. And with romanticism, fondness of rhetoric, common to Brazilians and to Anglo-Americans of the two areas of the New World where slavery flourished with its most dramatic vigor: the South of the United States and the sugar and coffee regions of Brazil. As in the South of the United States, in those Brazilian regions rhetoric became "not only a passion," but, as Cash points out in his famous book, "a primary standard of judgment, the *sine qua non* of leadership." This love of oratory was associated in Brazil as in the southern region of the United States, with "the love of politics."

In Brazil even the campaign for the abolition of slavery suffered from an excess of rhetoric which was one of the causes of the fall of monarchy—a system of government that, being rather classic than romantic, was a powerful corrective, among Brazilians, to romantic excesses generally associated with republicanism in South America and in the South of the United States—excesses of individualism, paternalism, and familism. The monarchy in Brazil was also a healthy influence in favor of national unity and national culture and even in favor of objectivity (helped by an observance of proper diplomatic form and formal methods of diplomatic intercourse, uncommon among republican Latin and Anglo-Americans), in international, particularly continental, relations. For, being a sort of super-paternalism, with the prestige given to the royal family for the sake of the national role it had to play, the Brazilian monarchy stood above regional paternalism and above rivalries between powerful antagonistic families. It stood also as the basis for an international policy in which traditional methods and styles of diplomacy gave Brazil in this matter a clear superiority over the young romantic republics, whose diplomats made too many blunders for lack of diplomatic tradition. The presence in Rio de Janeiro of a royal family surrounded by statesmen and diplomats with a European training explains why dealing not only with *caudillo* republics like Paraguay, but also with the United States, the diplomacy of Brazil was in the majority of cases superior, for its objectivity and classic form, to the excessively romantic and anarchic republican diplomacy. In his book, *Diplomatic Relations Between the United States and Brazil*, Professor Laurence F. Hill brings out some interesting examples of discrepancy between the two types of diplomacy; and I think he would agree with me in describing one—the republican—as romantic, and the other one—the monarchical—as classic.

Familism, as an effect of the slavery system, was common to Brazil and the South of the United States, as well as to such other areas of America as Cuba and Peru. In Brazil, as in the South of the United States, in the isolation of plantation life, the home, the family, the small domestic world in and around the patriarchal "big house" became the "center of everything," and in both areas there grew, in this atmosphere, what Cash calls "an usually intense affection and respect for the women of the family—for the wife and mother upon whose activities the comfort and well-being of everybody greatly depended." In my 1934 essay I attempted to analyze this situation as it developed in the plantation area of Brazil, going into details; and in that essay and in subsequent essays that I have published on the subject, I have suggested that the Roman Catholic devotion for the Virgin Mary glorified as Queen—Regina—in no other Roman Catholic area of the world seems to have become more intense than in Brazil. This is a result, it seems to me, of that extreme idealization of aristocratic women and even of Negro women—under the shape of old Mammas—as vital or basic sentimental parts of the plantation family complex developed in slavery days.

In this particularly intense devotion to the Virgin Mary, characteristic of the old plantation area of Brazil, it is possible to detect a sublimation or idealization of the cult of women, which has found other means of expression in the United States, including an identification of the cult of the purity of women with the cult of race purity. This identification is not to be found in Brazil, where the cult of women has been associated more with family pride than with race pride. In Brazil one finds that the cult of the Virgin Mary was associated in so intense a way with the plantation complex that a large number of the old plantation houses, or "big houses," had their chapels named not after the owner's family, but with the name of his wife, or mother, or daughter, under the disguise of one of many denominations given in Latin countries to the Virgin Mary, respectfully preceded by the royal treatment of Our Lady: Our Lady of the Good News, of the Good Voyage, of the Good Hopes, of the Good Deliverance—a particularly maternal denomination—of the Perpetual Divine Assistance, of Grief, of Solitude. In many instances, it was this mystical Lady—a sort of goddess who more than God or Christ was supposed to take care of a whole plantation and to protect it against all sorts of enemies—who was made the godmother of the female slave children, born on the plantation and baptized in its chapel by the plantation chaplain, who generally was a subordinate rather of the plantation lord than of his bishop, baptized with the name of the particular Virgin Mary under whose protection the entire plantation lived, and whose name was also the name of the lady of the house and of her oldest daughter.

This indicates that patriarchal male power in Brazil during the slavery days was not absolute, there having been such an intense respect for women under romantic and mystic forms that were reflected in practical and everyday life. Men were the real lords in the Brazilian slavery system: the white men who were the owners of white women as well as of plantations and slaves. But their power was psychologically limited by the romantic or mystical respect they had for women: not only their mothers and their wives and daughters, but also the Virgin Mary, who to many of them was much more of a mystical power—this should be repeated—than God or Jesus Christ; and not a universal goddess, but a particular or domestic manifestation of the divine power that took care of a particular family or home.

In a very interesting book on South Africa written by a woman—*Color and Culture in South Africa*, by Sheila Patterson—an attempt is made to compare the slavery complex in South Africa with the slavery complex in the Old South of the United States and in Brazil. And a very intelligent discrimination is made in this book when Miss Patterson says that what prevailed in Brazil during the slavery days was a cult of "the purity of home" rather than a cult of the "purity of the race" (or blood) as in the United States and South Africa. She goes farther and suggests that in Brazil the slavery system derived from what she calls "a Portuguese prototype," different from the Anglo-Saxon or the Dutch. Here also, I am delighted to find in a 1953 English book conclusions strictly similar to the suggestions I made in my 1934 essay, in which I based my analysis of the Brazilian slavery system on the assumption that it was different from the Anglo-American, the Dutch, and even the French and the Spanish systems of modern slavery. It was an extension of the Portuguese system just as the Portuguese system was an extension of the Moorish or Arab or Mohammedan system of domestic rather than industrial slavery. For this suggestion I have found new and stronger evidences during my recent contacts with Africa and Asia, in the course of a long research voyage that took me through Mohammedan countries like Arabia, Pakistan, and Egypt, to India, and later to Negro Africa: not only to those parts of Africa deeply affected by Mohammedan culture or almost virgin of the Islamic impact, but also to the more or less industrialized parts of Africa under the influence of the French, the English, the Belgian, or of the Dutch, as in South Africa.

Everywhere I was impressed by the fact that a sociological kinship between the Portuguese and the Mohammedan systems of slavery seems to account for certain characteristics of the Brazilian system not to be found in other regions of America where slavery also prevailed. The fact that slavery in Brazil was less cruel than in English America and even in French and Spanish Americas seems to be a well-documented fact. Why was it so? Not, certainly, because the Portuguese are a more Christian people than the English or the Dutch or the French or the Spanish peoples—"more Christian" meaning here ethically better in morals and behavior. The truth seems to be the reverse: the more suave form of slavery developed by the Portuguese in Brazil seems to be a result of their contact with slaveowning Mohammedans who are known to have been particularly humane toward their slaves and to have had a domestic conception of slavery entirely different from that of industrial slavery.

We know that the Portuguese, though intensely Christian and, more than that, champions of the cause of Christianity against the cause of Islam, imitated the Arabs, the Moors, and the Mohammedans in a number of techniques and customs, and assimilated from them a number of cultural values. The Mohammedan conception of slavery, as a domestic system linked to family organization as a whole and including economic activity without being entirely dominated by an economic industrial purpose, was one of the Moorish values that the Portuguese applied to their Christian colonization of Brazil. When in 1938 I told my old teacher in Columbia University, the late Professor Franz Boas, that I had this in mind, he told me that this would probably be the basis for a new and better understanding of the Brazilian situation, that I should go on with research in this connection between the Portuguese and the Mohammedan culture and particularly the Portuguese slavery system and the Mohammedan one. He argued with me on this: that the Mohammedans—Arabs and Moors—had for centuries been superior to the Europeans and Christians in their methods of assimilating African groups and cultures into their civilization.

Another anthropologist of the same generation as Boas, and equally an authority on race and culture contacts—Professor Fox Pitt-Rivers, of England—in one of his books on what he calls the clash of cultures, points out the fact, generally neglected by Europeans when they present the Arabs and the Mohammedans in Africa as terrible beings and even monsters specialized in enslaving Negroes—that their system of slavery was different from the European systems of slavery. In the words of the well-known British anthropologist: "Orient slavery is something quite different, nobler and less degrading than it was in Europe and the United States." [1] Even its "polygamy"—Fox Pitt-Rivers thinks—deserves the respect of the Westerners.

This is the type of slavery which the Portuguese adopted in

[1] *The Clash of Culture and the Contact of Races* (London 1927), p. 238.

the East and in Brazil: a suave form of slavery that, as part of a social whole, included polygamy to increase population. Some say to increase the number of laborers, but one should remember that from the fifteenth century on the Portuguese used slavery for eugenic selection of good human elements that, once Christianized, domesticated in the sense that they became a part of domestic, patriarchal, family systems, were liberated and given an opportunity to be the social equals of the white Europeans. As early as the fifteenth century, African youths were given the opportunity in Portugal, through a eugenic selection that did not mean race exclusiveness, of becoming priests, then a high position in Portuguese society. This opportunity for social advancement was increased when the youths were not African youths brought very young from Africa as slaves, but the sons of Portuguese men and African slave girls. Here, again, the Portuguese, perhaps under the pressure of a problem they had to face—that of scarcity of population for the tremendous task of expanding in Asia, Africa, and America, in the tropical regions of these continents—followed the Mohammedan or Arab method or example. According to the Mohammedans, the offspring of Arab men and slave women had only to adopt their father's faith, rituals, and customs to be considered their father's equals in social status.

The Portuguese did not go that far, when they developed in Brazil a slave system on a larger scale than the one they had developed in India, following—it seems evident to some of us —Mohammedan suggestions. But as soon as they established themselves in Brazil, they began to add to their plantation system a disguised imitation of polygamy, allowing for the legal adoption by a Christian father, when he wrote his will, of "natural" and illegitimate sons not only by Indian girls, but also by African slave girls—that is, the "natural" and illegitimate children chosen by him to be the social equals, or almost the social equals, of his legitimate children, and educated in his "big house" by the priest or chaplain who educated his legitimate children.

Here I should point out that legal marriages of Portuguese planters with Indian girls, after these girls became Christian women, were not rare in colonial Brazil. Some of these girls, like the North American Pocahontas, were Indian princesses; and being the descendant of an Indian princess and a Portuguese nobleman has remained a matter of special pride for many Brazilians. The first cardinal, not only of Brazil but of all Latin America, was a descendant of a sixteenth-century Albuquerque who, besides marrying a Portuguese girl of good origin—a Mello—sent to Brazil to marry him by the Queen of Portugal, adopted and legalized the children he already had had by an Indian princess. So the Cardinal was a product of this suave polygamy tolerated by the Church whenever good Catholics (as most of the aristocratic planters were) adopted their illegitimate children when writing their wills. I have read a large number of such wills—of the colonial period of Brazil —and know how this suavely disguised polygamy contributed to the increase of the Brazilian population along lines that would have met with the approval of eugenic specialists, for the fathers were in many cases first-class men, not only from a sociological, but also—judging by their achievements and by their legitimate children and grandchildren and later descendants—from a biological point of view.

Slavery of this type was not only useful in many ways to Brazilian social development: it also proved valuable for national political unity and social discipline—the patriarchal discipline—in such an immense country as Brazil, for it was a system common to different provinces and sub-regions. In "big houses," children grew up surrounded by relatives—grandmother and grandfather, an unmarried aunt, a cousin, even a close friend of the family—so that from the time they were born, such children saw, as the anthropologist Margaret Mead has pointed out in regard to children in the old Anglo-American patriarchal families, "many ranges of ages and human experience, right in or near their own home." (On the other hand, patriarchalism in Brazil was, and has been in some ways, harmful to the national development and to the Brazilian character in general. It has made Brazilians too much dependent upon paternalism and paternalistic government. It has made it difficult for manual labor to be considered a decent occupation for free men. It gave too much value to such careers as the priesthood—even when one did not have the vocation for so noble a career—the military and the academic, with a neglect or disdain for industrial, technical, and commercial activities— a deficiency that only today is being overcome by Brazilians. It contributed to make some Brazilians sadistic in their exercise of power. It contributed also, as in the South of the United States, to the association of politics with rhetoric, rhetoric being the easiest way for leaders to impress emotional people.

But unfortunately for Brazil, slavery did not act entirely by itself upon the Brazilian social development and the shaping of the Brazilian character or ethos. Here we come back to the point that slavery in Brazil was corrected in some of its excesses by another powerful institution that the Portuguese brought to Brazil and the Brazilians were wise enough to maintain, even when they separated politically from Portugal. This institution, the monarchical system of government, deserves as much attention as slavery from students of the Brazilian development.

While the various "big houses" of sugar-cane, and later of coffee, autocrats had a tendency to separate Brazil into sometimes violently antagonistic patriarchal blocs—each one protected by a particular Virgin Mary or saint, in such a way that the field slaves of one plantation more than once engaged in fights when they met the slaves of another plantation—monarchy acted as a force by nature too national to take sides with local or provincial autocrats or to take sides with saints who protected only particular patriarchal families. It acted also in defense of law, of justice, of morality against paternalistic abuses of power. Because the autocrats of the "big houses" wanted to show their prestige by participating in political life and being recognized by the Crown with titles—barons and viscounts wanted to be marquises and, if possible, dukes—it was in their interest to behave in such a way as to please the Emperor and his counselors. Fortunately for Brazil, the four monarchs who ruled from the day when Rio de Janeiro became the seat, first of the Portuguese monarchy, later of the Brazilian monarchy, were individuals who had a high sense of national and royal responsibilities: King John VI, Emperor Pedro I, Emperor Pedro II, and Princess Isabel.

They were greatly respected by the Brazilian people, and this respect was to a large extent a result of the general Brazilian attitude toward paternalistic authority: only the King, the Emperor, and the Princess were understood by all, or really by all, to be more powerful than local autocrats. On the other hand, monarchical authority in Brazil felt for a long time that it had to depend upon the loyal co-operation of these local autocrats. The interdependence between the two was complete. So much so that when the Crown took the side of abolition of slavery, and played an important part in the movement to free the slaves in the Empire, the Empire immediately lost its vitality and was able to survive slavery—which disappeared from Brazil in 1888—for only one year. In 1889 the Republic was established.

A fraternalistic republic, at first, it did not stay long as predominantly a fraternalistic republic: it had to imitate the monarchy it had replaced; it had to become somewhat paternalistic. It became paternalistic by acting as if presidents were strong men who had to protect their country almost as if they were kings.

The ironical thing about the simultaneous disappearance of the two institutions—slavery and monarchy—was that as free men former slaves found themselves men and women who had no Emperor and no autocrat of the "big house" to protect them. They became the victims of a deep feeling of insecurity.

Some of them became nostalgic for the Emperor and the "big houses." They were really insecure as free laborers. It took years in Brazil for political leaders to understand the real psychological and sociological situation of these former slaves, disguised as free laborers and deprived of the patriarchal social assistance that they had been given by the "big houses" in their old age or when they were sick. By the "big houses" and, when the big houses failed to do them justice, by the Emperor or the Empress or the imperial Princess, so paternally and maternally attentive to the welfare of slaves. The Emperor was called or considered by most of them their "big Father," the Empress their "Mother," in a sense similar to the Virgin Mary, who, as Queen (Regina), was also their Mother.

This explains—to come to modern Brazil—the great popularity of Getulio Vargas, when, as President for some time with dictatorial power, he decided to give the Brazilian underprivileged social legislation that has meant for a large part of the Brazilian labor population, protection against old age, against disease, against commercial or industrial firms with whom the laborer formerly had no rights. This explains why Vargas became known as the "Father of the Poor" and won a popularity among the common people which surpassed even that gained by Pedro II in forty-eight years of good, honest, paternalistic government.

Perhaps one may conclude from this that in Brazil the monarchical tradition, correcting some of the excesses of the paternalistic tradition that had developed as a consequence of a strongly patriarchal, familist plantation system, has expressed itself, down to the present day, in positive values, and not only through negative traits. This seems to be the conclusion of everyone who analyzes the relations of administration and government with other parts of the general social organization of Brazil.

Years ago, in an essay that became classic, Woodrow Wilson wrote that in regard to administrative adjustment the United States was "at a signal disadvantage as compared with the transatlantic nations." Why this? To a certain extent, because in such nations much that became more efficient in their administration systems than in the United States system had been developed by "kingly initiative." Kingly and, one might add, paternalistic, as in Prussia and, to a lesser extent, England, where there was a sort of anticipation of the United States political history: a history, as Wilson pointed out, not of administrative development, but of legislative overseeing; not of progress in governmental organization, but of advance in lawmaking and political criticism.

Brazil seems to be in a unique position in the political history of the republican Americas—North, South, and Central. This has been a history influenced to such an extent by the Anglo-Saxon and the Revolutionary French examples of democratic lawmaking and sometimes overliberal political criticism, that governmental organization of the efficiently paternalistic, kingly type, responsible for much of the European advances in measures of protection of the common people against the privileged groups, has required an abnormal effort, an effort through frequent revolutions and frequent dictatorial republican governments. This is a repetitive situation that Brazil, with its tradition of paternalism and monarchism combined—a tradition assimilated even by its republican regimes when theory has had to be superseded by practice—has not known. This seems to explain why Brazil—a country that has added to the tradition of paternalism and monarchism a slow, peaceful imitation of parliamentary lawmaking, as in Great Britain, and of legally free political criticism, as in the United States—stands today as the very complex case of a nation that, being very American, very liberal, very democratic in some of the most expressive traits of its social organization of its political system, is, on the other hand, very classically European—more than Argentina, Uruguay, or Canada—in being sensitive to a paternalistic-monarchical tradition that is its peculiar inheritance in America. This tradition, instead of giving Brazilians only a predisposition to remain archaic against so-called Progress with a capital P, has acted as a constant stimulant, specially in critical days, to the legalistic, peaceful, civilian solution of problems that other Latin American republics—even Argentina and Chile—have faced only through open and sometimes brutal military, though republican, dictatorships—republican in form and sometimes in substance. Through violence and through the most complete disregard for written laws.

It is a fact that in Brazil the Crown always acted as a force or an influence above parties and the political antagonisms between groups; and also as an influence—as already suggested here—in favor of an objective international policy carried on by Brazil through a Foreign Office whose specialized knowledge of international matters, training, and awareness of European styles and techniques in art—like diplomacy and applied international law, much more monarchical than republican until the nineteenth century—have given the Brazilian nation a generally recognized superiority over other American nations, even the United States. It also seems to be a fact that the Brazilian army, since the establishment of the Republic, has considered that one of its great responsibilities as a national force is to take the place of the Crown as a super-party influence in Brazilian national life. Joaquim Nabuco, the distinguished Brazilian publicist and diplomat, was perhaps the first to rejoice in the fact that the army in Brazil, and not any political republican party or republican ideological sect, took effective control of the Brazilian situation when the monarchy was overthrown mainly as a consequence of the abolition of slavery, a measure perhaps unwisely enacted by Princess Isabel during the absence of her father, Dom Pedro II, who was then in Europe.

One may generalize and say that from the end of the nineteenth century to the present day the army in Brazil—in the last decades, the entire armed forces of Brazil, army, navy, and air force—has acted as a substitute for the Crown during the monarchical days—that is, as a corrective influence acting, especially during critical days, to prevent abuses of power by any single individual or by any particular political, economic, ideological, or religious group within the national organization of Brazil. This seems to explain why the presence of military leaders in Brazilian life as *caudillos* or dictators has been rare, exceptional, abnormal; and also why Vargas, when a semi-dictator in Brazil (for he never was an absolute dictator, but voluntarily surrounded himself with legal controls that made of him a sort of active regent in a limited monarchy), was an exception to purely constitutional normality, and as such was tolerated but supervised by a socially democratic, though politically protective, army. Vargas's dictatorial paternalism was not of the common Latin American republican *caudillo* type, but an effort toward administrative adjustment within the Brazilian monarchical and paternalistic tradition.

The better organization of civil service was one of Vargas's great accomplishments, the other being his initiatives in favor of the common people, specially the urban laborer. Most of the army leaders who supported Vargas regarded these efforts as a necessary adjustment in Brazilian life and one that the lawmaking elements had been unable to accomplish during almost half a century of congressional activity in a presidential republic of the United States type, more fraternalistic than paternalistic so far as Brazilian reality is concerned.

"It is harder for democracy to organize administration than for monarchy," Woodrow Wilson has written in his essay already referred to. The Brazilian case seems to favor his opinion. Being definitively a democracy that is one of the most advanced communities of the continent and of the modern world in social and ethnic democracy, Brazil in its political development has been a singular country on the American scene in having begun its independent political life as a monarchy. Paradoxically, the monarchy was a liberal, democratic, national corrective influence to aristocratic or autocratic regional and local excesses stimulated in a vast space by the dominance of a plantation, slaveowning, economic system and social organization.

This is why, since becoming a republic, Brazil, in its critical political days, instead of acting as a typically Latin American republic—through revolution, *caudillismo*, military dictatorship—has acted differently, peculiarly. One has to seek the reasons for its unique behavior in its unique political-social development as a society in which aristocratic excesses of private groups were, or have been, moderated, not by radical republicanism, but by democratic monarchism, and where important initiatives in favor of the so-called underprivileged groups have been taken not so much by congress or parliament as by creative individuals acting within a monarchical tradition of executive initiative, preserved by a presidential, civilian, legalistic republic in which the army has usually played a role similar to that of the Crown during the monarchical period.

[V I I I]

The Modern
Literature of Brazil:
Its Relation to Brazilian Social
Problems

Literature and art are not the field of the literary or art critic
only; they are also the concern of the sociologist, the social historian or anthropologist, and the social psychologist.
For through literature and art men seem to reveal their personality and, when there is one, their national ethos. Through the
arts they describe the most crushing social conditions and
breathe their most revolutionary wishes. And through the arts
they portray the particularly oppressed as well as the most vig-

orously dynamic aspects of their personality and their national ethos. In this chapter it is not my purpose to deal with modern literature and art in Brazil as purely aesthetic forms, but only in their relations to Brazilian social conditions or social problems.

For a long time Brazilian art and literature remained almost inarticulate and passively colonial or sub-European. Aleijadinho, the mulatto sculptor of eighteenth-century colonial churches in the gold-mining region of Brazil, was one of the few artists to appear with a socially significant artistic message and a technique distinguished by creativeness, audacity, and non-European characteristics in a century marked, in Brazil, by academic literature and imitative art. Aleijadinho, the son of a Portuguese artisan and a Negro woman, was born under the shadow of slavery; and a terrible disease that ate away most of his fingers seems to have increased his consciousness of belonging to an outcast part of the population and his tendency to social revolt. He worked assisted by loyal slaves. It is easy to see how significant were the material and social conditions that favored the technically non-European and sometimes socially anti-European qualities in his sculptures. If I rightly interpret his work, it was and remains an expression of social revolt and of the Brazilian native and mestizo wish for independence from white or European masters and exploiters of slave labor.

Religious art was his medium of expression. Sometimes as I look at his work, it seems to reveal very clearly his conscious or unconscious identification, as a highly sensitive and potentially revolutionary mulatto, with, on the one hand, Christ and the primitive Christian martyrs (masochism) and, on the other hand, with the most terrific Old Testament prophets who preached against social sins and made personal sinners suffer mentally, if not physically (sadism). His satirical or sarcastic way of brutally exaggerating, in the Roman officers and soldiers and in the Jewish high priests who persecuted Jesus, their noses and other racial characteristics seems to be also an expression of his revolt against the domination and exploitation of a rich region, like the gold-mining region of Brazil, by arrogant Portuguese officers and soldiers and, according to some students of the period, by priests and friars as well as by Jewish merchants attracted by the presence of gold and diamonds. In Minas Gerais, on account of the large profits from the gold mines, there was, beginning in the seventeenth century, a particularly dramatic rivalry between the Portuguese of Portugal (a large number of whom in the eighteenth century were arrogant officers and soldiers) and native Brazilians, some of whom were white-and-Indian mestizos and, later, mulattoes. For the slave population in that region rapidly became one of the largest in Portuguese America.

It is also to be noted that in the gold-mining region, relations between master and slaves were, from the beginning, different from what they were in the plantation region: less patriarchal, more impersonal, and (according to reports from travelers and from other sources) more cruel.

Aleijadinho was a natural, if not a logical, product of his region. In all his work there seems to be a symbolic intent, probably well known to some of his contemporaries though it has escaped the notice of most of his critics and interpreters. It seems to me that the sculptor's physical vision was distorted by his desire to convey a political message through a then-popular form of art—religious sculpture. If I am right, he was a pioneer. A sort of mulatto El Greco in his daring distortions of the human form, he anticipated by two centuries the work of Rivera and Orozco, of Portinari and Cicero Dias

—modern Latin Americans in whose art there is frequently a symbolic political intent as well as a tendency toward exaggeration, distortion, caricature.

Aleijadinho also was a pioneer of the modern literary art of Brazil—the art of such novelists as José Lins do Rego, Jorge Amado, and Raquel de Queiroz, to mention only three of the most characteristic ones; the art of poets like Manuel Bandeira, Carlos Drumond de Andrade, Jorge de Lima, Murilo Mendes, Venicius de Morais, and Odorico Tavares, to name six of the most daring in their association of social problems with poetical art and in their eagerness to be the expression of an extra- or ultra-European Brazil rather than merely the colonial echo of a purely European philosophy of life and a purely European literary or musical technique—an eagerness to be found also in Heitor Villa-Lobos, the composer.

For although the younger writers of Brazil have grown up under European literary influences and some of them have imitated, or still imitate, Europeans on the mechanical or technical side of their art, they are powerfully Brazilian in their characterization, exaggeration, and interpretation of life, in their freshness of visional truth and essential (not formal or conventional) fidelity to the living actuality and the living past of Brazil. Some of them are also masters in the style of El Greco: they like distortion of reality when they feel the need to make reality more real or more Brazilian than it appears to be. Such distortions are to be found in some of the pages of Jorge Amado, for instance, where purely visional truth is freely exceeded by the poetic and sometimes political dramatization of situations.

Satire and an interest in social problems and revolt against political abuse were early characteristics of Brazilian literature. Though no viceroy of Brazil, no king, no emperor, no president, no bishop has been assassinated in the history of the country, some have suffered almost the equivalent of death at the hands of literary and popular satirists. As early as 1666 a colonial governor sent to Pernambuco by the king of Portugal was given such a ridiculous nickname and satirized so unmercifully in literary and popular verse and prose for his graft and his incompetence that it was easy for a group of Brazilians to assault him one day as he was walking through a street followed by his military aide. They took his spectacularly large sword from him, quietly put him on a ship, and sent him off. This would probably have been impossible if the moustaches he wore—copied from those of German generals of the seventeenth century—had not made him such a perfect butt.

In the same century there lived in Bahia and Pernambuco a brilliant man, Gregorio de Mattos, noted for his satirical talent in verse. More than that, he was a social critic of considerable importance. Some of his verses describing the local types are the work of a master caricaturist and a penetrating social critic. At the same time, he was the first Brazilian poet to interpret the sorrows and joys of Brazilian life in its first phase of transition from almost purely European standards of culture to a mestizo, extra-European culture. There is little pity in his representations of bishops, governors, planters, women, and priests, in whom he always found some human weakness to laugh at. Some of his verses became popular. I think that he should be considered a pioneer of social literature, social art, and social or political caricature in Brazil. From this point of view he was as important as Aleijadinho, the sculptor. Mattos was more intellectual, but Aleijadinho had more emotional vigor in his art and more symbolism in his distortions of the human form. The sculptor was probably influenced to a greater extent than Gregorio de Mattos was by popular art and by popular verse, for, as I said above, he was the son of a Negro woman and consequently came into closer contact with the peasants and the slaves than the sophisticated Mattos did.

The great popular art in colonial Brazil was that of ex-votos, or votive tablets, hung in the churches, with their naïve exaggeration of miracles—for instance, deliverance from shipwreck. This art was various. Wood, clay, or wax sculptures of heads, torsos, hands, feet, hearts, livers, eyes, and other members were offered to the saints whose help had been asked—effectually—in the cure of this or that infirmity or disease. The burning of the Judases was another aspect of this popular art; the crowd had an opportunity to satirize the un-Christian behavior of some local lord, represented by a grotesque straw figure of Judas in old clothes. Even native pastry and Brazilian popular confectionery had an element of caricature in them, caricature of such sacred things as rosaries and such respectable beings as nuns. Cakes and sweets had—some of them still have —names that orthodox Catholics of Anglo-Saxon countries would probably consider sacrilegious. "Rosaries" was the name of one, a delicacy mentioned by the American Ewbank in his list of popular articles of native pastry that he knew in Brazil when he was there in the middle of the nineteenth century; [1] "Celestial Slices" the name of another; and "Angel's Hair" the name of still another. "Nuns' Bellies," the name of a fourth one, is a terribly sacrilegious name; so is "Heavenly Bacon," the name of a light pudding composed of almond paste, eggs, sugar, butter, and a spoonful or two of flour. But sacred and worldly things were mixed in many ways, as if caricature was ubiquitous in Brazilian life. Some of these cakes and sweets with sacrilegious names were made in convents by the nuns themselves. And the vendors of confectionery were also the

[1] Ewbank: op. cit., p. 136.

vendors of the coarse wooden images of saints. Each of these two arts, confectionery and the sculpture of saints, was a popular art distinguished by caricature. The sculpture of saints tended to exaggerate, distort, and magnify this or that power of the saint, and thus resembled the ex-voto described above. Because they were born under such influences it was natural that Aleijadinho and, to a lesser extent, Gregorio de Mattos should develop into masters of social caricature.

The same tendency is to be found in the songs of the illiterate Brazilians and in popular verse written by popular poets for laborers and peasants who can read only simple words. These songs and poems recount episodes that have made a deep impression on the popular mind; and they often tend to exaggerate or distort facts and personalities—in an effort not to hide the truth, but rather to make clear, violently and brutally clear, the most important characteristics of a personality or a fact from the point of view of the popular reader or hearer. This, also, is the technique of caricature.

This technique has also marked what there is of a national stage in Brazil: the so-called *revista*. Amazed at the freedom enjoyed by the authors of *revistas* in their bold caricatures of political personages, a foreign observer in Brazil thirty years ago remarked that he supposed that on the stage, as in the Brazilian press, there must be some limit beyond which the libel law became operative, but that he could not imagine where it was drawn—he saw theater audiences rocking with laughter when well-known political personages were caricatured.

It is a fact—and not a legend—that some Brazilian politicians and even statesmen have considered it a disgrace not to be caricatured in *revistas*, newspaper cartoons, and café stories. One of these, when nothing unpleasant or caustic was being written or said about him, took the trouble himself to write something of that sort about his political ideas or his personality, and sent it under a false name to an opposition paper. Then, and only then, he felt well: he was alive, he said—not harmless.

Students of Pareto's psychological sociology will realize how wise this attitude of Brazilian leaders was in the days of political liberalism. A sort of political fatigue seems to descend sometimes on the people vis-à-vis their leaders, like industrial fatigue among workers; and, according to a specialist in the human problems of an industrial civilization, Professor Elton Mayo (to whose ideas and work I have recently had the pleasure of being introduced by one of his former students), a scientific investigation of industrial fatigue suggests that merely listening to workers' complaints, even without acting on them, lessens the workers' fatigue and so increases their efficiency. There may be something of the same situation among politically conscious people with regard to their leaders, who—if that is true—make a mistake when they try to suppress literary or popular criticism, satire, and caricature directed at their acts and personalities.

King John VI of Brazil was ridiculed by many because he ate too much and sometimes carried fried chickens in his pockets, but he seems to have tolerated the true as well as the false stories circulated about him. The same tradition was followed by his grandson, the Emperor Dom Pedro II, who was freely criticized and caricatured in the Brazilian press on account of his devotion to astronomy and Hebrew while so many popular needs and social problems went neglected; on account also of his almost feminine suavity when problems pressed whose solution, some of his critics thought, demanded the iron hand. As I have mentioned, Dom Pedro was called "Pedro Banana"—a nickname generally attached by Brazilians to people who are soft and lazy, but one that, applied seriously, was and is (as even foreigners have found out) a gross insult. Among the presidents of the Republic, a marshal of the Brazilian army, Hermes da Fonseca, was given the nickname of Dudú, and during his four years as president a number of articles and cartoons appeared in the press making fun of him and of his alleged power to spread bad luck. All three—John VI, Dom Pedro II, and President Hermes da Fonseca—have become, if not national heroes, at any rate well-loved characters whom Brazilians regard with esteem and even affection. Even Senhor Washington Luis, when President of the Republic, though known as "Strong Arm," let himself be caricatured in *revistas* as a good eater and an old bohemian, and he was the butt of much satire and many caustic remarks in the daily press.

Such is the atmosphere in which Brazilian literature and painting have developed into an expression of social criticism and sometimes of social revolt. Both José Lins do Rego and Jorge Amado are master caricaturists, not photographic realists; their novels remind one of the Aleijadinho sculptures, of Gregorio de Mattos's satirical poetry, and of Euclides da Cunha's *Os Sertões* in that, though keenly alive to reality, each of these two most famous novelists of modern Brazil is a mixture of the artist and the social critic; each is a poet in prose; each, though possibly deficient in sophisticated humor, is a powerful master of caricature and satire of the kind that simple men can understand. Sometimes José Lins do Rego [2]—a sort of Brazilian William Faulkner—writes as if he were copying from life; and he has copied from life to such a degree that some of his pages are rather those from some vivid and powerful memoirs than those of a pure novelist. But he has a tendency to distort or exaggerate some of his characters so as to give them a symbolical value; one of these, Vitorino Carneiro da Cunha, has been acclaimed by critics who know Brazil well as a sort

[2] Died in 1957, a few months after being made a member of the Brazilian Academy of Literature. He was born in 1901.

of Don Quixote of the sugar-cane plantations of Paraíba—a symbol, not a mere character.

The same thing has been accomplished by Jorge Amado in some of his best novels; in them he has adapted to literature part of the technique of the "A B C" or story-songs through which news is propagated and men exalted or insulted among the masses of illiterate and semi-illiterate peasants of Brazil. His Balduino is a hero, the symbol of Negro vitality in Brazil. In this connection it is interesting to note that the name Balduino, as used by numerous rustic Brazilians, is not taken from the Christian calendar, from which so many Brazilians take the names they give their children; if I am not mistaken, its origin is popular and, at the same time, Anglo-American—it is a corruption of Baldwin, from the Baldwin locomotive! When Brazilian peasants talk of some powerful machine they call it a *balduina;* and Senhor Jorge Amado's Negro hero seems to have something in him of the locomotive so admired by peasants and small boys, in that he is a human power, the symbol of the people's vitality, Afro-Brazilian vitality.

Of the modern Brazilian novelists who have dealt with social problems—authors like Lins do Rego, Jorge Amado, Raquel de Queiroz, Amando Fontes, Vianna Moog, José Americo de Almeida, Herberto Sales, and Erico Verissimo—one may say that, though realists, they are also romanticists, with a romantic yearning not so much for an imaginary past as for an imaginary future. Some of them come from the oldest and most feudal regions of Brazil: Pernambuco, Bahia, the northeast. And at least one, José Lins do Rego, is connected with an old, but now decadent family of feudal Brazil. Nevertheless, they are doing more than economists, more than politicians, more than demagogues to carry not only Brazilian literature, but the Brazilians themselves, away from an excess of colonial tradition in their behavior and from oppressive colonial complexes of inferiority to Europe. In literature such excesses have meant the writing of novels, poetry, and essays in strictly academic Portuguese and according to academic prescriptions and rigid European techniques, with the result that the literature has failed to express or interpret Brazilian reality.

As a consequence of their revolt against conventional techniques, their criticism of Brazilian life, and particularly their frankness in regard to sex and to the relations between whites and blacks and between rich and poor, the young Brazilian novelists have encountered opposition. They have come into conflict with the optimism of some Latin Americans and Anglo-Americans who seek to give outsiders and themselves the impression that everything is well with young America, that nothing is wrong in Brazilian life; they have encountered the theory that literature should be an instrument of propaganda for the good and pleasant in that life, that it should avoid mockery, satire, or criticism of the sort that might convey the idea that Brazil has many Negroes and that it also has serious problems of maladjustment, poverty, and misery.

The same thing has happened to some of the modern Brazilian poets, historians, essayists, literary critics, and painters who are taking Brazilian culture and the mind of young Brazil out of that passively colonial and rigidly academic tradition in which there was no place for a literature or an art different from Europe's. This tradition made Brazilians afraid to express themselves freely. They were afraid to reveal how different Brazil was and is from Europe—a Europe considered socially and intellectually perfect by many Latin Americans with a colonial psychological complex of inferiority.

Some years ago a novel was published in Rio which may be regarded, in some of its aspects, as an anticipation of the modern social novel of Brazil. I refer to *Canaan*, written by Graça Aranha, an aristocrat descended from an old family of northern Brazil. Its plot has been summarized by the famous Italian historian and critic, Signor Guglielmo Ferrero, who says that its real subject is "the encounter of the races, the mixing of cultures, the disturbance caused in the social organization of all American countries by the masses of men arriving from overcrowded Europe." [3] But I think that *Canaan* is also the drama of Brazilians under the pressure of that old colonial complex from which only now their historians, essayists, novelists, poets, and critics are vigorously liberating them.

One of the most significant characters in *Canaan* is Paulo Maciel, a young Brazilian lawyer. The way that he talks throughout the novel is the way that many Brazilian lawyers, intellectuals, and artists talked thirty or forty years ago, when they felt that Brazil was nothing more than "a colony of Europe." They saw no hope that Brazilians might overcome their colonial condition. At that time men like Paulo Maciel, though conscious of the dependence of Brazil upon Europe, did nothing to counteract it. When one of these men made a speech or wrote an article or a dissertation, a book or a poem, he wrote as though he expected to have to submit his grammar, composition, style, vocabulary, and ideas to a committee of Portuguese professors of grammar and to a committee of professors of literature, law, or sociology from Paris. Nearly all of these men derived their ideas about Brazil, not from direct study of conditions, but from what remote and sometimes ignorant or second-rate French sociologists, like Le Bon, wrote about race mixture in Latin America. The best of the writers followed such European social theorists as Spencer and Comte, ignorant of extra-European conditions and problems. Consequently their attitude toward Brazil was one of pessimism, though very few dared to express themselves in public in such

[3] Guglielmo Ferrero: "Preface," *Canaan*, by Graça Aranha; translated from the Portuguese by Mariano Joaquin Lorente (Boston, 1920), p. 7.

a way as to conflict with Brazilian official philosophy—the philosophy of those in power, an emphatic and superficial optimism as long as those who expressed it remained in power.

The following words are spoken by Paulo Maciel, the character in *Canaan* to whom I have referred, as he talks to some Brazilian colleagues:

"You gentlemen speak of independence, but I don't see it. Brazil is, and has always been, a colony. Our regime is not a free one. We are a protectorate. . . . Tell me: where is our financial independence? What is the real money that dominates us? Where is our gold? What is the use of our miserable paper currency if it isn't to buy English pounds? Where is our public property? What little we have is mortgaged. The customs revenues are in the hands of the English. We have no ships. We have no railroads, either; they are all in the hands of the foreigners. Is it, or is it not, a colonial regime disguised with the name of free nation? Listen. You don't believe me. I would like to be able to preserve our moral and intellectual patrimony, our language, but rather than continue this poverty, this torpitude at which we have arrived, it is better for one of Rothschilds' bookkeepers to manage our financial affairs and for a German colonel to set things in order." [4]

And later, speaking not to a fellow countryman, but to a German, Milkau, to whom Brazil was "Canaan" and Europe the reverse of "Canaan," young Maciel in a still more pessimistic mood says:

"My only wish is to get out of here, to exile myself, to leave the country and go with my people [family] to live in some corner of Europe . . . Europe! . . . Europe! . . . Yes, at least until the crisis is over." [5]

[4] *Canaan*, pp. 196–7.
[5] Ibid., p. 293.

All this was typical of the psychological attitude of Brazilian intellectual youth forty and even thirty years ago. In contrast to a strictly official optimism, there was a Russian pessimism among writers, lawyers, and students, caused by the impact of a deep complex of colonialism on their minds and their entire personalities. For most of them Europe—Paris, or London, or Berlin—was the ideal place of escape, actual or imagined, from Brazilian colonialism. For some did take imaginary refuge—even the old historian and critic João Ribeiro did—by living intellectually in Europe; that is, by being *in* Brazil but not *of* it, attaching themselves mentally to Europe—to France, particularly—as colonials, as exiles.

It is curious that in Graça Aranha's novel the best explanation of Brazil's critical condition as felt by some of her intellectuals is given not by one of the Brazilian characters, but by the German, Milkau, whom the author represents as a European with a philosophical turn of mind. It is he who tells the typically pessimistic Brazilian intellectual of the early 1900's that Brazil, having originated as a conglomeration of races and castes, masters and slaves, had created through master-and-slave contact an intermediate race of mestizos which was really the link between classes, the national tie. Their numbers increasing every day, these mestizos were appropriating the best positions. When the army (very important to a German as to a Latin American) had ceased to be "the appanage of the white man" and began to be taken over by the mestizos, a social revolution had started—"a revenge of the oppressed."

This generalization was only partly true, for, as I have pointed out, most of the mixed-bloods who became prominent in early republican Brazil had done little more than take the places and carry on the leadership of the monarchist leaders, some of whom were already men of Negro blood.

But, according to Aranha's Milkau, whatever shock of conflict there was between the white and the heterogeneous leadership as a result of the republican revolution was "absolutely necessary to bring about what other means had not been able to accomplish for centuries; the formation of a nationality." [6]

This again is a generalization only partly true, for after their successful struggle against the Dutch in the seventeenth century, some Brazilians began to feel and even to act as if they were capable of being a nationality. And since that early war for independence, leadership has been heterogeneous as far as military action was concerned. The four great heroes of the Brazilian war against the Dutch belonged to different races: one was a Portuguese, another a white Brazilian, the third an Indian, the fourth a Negro. During the war against the Dutch, various men of African blood or modest social situation distinguished themselves by acts of bravery or by valiant services in the defense of Brazil. These services were recognized, and they contributed to the social elevation of the men and in some cases to their entrance by marriage into the ranks of the highest Brazilian society. It was also during the war against the Dutch that Father Vieira—born in Portugal, but educated in Brazil, where he arrived as a child—distinguished himself as an intellectual leader whose sermons and writings have not only a religious interest and a literary value, but also a deep psychological and sociological significance as a sort of manifesto—an ethnically democratic manifesto—against the idea of superiority of men over men based upon skin-color. If this idea were true, he said once, the Dutch would have to be considered a superior race that could not be defeated by the Portuguese and the Brazilians; but it could not be true, for the Dutch were Protestant heretics and the Portuguese and the Brazilians were orthodox Catholics. Vieira thus made anthropology dependent upon theology and Catholic orthodoxy.

[6] Ibid., p. 295.

Although his father had been made a nobleman by the king of Portugal, Vieira was the grandson of a dark woman. When he preached race equality, he spoke *pro domo sua*. He was in a logical position to be the psychological and intellectual link in a social revolution that began in Brazil, not with the Republic in 1889, but during the wars against the Dutch in the seventeenth century, a revolution looking toward the admittance of mixed-bloods to leadership in Brazil and toward the formation of a Brazilian nationality through an at first vague, and only today clear, consciousness or feeling of ethnic as well as social difference from Europe. But difference—not inferiority.

All this seems to have been forgotten by Graça Aranha's German philosopher on Brazilian history, Milkau, when he tells Maciel that the revolution against Europe in Brazil had begun with the Republic, with the 1889 victory of the Republican leaders who were army officers—some of them, as we know, men with Indian and Negro blood. But in the dialogue between Maciel and Milkau it is the Brazilian who is the Aryanist or racist, the German who is the believer in the advantages of race mixture. It is the German (copied from life, and not a purely literary invention) who tells the pessimistic Brazilian intellectual (representing the feeling of some of the best Brazilian intellectuals of one and two generations ago, including Euclides da Cunha, Sylvio Romero, and Graça Aranha himself) that "there are no races capable or incapable of civilization," history being "nothing but a record of the fusion of races." And, Milkau continues, "in Brazil, you may be sure, culture will flourish in the soil of the half-caste population because there has been there that divine fusion which is the creative force." In "a remote future, the period of the mulattoes will have passed," to be succeeded by "the period of the white people." The "white people . . . will accept the patrimony of their half-caste predecessors, who will have built something, for nothing passes uselessly over the earth." [7] As to Europe: "That Europe toward which you people turn your longing and dying eyes and which you love with your tired souls, hungry for happiness, culture, art, and life, that Europe also suffers from the malady which disintegrates and kills. Do not allow yourselves to be dazzled by her empty pomp, by the useless strength of her armies, by the brilliance of her genius." [8]

I repeat that two contradictory views of philosophies of life and of Brazilian history were powerfully reflected in Brazilian literature until, soon after the First World War, new voices began to be heard, first from São Paulo, and then from the northeast. Of the two traditional views, one expressed an almost absolute optimism concerning Brazilian past, present, and future, and particularly the Amerindian basis of its "race" and "ethos." The extreme expression of this philosophy is to be found in a book entitled *Porque me ufano do meu paiz* ("Why I Am Proud of My Fatherland"), written by Afonso Celso, a good and distinguished, though naïve, Brazilian who was given the title of Count by the Holy See. The other philosophy combined an almost suicidal pessimism over Brazilian ethnic and social conditions with a longing for Europe, viewed with a sort of filial veneration as if London and Paris, Lisbon and Berlin each had a pope whom the Brazilians must follow blindly when studying law or sociology and writing poems or novels. Between the two extremes there had appeared a few books like *Os Sertões* by Euclides da Cunha and *Canaan* by Graça Aranha, and some of the best pages of social and literary critics like José Verissimo, Sylvio Romero, and Alberto Torres. These were the harbingers of a new phase in Brazilian literature, the modern phase.

In 1919 a book was published in São Paulo, *Urupés*, which,

[7] Ibid., p. 296.
[8] Ibid., p. 297.

though pessimistic in its views of social conditions, nevertheless was far from colonial, academic, sub-European, or orthodox *à la française* in style, form, or language; it was vigorously Brazilian, full of native idioms, and marked by departures from rigid grammatical rules. Its author was Monteiro Lobato. *Urupés* is a collection of tales about the poor or decadent populations of rural Brazil generally neglected by politicians and by conventional *literati* (though Euclides da Cunha's *Os Sertões* had been a powerful pioneer study of central Brazil as a dramatic subject not only for literature, but also for sociology, anthropology, and human geography). The personality of the author of *Urupés*—even more than his first book or any that followed it—was to be a center of intellectual and cultural revolution in Brazil. Dynamic, suggestive, stimulating, Lobato became a literary and social critic and creative artist, as well as a publisher. For years he published essays, novels, poems, and sociological and historical studies written by promising young writers, the best of whom exhibited vigorous intellectual honesty and realism in dealing with Brazilian subjects and followed Lobato in his courageous use of native idioms and even in his disdain of Europe as Brazil's intellectual and cultural master.

In São Paulo, and later in Rio, there followed another literary revolution, significant as an attempt to express the Brazilian ethos and, to a certain extent, to reflect extra-European social and ethnic conditions. I refer to the movement called "Modernism" in Brazil. One of its most interesting leaders, the late Mario de Andrade, significantly regretted, when he analyzed Brazilian "Modernism" a few years before his death, that it remained too exclusively a literary or narrowly artistic revolution: that it did not go far enough in developing its social implications. But there is no doubt that Brazilian "Modernism" did much to bring Brazilians to an awareness of their country.

Fearless of the unapproved, in its reaction against academic artificiality "Modernism" sometimes became artificial itself. But it opened the door to a new Brazilian way of writing which has influenced and is still influencing the Portuguese written in Portugal.

Independently of the "Modernism" of Rio and São Paulo, a similar movement started in the oldest region of Brazil, the northeast. This also was a revolt against narrow colonialism, though it did not repudiate Brazilian experience and the integration of European with extra-European values during the colonial era. It proclaimed the need of extra-European attitudes and values without failing to recognize the need in Brazil of a close contact with Europe and with its European past; Brazil should select from its colonial heritage a series of values in harmony with the tropical landscape and with Brazilian conditions of life. Hence the importance attached by some of its leaders, in a way that was not that of the "Modernists" of Rio and São Paulo, to traditional cookery and pastry, traditional architecture, furniture, and popular art—not to preserve them as sacred things, but to use them as honest beginnings for a really Brazilian art and way of living. Not a single or exclusive tradition—that of Aryan Europe—but a combination of traditional values, from the Arabs and Moors, from the Jews, from Africa, from Asia, should be followed, having as a basis the experience of the Portuguese and the heritage of the Amerindian.

Opposing the reaction against this combination, which had taken place during the nineteenth century when sophisticated Brazilians began to be ashamed of some of their best extra-European values and traditions, the leaders of the northeast movement argued that Brazil ought to maintain and develop the extra-European values and traditions already harmonized with tropical and Brazilian conditions of life, instead of neglecting or abandoning them in order to become a cultural province of

Europe or of the United States. Impelled by this idea, the Congress of Regionalism met in 1925 in Recife, intellectual capital of the northeast, with Odilon Nestor, José Lins do Rego, Morais Coutinho, Annibal Fernandes, Luis Cedro, Julio Bello, and others as its leaders or followers. It was the first Congress of Regionalism in Brazil. Its manifesto was literary and artistic, but also sociological and political. Variety in unity characterized the proceedings, not only in the basic ideas of the program itself, but also in the personnel, which included men of various ages and generations, temperaments, and professions. It is safe to say that the group that met for this Congress—some of them still students or very recent graduates from universities—and those who since have been directly or indirectly influenced by them have produced some of modern Brazil's most interesting and vitally significant literature and social and literary criticism.

Resisting the idea that material or technical progress should be taken as the measure of Brazilian greatness, the Regionalists stand for that love of locality which to them seems to be a prerequisite for honest, authentic, genuine creative work—not an end in itself. These are no narrow nationalists; they realize that interdependence is, throughout the world, an essential condition for a more humane and more co-operative intellectual and artistic life. Some of their earlier critics accused them of being reactionaries; others called them "Communists" or "Anarchists" who refused to acknowledge the need for centralization, for rigid uniformity, in a country like Brazil. The truth is that the work done by the most creative of them—among them José Lins do Rego, José Americo, Cicero Dias, Luis Jardim, Julio Bello, Olivio Montenegro, Annibal Fernandes, and more recently, Mauro Motta, João Cabral de Melo Neto, Perminio Asfora, Carlos Pena, L. Cardozo Ayres, A. Suassuna, F. Brennand, and A. Magalhães—is vigorously constructive. It has done much to generate real unity and interregional understanding as well as to make Brazil a vital part of a new and more cooperative world.

The same might be said of the cultural revolution effected with a more immediate literary and artistic success by the "Modernists" of Rio and São Paulo—Mario de Andrade, Oswald de Andrade, Graça Aranha, Alcantara Machado, Manuel Bandeira, Sergio Buarque, Prudente de Morais Neto, Carlos Drumond de Andrade, Ribeiro Couto, and others—whose movement at once initiated a new era in the intellectual and artistic development of Brazil without overlooking Brazilian social conditions. Southern Brazilians of the central state of Minas Gerais have recently become more vigorous in literature than those of São Paulo. Senhor Guimarães Rosa is the outstanding representative of a new type of literature in Brazil which, being regional, is psychological. He seems to have been influenced by Mario de Andrade, in his preoccupation with a language at once artistic and telluric, by the northeast Regionalists, in his interest in regional types, and by Simoes Lopes Neto, a pioneer Regionalist from Rio Grande do Sul, who was a master of the folk-tale (*conto regional*). But there is something in him as in other younger writers such as Antonio Callado, Mario Palmerio, and Osman Lins, that is distinctly new.

These two movements—the "Modernistic" of Rio-São Paulo and the "Regionalist" of Recife—will probably stand as the most significant in revolutionizing the letters and life of Brazil in the direction of intellectual or cultural spontaneity, creativeness, and self-confidence set against the tradition of colonial subordination to Europe or the United States.

Brazilian Architecture: "Moorish" and "Roman"

A French writer who has been in Brazil more than once, M. Blaise Cendrars, and who is also acquainted with the Far East, has included Brazilian cookery among what he considers the three best *cuisines* of the world, along with the French and the Chinese. Other foreign observers of Brazilian civilization are inclined to give an equally high place to Brazilian architecture: to include it among the best in the modern world. And still other foreigners seem to think that even today Brazilian women, though considerably "Americanized" in the most progressive towns, may still be included among the best housewives to be found anywhere.

If one takes these three generalizations as real or as close approaches to real facts, and adds to them the circumstance that

Brazil is only now beginning to have tolerable hotels outside of Rio and São Paulo—one good one in Salvador de Bahia is a brilliant exception—this group of Brazilian pre-eminences seems to express something essentially and characteristically Brazilian. Perhaps the root of the matter lies in the patriarchal past of Brazil. Its civilization has been rather the effort of a familistic organization than the achievement of state or church, of kings or military leaders. Hence its development as a civilization that has had as its basic values domestic, patriarchal, sedentary values: (1) the residential and the agrarian buildings associated with a family economy of a permanent, and not a nomadic, character; (2) the cookery, always complementary to a family sedentary civilization like the Chinese in the East; (3) the housewife, as an administrator of cookery and other important domestic activities.

And as is always the case with civilizations of this type, hospitality was in Brazil through the three centuries of its development as a patriarchal system, a duty of the patriarchal families. This seems to explain why private residences for a long time were the proper places where strangers were made to feel at home while traveling through Brazil, with rooms of their own, slaves to take care of them, and a place at the vast, well-provided patriarchal table. Inns, when inns existed in colonial Brazil, were only for strangers or foreigners so insignificant as not to be admitted as guests into the patriarchal residences. Hence the fact that Brazil does not have a good hotel tradition: some of its new hotels are beginning wisely to associate a certain family, domestic atmosphere with international styles of hotel organization, so as to keep up with tradition. In one of these new hotels guests are taken care of by servants dressed as African girls and pages dressed as in old patriarchal Brazil; and the food, instead of being only international hotel cookery, is made up also of Brazilian national and regional patriarchal dishes.

One has the impression that the manager behind this compromise between international and national styles of hospitality is also a double personality, half Swiss *ménagère*, half Brazilian housewife.

The same compromise seems to be taking place in regard to architecture in Brazil. It is emerging from the Brazilian patriarchal past as a building-system capable of being adapted to modern conditions and modern styles of living without losing its basic traditional values. These basic traditional values are domestic, private, familistic—that is, "Moorish," but not narrowly domestic, because they are also "Roman" in their patriarchal roots and, as Roman, inclined to contact with the outside world. Combined, the two elements—"Moorish" and "Roman"—seem to be responsible for a tendency in typically Brazilian modern buildings to be peculiarly humane and personalistic, instead of efficient or "functional" only from the point of view of their use as official, industrial, impersonal, commercial, and collectivistic buildings.

The extension of architecture in Brazil from what it was as an architecture for private, domestic, patriarchal, personalistic, rather than impersonally collectivistic conditions and needs to an architecture of a modern type and for conditions that are collectivistic and public rather than personalistic and private has been possible because the old colonial type of Brazilian house or residence was more than a mere residence. As students of social history have shown, that house—the "big house" of sugar- and coffee-planters—besides being a residence for a large family with its many domestic slaves, was also hospital, church (for its private chapel with a private chaplain amounted to this), orphan asylum, fortress in case of attacks from wild Indians, and bank in whose thick, solid stone or brick walls jewels, money, or other values were kept. Consequently, it was a building of large dimensions, and its architects had to solve problems that in other countries had to be faced by builders of official palaces, of churches or monasteries, of fortresses, and not of mere private residences.

Some of the old plantation "big houses" of Brazil were indeed, in their appearance, their dimensions, and the number of their rooms, more like monasteries than like private residences. One of them has been described by a Brazilian writer as a Brazilian "rustic Escorial" on account of its many rooms and also of the many tombs in its vast chapel—for the dead of the family, an old patriarchal custom in Brazil. In this particular house described as an Escorial, it is interesting to note that some of the tombs in the chapel were of the wives of the last planter who lived there as a real *grand seigneur*, and who had not only three wives—one after the other, of course, for he was an orthodox Catholic and officially, at least, monogamic—but many children and grandchildren from his successive wives. This was not exceptional, but typical.

This so-called Escorial was typical of a Brazilian plantation "big house" or *casa-grande* of the colonial days, whose architecture seems to have been in Brazil almost as important as church architecture; and certainly its superior as an ecological type of architecture in the development of which the Portuguese seems to have done his best to adapt to Brazilian tropical conditions his European ways of building (even in Europe touched by a certain Moorish or Oriental influence) and the lessons as to building residences in the tropics that he learned from East Indians in the East itself and even from China. Hence the long low structure of a typical Brazilian "big house" of the colonial days, containing sitting-room, dining-room, sometimes twenty bedrooms, a protective, large veranda, roofed in such a way—an Oriental way introduced by the Portuguese in Brazil—as to exclude excesses of light and to protect the house against heavy rains. Most of the windows were of wood, in a

Moorish style; the rooms for unmarried girls were in the interior of the house, with no windows to the outside. A *pateo* usually provided the aristocratic ladies and girls of the house with space for recreation without any need of contact with the outside world: a world that according to the patriarchal social orthodoxy was a world for men and not for women. The great mission of women in the patriarchal system of Brazil—a system that developed such a valuable type of domestic architecture—was to be the managers of a variety of domestic activities that included the welfare not only of the aristocratic old people and children of the family, but of its slaves as well, and also of small farmers of the neighborhood, who, though not slaves, depended upon the master and the mistress of the "big house" for a number of things, not only for religious assistance, but for medical aid as well.

It is only when one considers how complex were the activities of a typical plantation "big house" in patriarchal Brazil that one sees why its type of architecture did not die entirely with the old social order, but has become a valuable inspiration for experimental modern building, which in Portuguese America is an art as well as a science, and which is already known for its practical, effective, and not only theoretical advances. This art, as well as science, has probably its greatest creative expression in the work of Senhor Lucio Costa, though some claim this pre-eminence for a younger architect of great talent: Senhor Oscar Niemeyer. Costa's achievements seem to be the result of the fact that he is a man who has carefully studied the social past of Brazil and Portugal as reflected in their traditional architecture. He even has shown in his most recent work a tendency to use color boldly on the exterior of his buildings, so associating his modernism with the Moorish, Portuguese, Brazilian tradition of freely using tropical, vivid colors, and not only the conventional blues and greens of tiles (*azulejos*) with religious motifs in the outside decoration of buildings. Even large apartment buildings, where this use of vivid colors asks for a particular care in the combination of blues with reds, are now being built in Rio: a victory for Brazilian writers who have clamored for this since the beginning of the present modernistic movement in architecture in Brazil.

Another recent preoccupation is to associate tropical vegetation with modern architecture, also a tradition of the old domestic, patriarchal architecture of Brazil, famous for its flower gardens [1] sometimes linked to gardens of vegetables useful for domestic consumption. Not only for kitchen or cookery purposes, but for medical, hygienic, and prophylactic purposes as well, or only to decorate and perfume the interior of the house when a birthday or other family event was celebrated with a great dinner. For this purpose, leaves of palm trees were freely used and also aromatic and brilliantly green leaves of the cinnamon tree.

One should not forget that the domestic, Moorish character of some of the most modernistic apartment buildings in Brazil seems to be a new expression of the vitality of an architectural tradition inherited by the Brazilians from Moorish—as well as Roman—Portugal. As a result of its expansion in as large a tropical space as Brazil, this tradition first modernized itself in the eighteenth century, when the manor houses of the northern part of Portugal became larger and more elaborate, thanks to the immense impulse given to their reconstruction—or to the construction of new ones—by what an English student of the

---

[1] Of "private mansions" in Belém, a characteristically tropical city of Brazil, Charles W. Domville-Fife, in his book *The United States of Brazil* (London, 1910), gives the following description: "The private mansions—for, in most cases, they can be so termed—are well built, with imposing entrances, flanked by broad stone columns. They stand in their own tropical gardens, are seldom more than two stories high. The second floor is always surrounded by a veranda, which is usually covered with creepers of tangled growth and with flowers" (p. 121).

subject, Mr. Rodney Gallop, calls "the Brazilian gold." It was then, according to the same British observer, that such manor houses took "definite form"—something that happened also in Brazil with the plantation and city "big houses" of the most advanced regions. In Portugal, as in the most advanced regions of Brazil, one may agree with Gallop that a number of factors— not the same in Europe and America—acted then to nullify, in domestic architecture, the influences of the Moors, and, coupled with the classical tendencies of the epoch, bred qualities of solidity and sobriety—Roman qualities, one is tempted to add. According to Gallop, "the façade of the Portuguese country house is notable for its harmonious proportions and for the symmetrical distribution of the many windows with their more or less ornate enclosures of unwashed stone." [2] Both the "symmetrical distribution" of windows and their large number became characteristic of Brazilian domestic architecture as it became less Moorish—that is, less orthodoxly private—and more Roman or more classic—more public. And this type of domestic architecture, made possible not only by gold, but also by sugar and coffee, seems to have developed in Portugal under a certain Brazilian influence.

Some think that classicism endowed the United States with an architectural tradition unsurpassed in the qualities of monumentality and dignity. In Brazil, classicism has been modified by an experimental tendency that is felt even today in an impulse toward what the late Fiske Kimball—the well-known historian of domestic architecture in the United States—would probably have considered "original forms expressive of the novel elements in modern life." The Brazilian seems to have acquired this experimental tendency from the Portuguese, who became experimental in his architecture in the East Indies, where he had to face "novel elements" in life: tropical and ex-

[2] *Portugal: A Book of Folk-Ways* (Cambridge [England], 1936) p. 42.

tra-European elements. He adopted them experimentally, assimilating East Indian and Chinese Orientalisms, besides the Moorish ones already assimilated in the Iberian Peninsula, but without ceasing to be classical in his attachment to the elements of continuity within his European, or Roman-Moorish, past.

Of course, under present conditions, some of the desirable combinations of tradition with modernity in the architecture of Brazil are made extremely difficult, so far as the urban areas are concerned, by the fact that though architects are developing an art that is genuinely Brazilian, ecological, and tropical, city-planners do not follow the same method: they are too imitative of such "modern" as comes to them from Europe and the United States, and too indifferent to planning according to conditions peculiar to tropical Brazil. One of these desirable combinations is, of course, the association of vegetation and building. But land is becoming too expensive and proper care is not being taken by city-planners in Brazilian capitals for the necessary presence of vegetation in urban areas except under the conventional form of public purely ornamental gardens, usually of the Versailles artificial, symmetrical type, exactly the type least adapted to a tropical country like Brazil. Even Petropolis, near Rio de Janeiro—which since the days of Dom Pedro II has been for the capital of Brazil what Newport was for Washington, Alt-Aussee for Vienna, and Yalta for St. Petersburg—is being badly affected by the divorce, so sharp in modern Brazil, between architecture and town-planning. Even there, vegetation is ceasing to be defended from narrowly commercial building. As to Rio itself, no European or Anglo-American finds there, at present, as he would have found until the first two decades of this century, "restful by-ways, like those of the sea-bound towns of northern Portugal," so highly praised by an Englishman who visited Brazil during the First World War, "little *plazas* slumbering in the sun, past old-

world gardens where children laugh and play, and shaded
patios, whose marble pavements glisten and gleam amidst
white and purple flowers and cool ferns." Even in the heart
of the city, he found spots—one of them the Largo da Carioca
—that were restful and "full of the ethereal fragrance of
tropic days and nights." [3]

One of the tasks of city-planning in Brazil is to preserve this
fragrance, this atmosphere, or this tropical charm in cities that
are losing their souls in order to become modern. What Brazilian architects are successfully doing with buildings is this: they
are showing that it is possible to have perfectly modern buildings that are at the same time Brazilian in the way that they re-
tain something of the patriarchal, personalistic, familist past of
Brazil in their present-day forms, something of that past which
represents a long process of adaptation of European values to
tropical conditions.

Some time ago, a geographer pointed out that many beautiful orchids were sent home—that is, to Europe—from businessmen residing in South America, especially in Brazil, and
thus introduced in European gardens. It is a fact that European, especially English, businessmen became famous in Brazil
for their preference for living not in newly built houses, but
in old ones, usually old *"quinta"* or *"chacara"* or suburban
houses built by Brazilians according to old Portuguese tradition. In Brazil Englishmen and other European residents became enthusiastic about plants, ferns, and cacti that they usually found already associated with the houses that became
their Brazilian residences, sometimes for long years. Theirs is
the merit of having perceived that the problem of European
residence in tropical Brazil had already been solved by the
Portuguese: what some of them added to these ecological

[3] J. O. P. Bland: *Men, Manners, and Morals in South America* (London,
1920), p. 54.

houses was improvement in their sanitary conveniences and, in some cases, development, more than the Brazilians had done or were doing, of the space given, in their residential gardens, to orchids, the evening primrose, and other beautiful plants.

It seems that Englishmen and others who at first criticized Brazilian residences for not being floored with wood almost always were converted to the Brazilian way. One of them, having arrived in Brazil in the late sixties of the nineteenth century, found out that the houses had no wood flooring: the better ones had marble flooring or a tiled pavement according to the owner's taste and means, and the humbler ones had no flooring at all. He was shocked at first, but in a book written after a forty years' residence in Brazil, this same Englishman—a Mr. Bennett, who lived first in Pernambuco and later in Rio Grande do Sul—wrote that marble flooring or tiled pavement such as he found in the houses of Pernambuco was "much more suitable for the climatic conditions that prevail there." It was in these patriarchal houses that Mr. Bennett made his direct acquaintance with Brazilian slaves and found with his own eyes that they had had board and lodging and were clothed at their master's expense and were, a great many of them, "better off than some free-born people . . . in England in the present day, who, with all their hard work, do not get sufficient to keep themselves in good working condition. . . ." Therefore he was not entirely indignant against slavery as a domestic, patriarchal institution, when he observed that in Brazil, the Brazil that he first knew, about 1868, "there was one very fine house [in Pernambuco] built by a man who had made a great deal of money in the slave trade, and in the garden there several statues, which were found all painted black one morning!" [4] Mr. Bennett was simply amused by the fact, which incidentally reminds us of the prevailing custom among architects of Brazil

[4] Frank Bennett: *Forty Years in Brazil* (London, 1914), p. 10.

during the Empire of having not only residential but also commercial and official buildings decorated with statues, most of them made in Oporto, in Portugal. They represented—some of them are still to be found—the four seasons (spring, summer, autumn, and winter), the four continents (Europe, Asia, Africa, and America), Jupiter, Neptune, and other classical gods. Busts of great men also were sometimes used for the same decorative purpose, the whiteness of the marble or of the ceramic harmonizing well with the vivid colors, red, blue, purple, yellow, pink, of the building and the green of the tropical vegetation. Among these great men, whose busts are still to be seen decorating old buildings in Brazil, were Camões; the Marquis of Pombal, the Portuguese statesman; and Dom Pedro II, Emperor of Brazil.

Europeans who visited Brazil as late as the beginning of the present century were agreeably impressed by the harmony of colors offered by the old buildings, some of them faced or painted with green, blue, yellow, pink, and brown tiles, surrounded, as most of the patriarchal residences and even some of the public buildings still were, by vegetation: plants, trees, gardens of a brilliant green. Some of the Brazilian towns in which vegetation was complementary to the architecture of residential houses gave one the impression of being built in the midst of what another English traveler, a Mr. Martin, described as "several small park-like plantations." [5]

Like his fellow countryman Mr. Bennett in regard to wood flooring (unusual in Brazil, Brazilians having come to consider marble a better material for residential, and not only official, floors in a tropical country), Mr. Martin became converted to the Brazilian custom of having in residential buildings numerous doors and windows opening onto those "park-like planta-

[5] Percy F. Martin: *Through Five Republics of South America* (London, 1905), p. 167.

tions." Writing particularly of Belém, Mr. Martin observed that both doors and windows in residential houses were "as lofty and as wide as possible, so as to afford a continuous current of air through them. Above the doors are built open ventilators, the doors themselves being often half open-latticed."

Other Brazilianisms in domestic architecture attracted his attention and seem to have deserved the approval of Mr. Martin, a very typical Britisher of the end of the nineteenth century in his upbringing, but cosmopolitan enough to admit that Brazilians were developing an ecological architecture. One, the fact that the walls of the houses "are never papered. . . . Even in the most luxuriously appointed residences," he found the walls "distempered usually white or green." Another architectural Brazilianism was the fact that "the ceilings are of wood painted a similar color or varnished." Still a third one: he observed that the wooden staircases were invariably left uncarpeted, which gave a somewhat bare but decidedly cool appearance to the interiors. And a fourth one: all the windows he observed to be provided with Venetian shutters, designed to keep out the strong sunlight, but to admit the air freely.[6] The same, or similar, function was that of the veranda, sometimes around the entire house.[7]

[6] Ibid., pp. 168–9.
[7] According to Mario de Andrade, in his essay "Art," included in *Brazil* (edited by Lawrence F. Hill, Berkeley and Los Angeles, 1947, p. 184), the rectangular plan of building, in the colonial architecture of Brazil, "seems to reveal a certain class promiscuity which had arisen through the necessity of defence. . . . Class distinctions, however, led eventually to corresponding distinctions in building plans. The most characteristic examples are terraces and covered porches, which are found in chapels as well as in the *casa grande*. . . . Although their cool shade was a protection against the tropic intensity of the climate, the function of balconies and terraces was primarily social: they served for communication between master and slave or for business transactions." It is doubtful if the function of such terraces was primarily "social." Porches in chapels seem to me to have been a Luso-tropicalism developed by the Portuguese, first in India, later in Brazil, though they may have been preceded in rare cases by European churches

Such Brazilianisms were not peculiar to the northern part of Brazil, but might be found, in the early years of the present century, in the most typically Brazilian residences of Rio and São Paulo: in those where carpets, wood floors, wall paper, and other North European customs, then generally considered refinements by passive imitators of Europe no matter what the climate was, had not been introduced as an imitation, either directly of Europe by Brazilians who went abroad or indirectly

---

with porches. (See, on this, Professor Robert C. Smith's chapter "The Arts in Brazil," in *Portugal and Brazil, an Introduction,* an excellent book edited by H. V. Livermore, Oxford, 1953, p. 370, note 13.)

As Richard Burton (*The Highlands of the Brazil,* London, 1869, II, 39) observed almost a century ago when writing of a "big house" he knew in Minas Gerais that he characterized as "a manor house in a normal style," this type of house, when orthodox, was "fronted by a deep veranda, from which the owner can prospect the distillary, the mill, (sugar cane) . . ." and, also, the chapel, the "Senzallas or negro quarters," and other activities. He forgot to mention that the owner stayed in his "deep veranda," sat or reclined on his throne—a hammock—though, in another passage of his book he refers to villagers in nineteenth-century Brazil—inhabitants of modest village houses—who spent the hot hours of the day in the hammock, "swinging, smoking, and eating melons" or sitting in a shady spot to the windward of the house "receiving visits" (II, 357). For one should not forget that it has been a tradition in the domestic architecture of Brazil for houses to have verandas, or shady spots, where the owner may sit to receive visits or look at the outside.

Recently, Professor Lynn Smith, a United States sociologist traveling in Brazil, noticed that in the best coffee and other modern *fazendas* or plantations of Brazil, a village arrangement is utilized for the homes of the workers and the essential establishments maintained on the *fazenda,* whose "point of orientation" continues to be, as in the old patriarchal days, "the casa grande" (or big house, originally of the patriarchal sugar-planter, later of the coffee-planter) ". . . usually well-constructed and comfortable . . . surrounded by well-kept lawns and gardens, which nearly always include a tiled swimming pool . . . drying floors for the coffee, the mill for cleaning and grading the beans, and the barns for livestock . . . the 'armazem' or commissary, the business offices . . . the slaughterhouse . . . often a school and chapel . . . not infrequently a station on the railroad . . . cottages of the *colonos* who perform the manual labor on the *fazendas*" (*Brazil: Its People and Institutions,* New York, 1954, 2nd ed., p. 324). On the relationship between the "big house" and the homes of less important people in a rustic tropical sub-area of Brazil, see *Amazon Town: A Study of Man in the Tropics* (New York, 1953), by Professor Charles Wagley.

of what some foreign residents did in their houses. For some of the foreign residents of other cities lived as if they were enemies of everything tropical and felt the need of remaining as loyal as possible to European styles and customs. Imitation of such customs and styles began to affect Brazilian domestic architecture in the early nineteenth century, when the use of glass began to displace the Moorish latticed windows and the Swiss *chalet* began to become a fashion for suburban residences, though usually a compromise was reached between this very European type of architecture and such of the already-mentioned architectural Brazilianisms as lofty, wide doors and windows and, later, Venetian shutters, which, in some of the older Brazilian houses, had been preceded by Moorish windows and East Indian light-shutters.

One should never forget that the Portuguese who colonized Brazil, making of Brazil since the sixteenth century a permanent home instead of a place for nomadic tropical adventures —as it was for the French, the English, and most of the Dutch in the sixteenth and seventeenth centuries—brought to America from the East a group of Orientalisms, some of them applied to domestic architecture or to domestic hygiene. The Chinese style of roof was one of them, the large porch another. With the extensive use of tile for both the interior and the exterior of houses, the Portuguese had already assimilated from the Moors and Arabs, since the days of the Moorish occupation of the peninsula, a few basic Orientalisms that were introduced into their domestic architecture in Brazil as a protection against the excesses—from a European point of view—of tropical weather. One of these basic Orientalisms seems to have been the thick walls, a protection against the heat. These walls, made of stone or brick, gave to some colonial residences in Brazil the appearance of fortresses, and fortresses some of them had to be during critical days when Amerindians attacked European settlements.

This should not make anyone think that Amerindians and Portuguese always fought each other and had no friendly intercourse in sixteenth-century Brazil during the heroic and difficult days when the bases for a permanent civilization—including a permanent domestic architecture—were laid. Friendly intercourse between the two rival groups alternated with hostility, but perhaps there was no other part of America where the two races, the European and the Amerindian, and the two cultures met with as much ethnic and cultural reciprocity as in Brazil, through the union of the Portuguese men with Amerindian women and through the adoption, by the Amerindians of European values, and of Amerindian values by the Europeans.

In regard to architecture of a permanent type, there was nothing that the nomadic or almost nomadic Amerindians could offer to a Portuguese willing to adopt tropical values from tropical peoples, and thus adapt himself to a tropical environment, following some of the techniques and methods of the natives. But it took little time and effort on the part of the Portuguese to make characteristic of their houses, in tropical and quasi-tropical Brazil—including São Paulo in the sixteenth century—the preparation of walls in the interior of the houses, and of pillars in the porches or the verandas, as places to hang or sling Amerindian swinging hammocks. With many of the colonists, these hammocks took the place of ordinary beds and even of nuptial or conjugal couches. Hooks and wall-space for hammocks became an essential characteristic of Brazilian houses. If one agrees with modern European observers that in a tropical climate heavy draperies and stuffed furniture are to be avoided, one has to recognize that in adopting the swinging hammock and making it an essential part of his house, the cal environments, through architecture as well as through furniture, cookery, dress—in various regions of Asia, Africa, and America similar in climate and physical conditions to Brazil, and are finding that valuable lessons can be learned from Brazil. The Brazilian pioneering work toward that adaptation stands, indeed, as an example to these Europeans, not only through its crude forms, but through the refined ones, adapted to modern conditions, by present-day Brazilian architects like Costa, Niemeyer, Mindlin, and the Roberto brothers.

All modern peoples are beginning to live in a civilization predominantly industrial and collectivistic which makes it imperative for modern men and women to live a great part of their existence in public. Brazilian architecture is flexible enough to allow men, women, and children to live a great part of their existence in tropical parks in which children can play freely, young men can have their lyrical, pre-nuptial contacts with young women, and tired workers and old men can rest, if not walking among the trees, then lying in cool, attractive hammocks or steel or wood substitutes for hammocks.

But Brazilian architecture seems to keep something essentially domestic which is perhaps its Moorish element in opposition to its Roman one; this essentially domestic intimacy is felt by some modern psychologists to be a need of some—if not nearly all—modern men and women, after a certain disappointment met by many in an entirely public life of going to games, movies, theaters, and churches, and after long hours in factories, offices, and other places of public activity. Radio and television are said by some students of these problems to be bringing a renewal of home-feeling and family gregariousness among super-industrialized populations. If this is really happening, the domestic element of intimacy characteristic of Brazilian architecture—an element generally associated only with

249

family reunion, but which may be extended to include non-family gatherings of groups whose private association is personalistic rather than mechanically collectivistic—makes the Brazilian architecture psychologically ideal as the scenery and environment for this type of "home" or "private" association. One has to visit some of the new—vast but cordial—apartment buildings in Rio to see how the conciliation between the Roman and the Moorish, the public and the private, elements of architecture, furniture, and town-planning are possible in an architecture like the Brazilian one, which since its beginnings has shown a tendency to adapt itself to tropical space—to its sun, its open air, its breezes—without ceasing to value "privacy" and personal "intimacy."

In a book about Brazilian architecture, Mr. Philip L. Goodwin has pointed out that "characteristic of old Brazilian houses is the fine contrast between the broad veranda with its sweeping view and the secluded court." It is as if he thus sensed the Roman element in the same houses, as represented by "the broad veranda with its sweeping view" [1]—in other words, a sort of public expression of the patriarchal system—as complementary to the Moorish element represented by the inner, secluded court, where privacy was assured against too much contact with the outside world. For the typically Brazilian architecture—the one developed during the colonial centuries and recently modernized by architects who, not being colonial in their spirit, know that they have to add to a bold attitude of experiment one of respect for what their predecessors have done in Brazil for the adaptation of European values to a tropical space—this architecture wisely harmonizes contacts, especially the two here simplified, for purposes of sociological classification or characterization, as the Roman and the Moor-

[1] *Brazil Builds: Architecture New and Old 1652–1942* (New York, 1943), p. 34.

ish elements, as they have been perceived or sensed in Brazilian architecture in particular and in Brazilian culture in general by a number of national and foreign observers.

Mr. Goodwin noticed in the modern apartment buildings of Rio which face the sea that hardly one is "without some form of partly sheltered outdoor space," continuous winds seeming to make screens (absolutely essential in most of the United States, according to the same specialist in architecture) unnecessary in Brazilian coast towns. "This encourages," Mr. Goodwin remarks, "a pleasantly open relationship between indoors and outdoors. The openness extends to the shops, which are often entirely without glass and protected by falling iron grills during the night." [2]

Here is an evidence of the fact that the old Moorish and Roman elements, the one making for privacy and intimacy, the other for open relationship between indoors and outdoors, continue to be characteristic of the most genuine Brazilian domestic architecture. As the same author writes, privacy and domestic exclusiveness have always appealed strongly to Latins, being "one of the conspicuous differences between North and Latin America." Hence his conclusion that one reason for "the enthusiastic acceptance of the sunshade, from the simple *rotula* to the most complicated type, is that they give the privacy which Brazilians have enjoyed for centuries." [3] Therefore, when a modern architect built in São Paulo two houses, one for Senhor Frontini, another for Senhor Arnstein, combining what Mr. Goodwin calls "the most complete and satisfactory use of a small ground area with all the privacy, yet all the openness that could be desired," it may be said that this architect built within the most genuine tradition in Brazilian domestic architecture.

[2] Ibid., p. 97.
[3] Ibid., pp. 98–9.

It was the value of this combination—perhaps an ideal combination—that many foreign critics, intolerant of *rotulas* in Brazilian houses, failed to perceive as a Brazilian solution for the problem of building in the tropics: a solution that Brazilians, preceded by the Portuguese who colonized Brazil after and during a fruitful experience in other tropical areas, reached through this permanent, not nomadic or transitory residence in tropical America, less as individuals or expatriates from Europe, than as the founders of a patriarchal society, men who decided to stay and to grow and to multiply in sons and grandsons in the tropics. Decided to stay and grow in a tropical space, as part of a patriarchal family system that had to safeguard its privacy but not to the extreme of closing itself off entirely from the outside world of sun, open air, trees, and human beings.

Modern foreign observers are showing a better comprehension of modern expressions of this really old Brazilian achievement in domestic architecture. One of them, Mr. Goodwin, remarks that, though it was Le Corbusier who, as early as 1933, used movable outside sunshades in his unexecuted project for Barcelona, "it was the Brazilians who first put theory into practice." He refers of course to movable external blinds that the French call *brise-soleil* and the Portuguese *quebra-sol*, and he praises not only the ones at the Ministry of Education in Rio, but also the horizontal blind in Correa Lima's Coastal Boat Passenger Station, also in Rio, the vertical, adjustable type of sunshade used by Senhor Oscar Niemeyer at the Pampulha Yacht Club in Belo Horizonte and at the Obra do Berço in Rio, and the equally vertical blind—different from the Niemeyer one—used by the brothers Roberto in the A. B. I. Building (Rio). These modernistic versions of sunshade come within an old Portuguese or Brazilian tradition—the tradition of colonial *rotulas*—still to be found, under a modern form, in the new hotel at Ouro Preto, and as fixed grilles of wood or cement and as Venetian blinds of various kinds, in a number of new Brazilian buildings, especially residential buildings.

Because of the value being given by modern Brazilian architects and foreign students of Brazilian architecture to elements in the same architecture which were created during the days of patriarchal plantations, when rustic vegetation fulfilled the role of parks, a new importance is being taken by the landscape gardener. He is the one to give to the typically Brazilian architecture—now that private plantations and even private *chacaras* or suburban "big houses" are practically gone—its place in the tropical vegetation of the country by an intelligent adjustment of building to vegetation. This is the work that is being done by an artist of superior talent, Senhor Robert Burle-Marx, not only for private residences in their relation to landscape, but also for hotels and casinos in their relation to public parks and public roads. Like the architects—the brothers Roberto, Lucio Costa, Henrique Mindlin—he is an artist whose boldness as an experimentalist is moderated by his conviction that the patriarchal past of Brazil was creative and not negative.

If Professor V. Ogden Vogt is right when he says that one of the characteristics of modern architecture is that it has "connected inner and outer spaces," [4] then Brazilian modern architecture must be considered characteristically modern. Through buildings Brazilians are beginning to say, architecturally, something that comes from their past, their experience, their American development in a tropical area, and which is, at the same time, what Professor Vogt would call their "total faith and practice" or—to come to the persistence of the two elements that have been always characteristic of the Brazilian

[4] *Cult and Culture* (New York, 1951), p. 126.

cultural and social development—their "wholeness of private spirit and social culture." Which, being true, seems to indicate that despite slavery, latifundium, and monoculture, that development favored wholeness, a wholeness that has found perhaps its best expression in an architecture that places Brazil, in this particular, among the most creative nations of our time.

Brazilian creativeness has its roots in a family system that has been, for four centuries, the center of Brazilian development as a new type of civilization. It was this family system that created Brazilian cookery, Brazilian music, Brazilian literature, Brazilian statesmanship and diplomacy, Brazilian re-interpretation of Roman law through the gigantic work of Augusto Teixeira de Freitas, a jurist who was an authentic product of Brazilian patriarchalism and its ethical realism. It was also this family system that laid the foundations of modern Brazilian architecture, perhaps the greatest Brazilian contribution to human welfare in the tropics. A United States sociologist specialized in the study of the relationship of family to civilization, Professor Carle C. Zimmerman, has written that "the creative periods in civilization have been based upon the domestic type." [5] Brazilian culture in general, and Brazilian architecture, in particular, as a creation of a family system peculiar to Brazil and as an expression of what may be considered a Brazilian civilization—the part of a larger complex, a Luso-tropical civilization—seems to confirm this sociologist's or anthropologist's generalization. [6]

[5] *Family and Civilization* (New York and London, 1947).
[6] Thomas Lindley, who published a *Narrative of a Voyage to Brazil* in London in 1805, was perhaps the first North European critic of Brazilian domestic, patriarchal architecture to express his ideas in the pages of a book. Lindley may be considered typical of the attitude on the subject taken by many of the authors who followed him. Although he admitted having seen in Brazil "large and elegant mansions" erected by "the superior class of inhabitants," most of them located "in the vicinity of the town" (Salvador),

he observed that as viewed from the street they had "a dull and dusty appearance." He noted that "the houses belonging to tradesmen and shopkeepers are still more disgusting: instead of glazed windows they have wooden drop lattices . . ." (247). It seems that their appearance to the eyes of Lindley was characterized principally by these "wooden drop lattices." As to "the lower order of soldiers, mulattoes, and negroes," they lived in "cabines" with "a single lattice window." These were examples of what modern specialists in architecture call "folk architecture," which Lindley viewed with complete disdain, so becoming the first of a multitude of foreigners, later imitated by Brazilians, to whom Brazilian folk architecture was good for nothing. Professor Goodwin, however, though in his *Brazil Builds* he seems to have taken as entirely wholesome certain Brazilian campaigns against coconut-palm cabins, for being "unsanitary" and "ugly," recognized in 1943 that Brazilian "folk architecture usually answers the elementary demands of use, site, climate, and materials more directly than buildings of greater architectural pretension" (p. 73). In this attitude I anticipated him: my *Mucambos do Nordeste* (Rio, 1937) was exactly a plea for Brazilian folk architecture as an answer to elementary regional demands of use, climate, and materials, just as *Casa-Grande & Senzala* (Rio, 1933, translated as *The Masters and the Slaves*, New York, 1945) and *Sobrados e Mucambos* (São Paulo, 1936) had included pleas for Brazilian patriarchal brick and stone architecture as a not altogether bad answer to the same demands on the plane of noble or quasi-noble architecture.

Perhaps the first writer on Brazilian architecture to point out from a technical point of view its virtues as well as its archaisms and deficiencies was J. B. Debret, in his famous three-volume book *Voyage Pittoresque et Historique au Brésil* (Paris, 1834). In Debret one also finds an anticipation of the idea that the most complex Brazilian domestic architecture contained Oriental elements beside the European ones. Debret was probably the first to describe typical Brazilian houses, pointing out their classical elements inherited from the Romans—*protyrum, oratorio* or *ararium, atrium,* etc., *hospicium, thalamus,* and also such of their Moorish or Oriental characteristics as the *alcova*. On giving the scheme of a typical Brazilian residence of the beginning of the nineteenth century, he points out that its analogy with the houses of the Moors in Africa and with the ancient houses of Pompeii is "extremely remarkable" (III, 215).

After Debret, it was another Frenchman of the first half of the nineteenth century, L. L. Vauthier, an architect, who treated the domestic architecture of Brazil with the highest competence in his diary written during his residence in Brazil (1840–6) and in his letters on Brazilian architecture written from Recife during the same period. The diary has been published in Rio, in Portuguese, translated from the French by Dona Vera de Andrade: it was never published in the original French.

Another very suggestive book on the subject is *A Arte Tradicional do Brasil*, by Ricardo Severo (1916). José Mariano Filko left some interesting pages on the Moorish influence in Brazilian architecture. As to the "Dutch" or north European influence on the urban architecture of Brazil, particularly of Recife—for some time a town occupied by the Dutch, whose governor-general, Count Maurice de Nassau, a German aristocrat with something of the character of a Renaissance prince, urbanized parts of it according to ideas of town-planning—the best pages written so far are by Senhor Aderbal Jurema, in his *O Sobrado na Paisagem Recifense* (Recife, 1952). On the same subject one finds valuable information in *Tempo dos Flamengos* (Rio, 1944), a study of some aspects of the Dutch influence in Brazil by Senhor J. A. Gonsalves de Melo. Considerable illustrative material on the history of Brazilian architecture has been gathered by Senhor Gilberto Ferrez of Rio de Janeiro. Also the *Revista do Serviço do Patrimonio Historico e Artistico Nacional* of Rio de Janeiro has published a number of good articles on the subject, including the letters written by Vauthier, also translated into Portuguese by Dona Vera de Andrade.

So far, however, no specialized history of the early domestic or civil architecture of Brazil has been written from a technical point of view which can be compared to *Domestic Architecture of the American Colonies and of the Early Republic*, by Fiske Kimball (New York, 1922). This is perhaps a task for Professor Paulo Santos of the University of Rio de Janeiro.

[X]

Why a Tropical China?

Why is it that some observers speak of Brazil as a tropical China when, aside from extension of territory, power of cultural absorption, and a few Chinese traits to be found in Brazilian civilization, Brazil seems so unlike modern or ancient China? Probably because there has always been in Brazil something Oriental in contrast to its Western characteristics; something "Moorish"—as it was pointed out *à propos* of its architecture—in contrast to its Roman or Latin traits; something different from Republican America, due to the fact that Brazil remained a monarchy until 1889 (even at present there are two inheritors to a Brazilian throne, two real princes, two authentic Orleans-Braganças).

Also, perhaps, because of the present tendency on the part of a considerable number of Brazilians to consider their tropical Amazonian forests and all that they contain, especially their oil and minerals, almost sacred values that only Brazilian hands should touch. For this sort of nationalism is taking the aspect of an intense Yankeephobia. Because, also, of the attitude of other Brazilians, not to be included among narrow economic nationalists, who think that there is something specific in certain values, social and cultural, peculiar to Brazil or to tropical America, which should be preserved from American standardization of a Yankee type.

If it is true that a member of the medical research staff of a United States pharmaceutical firm who has spent years studying diseases in Latin America—especially in central Brazil—is inclined to believe that there are places in that tropical part of the American hemisphere which are free of some of the diseases that so plague the so-called civilized world or affect other tropical areas, he is right when he points out the urgent need for the proper scientific study of this situation, a study to be carried on by a multi-talented crew of scientists: a biological chemist, an anthropologist, a zoologist, a clinician, and other specialists. This is an urgent need because settlements in which immunity to these diseases seems to exist are "in the path of rapidly advancing industrial civilization" and "their isolation will soon be over and their natural immunities may be a thing of the past." Now, what happens—if it happens—in connection with immunity to "civilized" or "tropical" diseases may happen in connection with the preservation of social and cultural values by certain Latin American communities of the less industrialized sub-areas of that part of the American continent. Proper scientific study of the conditions under which they flourish might indicate a way of saving them, or some of them, or parts of them, from blind standardization.

If a study of this type had been made in proper time of why Brazil became independent, remaining a monarchy and avoiding a republican form of government, monarchy might have been preserved in Brazil for the possible advantage of the Brazilian people in particular, and of the Pan American commonwealth in general. For it certainly meant immunity to some of the political diseases that seem to have been acquired by Brazilians when, to modernize or Pan Americanize their country, they adopted the republican form of government. Even today, the Republic in Brazil is safer from political diseases when its methods of dealing with Brazilian problems are a careful modernization of the traditional Brazilian monarchical and, at the same time, democratic methods instead of being a mere copy of what Anglo-Americans have done in the United States or of what the Germans did when they founded their lyrical, unrealistic Weimar Republic—also copied in some points by Brazilian idealists.

Some Brazilians think today that inter-Americanism should not mean a mechanical and narrow form of standardization with emphasis on the massive, quantitative or monolithic Pan American aspects of values and cultural styles, but a healthy, though difficult, combination of differences and even of antagonisms within a dynamic inter-American structure or system. Just as Latin Americans should take from the United States and adapt to their different regional or national conditions some United States values and techniques, so the Americans of the United States might profit from Latin American suggestions and examples instead of rigidly adopting the attitude that because they lead in industrial progress, they are, or should be, the absolute leaders of everything in hemispheric culture, that hemispheric culture should follow their example in every human or cultural activity.

There seems to be a tendency among certain Anglo-Americans to use disparagingly the words "Latin American," under the impression that in America what is Latin is always inferior

259

to what is Anglo-Saxon or Nordic. It is a tendency similar to the one of using disparagingly the adjectives "medieval" or "feudal" or "Chinese" or "Moorish" in their relation to modern civilization, as if the Middle Ages or the East had not given mankind values superior to the ones that came to man from the generally glorified age of Enlightenment or that have come to him only since the commercial and the industrial revolutions in the West, including, as Professor George Sarton, a specialist in the subject, reminds us, such apparently modern values as money, economy, banking, and extensive trade, an invention of the Crusades. In other words, a two-way cultural policy should be encouraged between the Americas, with reciprocal appreciation for Latin and Anglo values and inventions. If this is not done, Brazilians and other Latin Americans should close themselves against American standardization of a Yankee type to the point of appearing "Chinese."

When there is, as at the present time, a wave of "anti-Yankeeism" in Latin America, an acute manifestation of an almost always latent Yankeephobia—for as some Anglo-Americans know, to most Latin Americans, all Americans from the United States are Yankees—Americans of the United States should consider this situation a good reason or pretext for a really scientific study of their relationship with Latin America, investigations that should take into consideration not only political or economic matters, through statistics and figures, but also social, cultural, and psychological aspects of the same total and complex situation. One might say that the United States–Latin America relationships need a sort of Kinsey Report to magnify the intimate, hidden psychological factors that make them unhappy.

It may be that the present-day unpopularity of the United States in Latin America comes largely from the fact that the "North American colossus," as Latin Americans sometimes call the United States, is now, to Latin American eyes, a big power practically without competitors—the French, British, German, Japanese competitors, against whom the Latin Americans until some years ago might divide the somewhat feminine resentment of semi-colonial peoples faced by imperial, masculine, or economically aggressive nations. Now all the resentment is concentrated on or against the United States, with a weak France, a weak Germany, a weak Japan, a weak Great Britain considered almost angelic nations for whom some Latin Americans even begin to feel nostalgic, nostalgic for the days when they were powerful nations and, in their competition for Latin American markets used subtle, suave, and, at the same time, masculine, methods of economic penetration that some of the modern North Americans of the United States do not seem to consider necessary to use in Latin America, where they have no strong competitor to fight or destroy. Only in the Near East and in Africa do they feel that they have to deal with powerful Chinese or Soviet competition. Therefore, they seem to have neglected Latin America—a sort of legitimate wife—for exotic adventures of economic and political donjuanism in Africa, Asia, and Europe. Only now is Soviet Russia beginning to make its presence felt in Brazil as a strong competitor of the United States.

It is true that each one of us, Anglo- or Latin Americans, should consider some of these Anglo-American adventures in distant Eastern lands as activity essential for Pan American and even pan-human, democratic development, and not a mere adventure in the exclusive interest of the United States. But exclusiveness of action in this respect may do considerable harm to inter-American relations, in a phase still too plastic and delicate for Latin Americans to be left alone in their struggle to develop industries and an agriculture that depend, to a large extent, upon united financial help—a help that should not take the aspect of domination or imposition of Anglo-American values upon their Latin neighbors.

Would it not be possible for such Anglo-American activities to go on in the East and Africa as well as in Europe without an apparent or real neglect of Latin America by the United States, especially if one remembers that the United States had, during its tremendous war effort against Nazism, Fascism, and Japan the loyal and valuable co-operation of some of the Latin American countries—especially Brazil? Should not some United States leaders refrain from showing, in their relationship with Latin America, an immediacy of aim that has been disappointing to Latin Americans who are beginning to contrast what seems to them to be an extremely opportunistic, dynamic, restless, striving, or Faustian policy on the part of the United States or of the United States leaders with what they now idealize, through a nostalgic mood, as the reliable, classical, regular policy of the British, the French, or the Germans when they were powerful in Latin America and used methods —so the idealization of a recent past goes—notable for their sobriety and elegance and for their distrust of the unusual, the eccentric, the exuberant? Too often, it seems, United States forays into Latin America are almost immediately and totally followed by neglect or indifference or by a strict "business-is-business" or "time-is-money" attitude.

More than once the parent-child relation has been applied by sociologists and social psychologists to the study, analysis, and interpretation by analogy of the political, social, and psychological relations between human groups. Perhaps the male-female concept may be applied in the same way and with the same reservations to the study and analysis of the political and economic and social relations between the United States and the Latin American nations, with the United States as the male partner in this conjugal situation. These relations seem to be, on a national scale, those of a sociological male in regard to a sociologically feminine, that is, dependent, Latin America. The America south of the Rio Grande sees in the United States a masculine power that some of the most feminine Latin American nations are inclined to consider unstable, exuberant, and irregular in its masculine, that is, protective, behavior toward them. Hence the need of a careful scientific study of the situation, a task for not only a multi-talented, but also a multinational crew of social scientists from North and South America.

Sociologists tell us that in our time nationalism is one of the observed facts of life which no scientist can neglect. It is a potent fact in Latin American life, but so far no comparative study of the various expressions of nationalism in that part of the world has appeared. One of the results of neglect of this study is that outsiders have a tendency to oversimplify Latin American reality, neglecting its diversity.

Some time ago in Paris, in a UNESCO meeting of social scientists, I suggested not only a revision of history books used in schools—a suggestion already extended from Europe to Latin America by some of the late League of Nations idealists and pacifists—but also an attempt at a reinterpretation of the national heroes of Europe, Asia, and America, through comparative biographies, or through biographies written not by one single writer, but by three or four, representing two or three or four special sciences and two, three, or four areas more deeply affected by the projection of the hero considered, for sometimes a hero to one nation can be a villain to a neighboring nation. That has been the case of the Brazilian Caxias as viewed by most Paraguayans and of the Paraguayan Solano López as viewed by most Brazilians, the case of more than one Mexican hero when seen by Mexicans or considered by Mexico's Anglo-American neighbors.

A similar task might be attempted with regard to certain elements in the culture of a people considered noble by the Anglo-American group of Americans and inferior by the Latin Americans. They too might be studied, analyzed, and interpreted in a comparative and co-operative way. For instance, most of the modern Anglo-Americans seem to regard a political career as an inferior activity, while in countries like Brazil politics is still regarded as a high and noble form of human activity in which some of the best intellectuals of the nation are engaged or desire to be engaged. Brazilians and other Latin Americans still look down upon a purely business career and find it difficult to understand why the United States should send merely successful businessmen as ambassadors to Latin American Republics. Why the two attitudes? How do they affect the relations between the two Americas? For they are bound to affect these relations and to make them difficult and delicate.

Another study that I consider essential for the improvement of political, cultural, and economic relations between Anglo-Americans and Latin Americans is a careful psychological and sociological study of time: their different attitudes toward time or tempo. The rigid Anglo-Saxon attitude—"Time is money" —with an almost mystical cult of minutes and seconds on account of their practical, commercial value, is in sharp contrast to the Latin American attitude, a sort of "more-or-less" (*"mais ou menos"*) attitude. It is easy to understand why a Nordic was so shocked in Spain to know that a Spanish or Latin American guest in a hotel asked the desk to call him next morning not exactly at ten or ten-fifteen, as an Anglo-Saxon or an Anglo-American would have asked, but at ten or eleven: the "more-or-less" attitude in regard to time in contrast to the strictly mathematical one, a contrast that makes simultaneity as difficult between peoples or nations engaged in a common activity as between man and woman in love relations, for instance, when the male partner does not take into consideration the difference of time values of his female companion. When instead of a people or an individual enjoying as much as possible the flow of living, there is concern and eagerness for immediate achievement on the part of an individual in relation to another individual or on the part of a people in relation to another people, the relations between the two become extremely difficult. An adjustment has to be found between *speed-up* and *ralentie:* a sort of third *tempo*, a third psychological and sociological *tempo*, has to be found which will be lived by the two with full reciprocity.

According to the French sociologist Georges Gurvith, each national culture has its own time or rhythm. Anglo-Americans and Latin Americans certainly have two very distinct attitudes toward time, and this is important not only in political and business but also even in social and cultural activities. Anglo-American sociologists say that the predominant time dimension of the United States Americans "is the future." Most of the Latin American groups are inclined to celebrate the present, and some of them the past, rather than to "live in the future." São Paulo in Brazil and present-day Venezuela may be exceptions to this predominance and be as future-oriented as any progressive or faustian Anglo-American group. But São Paulo is only São Paulo and not all of Brazil. Present-day Venezuela is far from being typical of normal Latin Spanish America, where one generally finds, among some groups, an excessive attachment to the past, and among many a perhaps excessive taste for present enjoyment. As a result of this, one finds less inclination among Latin Americans than among Anglo-Americans to sacrifice almost everything in one's life to rapid collective progress, "mortgaging the present for the future," as an Anglo-American sociologist puts it.

It is easy to see how these two different attitudes toward time may cause social and psychological distance between two human groups, not only in regard to business and political matters, but also in dealing—I repeat—with diplomatic and cultural matters of the most subtle kind. A people taking a definite pleasure in mere activity in the present or in celebrating the past finds it difficult to understand, admire, and like a civilization that seems to specialize in disregarding the past and even the present, to value and glorify only the future. Perhaps the ideal Pan American time should be—I insist on this point—a combination of these two attitudes. But this combination will come about only if both groups become conscious of the problem through psychological and sociological analysis of each other's excesses. Hence the need of a scientific study of the differences that separate Latin Americans and Anglo-Americans as if they were two sociological, cultural sexes.

One hears more and more often that Africa is no longer an isolated, static continent, but what someone has aptly described as a quick-changing area whose fate is intimately connected with that of the free world and whose development has an immediate effect on the national interest of the United States and not only of Western Europe. Latin Americans agree with this: they too see the importance of Africa, as well as that of Asia. But they think that still more important in its social and cultural dynamics and in its closeness to the interests of the free world and particularly of the United States is now-neglected Latin America, if it be considered as an area or a region whose general development has been and is today, even more than African development, an expression or an evidence of the capacity of a group of peoples, largely non-European in their ethnic composition and in their folkway, to grow in modern civilizations and to organize themselves as nations of a modern type in largely tropical or semi-tropical spaces.

Books written on Latin America by Europeans and Anglo-Americans as recently as the first decades of the twentieth century hardly admitted, with one or two exceptions, that such a development was to be expected from non-European peoples, from peoples, like most of the Latin Americans, largely non-European in their ethnic composition, who added to this tragic deficiency—tragic to the eyes of a number of European and Anglo-American sociologists—the equally fatal inferiority of being inhabitants of tropical or quasi-tropical areas, a condition common to the majority of Latin Americans. That being so, it was natural for political and commercial Anglo-American leaders, and for missionaries and diplomats of the United States, when sent to tropical Latin America countries as to positions so difficult and unpleasant that they felt the need of being recommended to the special benevolence of God Almighty and of their almost as powerful governments or companies, to act in these positions like the British, the Germans, and even the French in similar situations. They considered themselves biologically, culturally, and totally superior to the strange peoples they found in such un-European and, to their eyes, absolutely inferior surroundings—physically and culturally inferior. There has been a considerable change of mentality in this respect both in Europe and in the United States, but even today one finds that Latin America suggests to the typical Anglo-American "inferior race," "unhealthy climate," "degenerate mestizos," "yellow fever," and "malaria," rather than any positive values.

I have just read in a New York magazine these words of a citizen of the United States apropos of a national problem now being widely discussed in newspapers and magazines of the dynamic Anglo-American Republic: "Look at South America, where all the races have intermarried, and what have they got? Lazy, unproductive, backward people." Latin Americans hesitate to express themselves on any strictly domestic problem of Anglo-America. But some of them feel inclined to remind Anglo-Americans or citizens of the United States who think of South America, Latin America in general, or Brazil in particular as being made entirely of "lazy, unproductive, backward people" that there are notable exceptions to this generalization. Anglo-Americans will find places in Latin America where people are so progressive, creative, and modern that even north Europeans or Anglo-Americans of the most dynamic type have been surprised at their progress and achievements, achievements obtained by them without doing violence to their essential Latin traditions. Of course, Latin or South America is no paradise. But is there a perfect paradise in the modern world? Are not orthodox Christians right when they consider the Paradise an unearthly reality?

Nevertheless, one finds persons in modern South Africa, for instance, who look at South America as if it were almost a paradise. Four years ago I heard from a South African in South Africa: "I wish we had followed the same ways as South America." As a South or Latin American I was greatly pleased to hear him, but I could not avoid telling him: "But do not think that in South America we live in a paradise." Of course, we do not. South or Latin America has had a tragic history. Earthquakes and revolutions have been numerous, some of them devastating. Great presidents of great republics—great on the Latin American scale—have committed suicide. Great political crimes have attracted the attention of the world even to small republics. But in spite of the generalization that Latin Americans are lazy and unproductive, incapable of self-government and civilization, positive values are increasing in number and quality among Latin Americans. Some of the Latin Americans have even reached political maturity.

Most of the Latin American peoples are going through an

aggressive anti-European or anti-Anglo-American phase of nationalism which places them in almost the same sociological situation as some of the modern Asians and Africans. And that fact gives some basis to the remark that Brazil is becoming a tropical China. But some of the Latin Americans have preceded by more than a century of political development these modern Asians and Africans who are now in the first and crudest phase of nationalistic adolescence, if not political childhood disguised by a few expressions of precocious modernity. National maturity has been reached by comparatively small groups in the Latin American populations, not by any of these populations as national wholes. Not even in a politically progressive country like the small Republic of Uruguay—a sort of Latin American Switzerland—is this the case. Argentina, after years of development as an electoral democracy that seemed to be so cosmopolitan in its spirit that one of its political leaders was enthusiastically applauded when thirty years ago he suggested that the "Argentinian Doctrine" surpassed the Monroe Doctrine—America for the Americans—in being a much broader claim: America for Humanity—a few years ago adopted a narrowly nationalistic policy. This is also the case of modern Brazil, whose tradition, developed under a democratic and politically advanced monarchy, was one of harmonizing national interests with international and continental responsibilities, so much so that as a very young independent nation it became famous for the opportunities it gave naturalized Brazilians, or to the sons of naturalized Brazilians, to rise to the highest positions in the Empire and even to become diplomats or officers in the international service of Brazil. This was the case of Varnhagen, for instance—he was the son of a German—who was given the very national title of Baron of Porto Seguro, and of Taylor, an Englishman, who became a naval leader at the service of the Brazilian national cause.

2 6 9

If countries like Brazil and Argentina have sometimes acted in international matters as if they were still adolescent nations excessively afraid of the maturer ones and eager to rival or surpass the maturer ones in the expression of their national "power" or of their national "vitality," that is because their process of becoming politically mature has not really advanced much beyond adolescence as far as their national wholes are concerned; and this may be true even of the United States in regard to international politics. And adolescence seems to be as difficult a phase in the life of a nation as in the life of an individual. As unpleasant to the adolescent as to the maturer members of his family who have to understand an individual who does not understand his own contradictions of feeling, thought, and behavior.

Still, this understanding is necessary, and Latin America has to be understood by outsiders—especially by Anglo-Americans who, as a national whole, are politically maturer than the other American nations, though not perfectly mature—as a dynamic, changing area whose problems are not entirely national, but international; but whose international behavior is to a large extent an expression of difficult national problems that each Latin American nation is facing, and has to face, through ways and methods that have to correspond to its culture, its past, and its particular psychology. In the midst of these difficulties—the difficulties of growing cultures, growing economies, growing national systems—they now see the United States as a fully developed nation that does not seem to know how to deal with adolescent members of the same continental family; or—to come back to a previous analogy—as a male nation that does not know how to deal with psychologically female nations, eager, as nations, for the equivalent of full sexual experience as well as for the sociological equivalent of a sexual equality that will not imply that female nations are necessarily inferior to male ones.

One of the recent expressions of this attitude of Latin American nations in regard to their powerful Anglo-American neighbor has been economic nationalism; and one of the manifestations of economic nationalism has been, in some of the Latin nations of the continent—especially in recent years Brazil—an eagerness for industrialization that has meant a systematic hostility to the super-industrialism of the United States. The United States, being, in relation to its hemispheric neighbors, a super-industrialized nation, must be treated as an enemy whose purpose, open or disguised, would be to preserve the same neighbors as inhabitants of mere agricultural areas so as to be only buyers and markets for its industries. Not only this, but the United States is seen by some Latin American nationalists as being diabolically active in Africa, doing much more than it should be doing, if it were a loyal member of the American community of nations, to stimulate African agricultural production to surpass that of Brazil and other Latin American countries. And this, with a United States financial help that some Brazilians think should have been given to Brazil. Thus stimulated and assisted by United States financial and technical help, Africa will become—Latin American nationalists fear— a competitor to Latin America, not by natural means but through the intervention in her favor of a nation whose duty should be to help its Latin neighbors in their agricultural production as well as in their industrialization.

However, restrictions against foreign—Anglo-American, included—enterprise in countries like Brazil, rather than being a Latin American reaction against this Anglo-American assistance to Africa, have to be considered acts that preceded the present-day United States policy of extraordinary economic activity in Europe, Asia, and Africa, with concomitant neglect of Latin America. Why these acts that seem to deprive Latin America of the right to complain against what is considered by many of them an unfair attitude of the United States, as an American leading nation, whose main activity as a stimulating economic force should be in the hemisphere and not outside of it?

One of the reasons is that Latin Americans were made to feel by some of their economists, as early as the thirties (when, during the effects of crisis the United States went through after 1929, some of the most respectable Anglo-American banks and industries with agencies in Latin America acted in these countries in what was considered by some Latin Americans a very inelegant and unethical way) that they were depending too much on foreign—especially Anglo-American—bankers, middlemen, industrialists, and shipping and insurance interests. They should free themselves from such a dependence instead of merely freeing themselves from European financial and industrial power to fall under the cruder dominance of "Yankee" industrialism and "Yankee" financial lords.

As the Second World War made clear that the United States would emerge as the great imperial super-power of a new phase in the history of capitalism, fear of "Yankee" financial and industrial lords began to increase among Latin Americans. Latin American nations should concentrate their nationalism in economic issues instead of satisfying themselves with mere political appearances of independence. Hence, the numerous Latin American restrictions and measures put into effect since the thirties and intensified after the end of the Second World War, measures against exploration of mines and water power by foreigners; against the establishment of deposit banks and insurance companies with shares held by foreigners; against the ownership by foreigners not only of agricultural land (until the foreigners have established permanent residence as farmers), but also of enterprises considered national in their purposes; of restrictions even against the practice by foreigners of liberal professions—restrictions that in some cases have been considered incomplete by some exaggerated and even morbid Latin American nationalists, because they do not include naturalized citizens of some of these young republics as well as pure foreigners.

Similar measures have been taken in Latin America during the last decades to protect native labor against foreign intrusion, a typical law specifying that foreigners shall not constitute more than one-third of the employees or receive more than one-third of the wages or salary of any industrial, commercial, or public-utility enterprise except in certain industries. Besides this, measures have been taken against foreign intrusion, to favor so-called industrialization programs, making them expressions of an intensive economic nationalism. Privileges of almost sacred value have been claimed by industrialists and patriots during recent decades, in Latin America in general, and in Brazil in particular, for domestic manufactures as opposed to imported commodities that once were exalted as angelic marvels and are now considered diabolical when imported from the United States. Through their influence in the press, industrialists have been able to create in some parts of Latin America a sort of industralist *mystique* or fad that has meant, in more than one case, the neglect of agriculture—for agriculture should be left to colonial peoples—and, almost always, hostility toward the United States, now the only super-industrial power whose influence is seen as an immediate "danger" by economic nationalists in some Latin American areas.

How have Anglo-Americans faced this situation in Latin America? With Franklin D. Roosevelt, the "Good Neighbor Policy" manifested itself through ways and means that gave even some of the most fanatic economic nationalists in Latin America confidence in the more experienced and economically and technically more mature neighbor. It is a fact that United States financial and technical aid was then extended to Latin America to assist not only non-competitive, but even competitive new industries—competitive with United States industries. The United States government made itself felt, through this assistance, as an influence—a corrective influence —that was above narrowly competitive or "imperialistic" private United States interests or groups in their relations with the Latin American republics eager to pass from a "colonial" status to a really national one, through industrialization. In connection with this, really constructive work—economically and psychologically constructive—was done through such agencies as the Export-Import Bank and the Inter-American Development Commission, organized in Washington in 1940, as a working unit of the Inter-American Financial and Economic Advisory Committee, to "assist in the development of the republics of the Western Hemisphere by promotion of trade, development of agriculture and industry, improvement of transportation facilities and conservation of forests."

As a concrete economic achievement of this now historical commission, the stimulation of interest in increased production of high-grade tapioca starch (manioc), a product so typical of tropical Latin America, including tropical Brazil, may be pointed out. Other concrete economic achievements might be pointed out in connection with vegetable oils and minerals. But the work of the commission was also successful from a psychological point of view because it gave Latin Americans, suspicious of United States economic imperialism, a healthy confidence in the United States government as a force that stood above narrowly private interests and threw all its influence in favor of a policy of continental economic co-operation.

It seems that those in the United States who have advocated the abolition of all governmental agencies as instruments for such co-operation, leaving private interests free to act, forget the psychological aspect of the problem as viewed by Latin Americans. The neglect of this aspect of the problem seems to be contributing, to a large extent, to the deterioration of inter-American relations. The recent pre-eminence of private interests in these relations has become an easy target for Communists—so active now in Brazil and so systematic in their efforts to stimulate a sort of nationalistic religion among Brazilians, especially among the Brazilian military forces—in their eagerness to do away with all the valuable remains of the "Good Neighbor Policy." Now, they point out, Anglo-American "big business" of "the worst kind" is free to do what it pleases with Latin America, and Latin America must intensify its economic nationalism so as to protect itself against this type of "big business."

At the same time, some Latin American nationalists point out that Europe and Africa have been receiving technical and financial assistance of a type that Latin Americans should not fear, but welcome, as really beneficial to its young industries and its archaic agriculture. A contradictory attitude. But the second attitude seems to indicate that there is, latent among Latin Americans, a feeling of solidarity with Anglo-Americans which reacts in a somewhat feminine way to what appears to some Latin Americans to be a sort of male disloyalty of the United States to its sister republics of the South, neglected for the sake of Europe, Asia, or Africa. This psychological situation—which makes some Latin Americans nostalgic for F. D. Roosevelt, and this is only one aspect of a complex problem—should not be overlooked by Anglo-Americans, but should be considered carefully and, if possible, studied not only through statistics, but also through more subtle, psychological methods. Psychological and ecological, for—being a European civilization developed in the tropics, adapted to the tropics, changed by the tropics, perhaps deformed, in some respects, and in other respects reformed, by the tropics—Brazil has to be studied, analyzed, and interpreted in the light of its tropical situation.

A prominent Brazilian business leader, Senhor Brazilio Machado of São Paulo, has recently expressed the attitude of a large number of Brazilian businessmen in regard to what they consider the neglect of Brazil by the United States in favor of a policy of an increasing concession of advantages to tropical Africa. Senhor Machado has anticipated the possibility of Brazilians refusing to co-operate with the United States if an international crisis similar to the 1941 crisis arises, on the basis that the United States should ask then, not Brazilians, but Africans for military co-operation and for the concession of naval and air bases, with all the serious disturbances to national life that such concessions mean. A similar stand has been taken by Senator Lourival Fontes, who was a close associate of Vargas and is an able specialist in international problems from a Brazilian point of view. These facts indicate that the present Yankeephobia in Brazil has sources besides shrewd Russian-Communistic propaganda against the United States in all tropical countries. Mistakes are being made by the United States in regard to Brazil that seem to be as effective in stimulating this Yankeephobia as Communistic propaganda ably carried on against the "Yankees" and "Imperialists" as if Soviet Russia were not an imperialistic power.

According to an Anglo-American author, Mr. Charles Morrow Wilson, in his book *The Tropics: World of Tomorrow* (New York, 1951), the tropics inevitably will have most to do with deciding whether the United States or Soviet Russia will lead the world tomorrow. He writes: "For at least twenty years past, the views and strategies of the Comintern have tended to accept this truth." Hence, a systematic policy of the Kremlin to penetrate the tropics and "win them, not by costly trade lines nor costly conquests, but rather by words, gestures, and implications, by exploitations of grievances, prejudices, and emotion, and by other superbly skilful devices of play-acting." Of course, this tropics-minded policy includes Brazil, considered by some a tropical China or, rather, *the* tropical China. Consequently, as Mr. Wilson points out, writing from a United States point of view in the final pages of his book, "now is the time to play well and look South."

Is the United States playing well in regard to Brazil? Scarcely a single Brazilian thinks so. Most Brazilians—even some of those who are known as sincere friends of the United States—think that their country has been, or is being, used by the United States for its narrowly national purposes without reciprocity or any special consideration for what has been Brazil's traditional policy of co-operating with the United States. Some Brazilians have even reached the conclusion that Argentina has been wiser in its policy in regard to the United States: a policy of roughness, arrogance, brutal "realism." They think that this policy seems to be more fruitful than the Brazilian one. For them, the United States takes Brazilian willingness to co-operate as passive submission allowing Anglo-Americans to consider Brazil a submissively friendly nation and then give special facilities to tropical nations that follow the Argentinian method of dealing with the United States.

There may be something in these arguments and there are facts that seem to back them.[1] One thing is certain: for the first

[1] In a recent book, *Um Estadista da Republica* (Rio, 1955), Professor Affonso Arinos de Melo Franco, a member of the Brazilian House of Representatives, pointed out a significant example of a situation in which the United States refused to take a stand in favor of Brazil in an international issue, as asked by the Brazilian Foreign Office in its traditionally suave way,

time in the history of the relations of Brazil with the United States, Yankeephobia is becoming a potent factor. The famous anti-United States letter signed by Vargas before his tragic death—I say signed by him because it is so badly written, so grossly demagogical, so deficient in the very qualities that made Vargas known and admired, that, having known him personally, I refuse to believe that he himself wrote it—has contributed enormously toward intensifying Yankeephobia in Brazil. It is time now for the United States to have an exceptionally able ambassador in Rio de Janeiro—a second Edwin Morgan, who will add personal charm to a deeper knowledge of economic and social problems—so that Brazil will not go on becoming a tropical China in some of the undesirable aspects of that concept.

Yankeephobia is becoming something of a religion among less well-educated Brazilians, well known for their predisposition to fall victims to emotional appeals. In connection with this, Vargas has become, after his death even more than while he lived, an example of the classic charismatic leader of Weber's definition: one who in an epoch of unrest stands at the beginning of a revolutionary, emotional, sectarian movement. He is finding adherents, as a typical charismatic leader would anywhere, because he is believed to have been the one who knew what was really needed for Brazil. And according to some Brazilian nationalists, nothing was more important in this knowledge than the fact that Brazil has been, or is being, exploited by the United States under the disguise of friendship. Hence the attitude of those sectarian nationalists who now claim for Brazil a position similar to that of China, that is, a

---

and then, immediately after this refusal, acted in favor of Argentina on the same issue (III, 1517–23). This is why Senator Lourival Fontes, in his *Discurso aos Surdos* (Rio, 1955), argues for the adoption by Brazil of an international policy that will go farther than "international courtesy" (p. 34).

position of aggressive resistance toward the United States and of receptive tolerance toward Soviet Russia, the only rival power of the United States at present.

One thing, however, should be taken into consideration in connection with an anti-United States *mystique* in present-day Brazil as part of a projection of Vargas's charisma over a large part of the Brazilian population, a charisma intensified by his tragic death. This is that Vargas reduced Communism in Brazil to a movement whose only hopes of attaining power are now through infiltration into the army, the navy, and the air force. As a force among the proletarian and the poor, the Vargas cult in Brazil became much more important than Communism; and perhaps to attain this, Vargasism had to outdo Communism in hostility to the United States as the symbol of the worst form of "bourgeois capitalism" and "imperialism."

When this is taken into consideration, one becomes prepared to accept the possible rise to presidential power of Vargas's successor as leader of the "worker's cause" in Brazil, Senhor Jango Goulart—now Vice President of the Republic—as a Brazilian Ngo Dinh Diem, to use an Asian, though not Chinese, point of reference. On the other hand, this may happen with another man, perhaps General Teixeira Lott, possibly Governor Janio Quadros or Mayor Ademar de Barros, taking the role of a President of the Republic who will probably be anti-United States in some of his nationalistic attitudes, though, like Vargas, any one of them will probably also be an obstacle to new attempts by the Communists, inspired by Soviet Russia, to transform Brazil into a tropical China according to their taste.

While Brazil waits for a new election for the Presidency, a physician who has become a politician, something unusual in the West, but not in the East—and in this, as at other points, Brazil presents a striking similarity to the Eastern world—is intensively engaged, as President of the Brazilian Republic, in establishing a new capital for the Republic in the very center of the country. This is indeed a monumental task, and if its foundations are definitively laid by President Juscelino Kubitschek during his presidential term, he will become a historic figure while still a young man with a face that reminds us of a Chinese or an Oriental with a European or Anglo-American training: he has non-European blood.

The plan to establish the capital of the Brazilian Republic in central Brazil involves a very complex group of problems. The architectural ones are being attended to by the two ablest modern Brazilian architects: Sehnor Lucio Costa and Senhor Oscar Niemeyer. Senhor Candido Portinari, the painter, will probably be asked to decorate new buildings with adequate murals. But some critics fear that urbanistic problems of a sociological character are not being considered as they should be, though one of the assistants to Senhor Lucio Costa has stated that the idea of a Brazilian sociologist that towns should have special zones for "social interpenetration" is being used by urbanists in the planning of the new capital. Nobody knows of any plans for European immigration of farmers—good farmers for tropical areas, such as the Portuguese of the Madeira Island—to provide for the needs of the new capital, establishing themselves as communities of families, an ideal opportunity for this type of colonization in an almost virgin part of tropical Brazil.

Numerous other problems of social relevance, for the orientation of whose solutions anthropologists, sociologists, economists, and educators should be consulted, seem to be neglected, with the risk of enormous mistakes being made by politicians with the help only of engineers and architects. Perhaps in the treatment of some of these problems, modern Chinese and Oriental leaders are being wiser than Brazilian politicians, most of whom have not yet realized that the task of modernizing such a tropical China as Brazil is in some respects is a very complex one, not to be accomplished only by politicians, engineers, and architects. A broader vision of problems is needed and also a technique of planning similar to that followed in the United States in regard to the Tennessee Valley.

As in China, industrialization in Brazil has meant, for a large part of the peasant population, the "physical and spiritual dislocations . . . that have undermined existing institutions" which an Anglo-American expert in non-Western problems points out in a recent book, *The Nature of the Non-Western World*.[2] In China, according to the same observer, these dislocations left "a vacuum" in which Communism "has proved the most powerful element of reintegration." Will Brazil have to depend upon so radical and violent a solution for its problems of social reintegration? Objective analysis of the problem seems to point to different means for Brazilians to achieve reintegration between rural and urban, industrial and agrarian activities. Here as in face of other difficulties, the choice would not be "either-or," between this and that, but in the direction of a complementary policy, for which a Brazilian student of the problem has adapted, from the English language, the word "rurban," giving it a new and broader implication than the one it has had so far; and meaning by it a dynamic adjustment between two apparent contraries.

Brazil would thus develop, in possibly a more dynamic way than China—for its population is in a more plastic condition than that of China—in a "rurban" civilization, more rurban than that of the United States. For this development would profit from ultramodern technical facilities favoring decentralization of industries, with modernisms usually associated only with cities taken to rural communities. The capital of Brazil,

[2] Chapter 11, *The Nature of the Non-Western World* (New York, 1957), by Vera Micheles Dean. An interesting book, though rather deficient on Latin America.

changed from Rio de Janeiro to Brazilia, would be a decisive step toward the development of Brazil as a "rurban" civilization of the most dynamic type, with agriculture and industry as complementary activities and not as the antagonistic ones they have been in Brazil and in other countries. This would be a check on the tendency of some Brazilian leaders to make the cause of "industrialization" and that of "national independence" a single cause, a messianic cause. Of course, it is not. Brazilian experience is already evidence in favor of what Mr. Eugene Staley writes in *The Future of Underdeveloped Countries*, that "unless agriculture does modernize substantially, industrial expansion in most undeveloped countries is likely to be cut short by lack of markets, for the great majority of the population will not have the necessary purchasing power."

Although apparently an absolute enthusiast for industrialization, Getulio Vargas was convinced that industrialism by itself was not the solution for a "tropical China" like Brazil. A few days before he committed suicide, his secretary telephoned me from Rio to Recife, saying that the President wanted to see me at once. It was very urgent. I took the first plane going from Recife to Rio, and was immediately received by Vargas; with him I had an old personal friendship, though not political affinities. He told me that he had for me what he considered a very important mission from a Brazilian or a national point of view, more important than any of a constructive character which he could think of at the moment. He told me that I should not fear that it would be a political mission: it was something far above politics. He wanted to begin at once an agrarian reform in Brazil. It would mean the modernization of agriculture and the decentralization of industries, which he knew I thought essential for Brazil. But to do this he wanted from me something more than suggestions or ideas: he wanted me as head of a national organism that would be more important than any post in his cabinet and that would give him the basis for a policy of immigration and colonization, for he agreed with me that nothing could be done in the way of an agrarian reform without European immigrants of the "right sort" who would stay as farmers.

I refer to this because it seems to indicate that Vargas had a clear vision of Brazilian problems even though at the end of his career he was a politician surrounded by politicians, some of whom saw only in him the charismatic leader they needed in order to stay in power. And the easiest way for politicians to stay in power in Brazil was then, and still is, to be, or to appear to be, narrowly nationalistic, to see a panacea in industrialization, and to flirt so much with Communism as to make it possible for Communists of the sectarian type who follow Russian instructions—and now so weak in Brazil among intellectuals, students, and laborers as to be insignificant as such—to attempt to take control of the country, through penetration of the army, the navy, or the air force. This is a risk; and an adventure of this kind may happen, a repetition of the bloody adventure of 1935, led by a Brazilian Communist trained in Russia and himself a former officer in the Brazilian Army. The technique followed then was Russo-Asiatic: it caused indignation among Brazilians—even among those who were leftist. But this was in 1935, and a small group of sectarian Communists under the same Russo-Asiatic spell of Communism may take advantage of present-day political and military leaders who think it a safe game for them to use Communism against "Yankee imperialism" and against liberals of what they consider a *démodé* type (and some of these liberals are really *démodé* in imagining that what is good for them is good for non-bourgeois Brazilians).

Communism, especially of an Oriental or Asiatic type, would be no solution for Brazilian problems. Brazilian civilization,

though not European or passively sub-European, is too Western and, from a sociological point of view, too Christian to
admit that solution. More than recent nations like India or
Pakistan or Ceylon, Brazil offers an example of a blending of
European with non-European ideas, customs, and traditions,
with a predominance of the European or Western ones. What
has been said of India and Pakistan—that their blend of non-
European ideas with modern Western ideas of social welfare
into a workable synthesis represents "the most telling challenge
yet discovered to totalitarian Communism"—may be said
much more aptly of Brazil. It is a nation in search of its own
solution for its own problems, a solution that socially is already
beginning to be a workable synthesis of the European and non-
European elements of its civilization. Only in its political aspect
is this synthesis still deficient.

But even under this aspect, the present Brazilian situation,
though damaged by an almost tragic absence of able leadership,
is plastic enough to admit a readjustment between advanced
thought in regard to labor—advanced here not meaning Communist—and a serious effort toward industrialization and
mechanization of agriculture, in which so-called free enterprise may take an active part. The 1946 Constitution of Brazil
is certainly wise on this point: the opening paragraph of its
paragraphs on the "social and economic order" is one of conciliation between those who wanted to give absolute emphasis
to the so-called "valorization" of labor and those who wanted
to emphasize free enterprise. As an independent member of
the National Assembly that was charged with the task of
drawing a new constitution for Brazil—entirely independent
from any political party, economic group or ideological sect,
for he was elected through the initiative of university students
—the author of this book took what he considers a decisive

part in the wording of that paragraph, a paragraph extremely important for the social and economic development of Brazil. He feels happy in having succeeded in defeating then a Brazilian version of Perón's "justicialism," in which there was also something of Communism—Soviet Communism—but he feels happy also in having contributed to defeat a "free enterprise" entirely antagonistic to the welfare state in a country like Brazil. Though this may sound like a sociological paradox, Brazil needs both. The conflict between the desire to preserve "traditional values" and the desire to live in harmony with "twentieth-century conditions," so well observed by a number of modern students of non-Western countries, is not peculiar to Oriental or African peoples. It is also found among Brazilians and other Latin Americans. And one of the expressions of this conflict is found in a Yankeephobia that identifies the United States with a capitalism considered to be disdainful of everything, including the improvement of the cultural conditions of workers, that does not mean profit for capitalists.

It is the conviction of some Brazilian students of the Brazilian situation that it will be possible through conciliation of technical development and some of the traditional values characteristic of Brazil and which may be preserved among workers, for this Latin American nation to develop a civilization that can be modern in its technical aspects without becoming in other aspects sub-European or sub-Yankee. Some of these students envisage this civilization—peculiar, in the American hemisphere, to Brazil, with this peculiarity not meaning absence of affinities with the other republics of America—as a Luso-tropical, that is, Portuguese-tropical, civilization that, if recognized as such, would be a vast civilization more widespread even than that of China—in America, Africa, the Orient, islands of the Atlantic, and Europe itself, in spaces either tropical or quasi-tropical. If such a unified civilization is really developing, then Brazil may be considered the potential leader of a significant modern civilization. A "tropical China" whose extension is considerable, and whose language—the Portuguese language—is spoken today by almost eighty million people.

Index

Abend, Hallett, 170n
Academy of Literature, 217n
Ademar de Barros (mayor), 279
Adeyemi, A. Adedokum, 34
Alagoas, 7
Albuquerque, Jeronymo de, 62
Albuquerque (Cavalcanti de) family, 49, 201
Aleijadinho (sculptor), 210–12, 213–14, 217
Alencar, José de, 135
Allen, Charles H., 130
Allston, Robert F. W., 91
Almeida, Alvaro Ozório de, 37, 122
Almeida, José Americo de, 218, 228
Almeida, Miguel, 37, 122
Amado, Jorge, 14, 212, 217, 218
Amaro, João, 75
Amazon region, 13n, 107–8, 112, 115, 154, 165, 178, 179–80
Amazon Town (Wagley), 242n
American Language, The (Mencken), 66
American Negro Slavery (Phillips), 92n
American Political Science Review, The, 96n
American Revolution, 184
Americo de Almeida, José, 218, 228
Amerindians, 7, 8–9, 21, 26, 49, 54ff, 71ff, 101, 107, 108, 110, 116ff, 124, 133–40, 142–65 *passim,* 172–90 *passim,* 211, 222–5, 227, 232, 244
Andrade, Carlos Drumond de, 13, 109, 212, 229
Andrade, Mario de, 226, 229, 241n, 248n
Andrade, Oswald de, 229

Andrade, Vera de, 255n, 256n
Anti-Semitism, 174, 187; *see also* Jews
Anti-Slavery Reporter, The, 130
Arabia, 198
Arabs, 26, 40, 42–4, 58, 98, 118, 198–200, 227, 243
Araquistain, 43n
Arcoverde, Cardinal, 134
Argentina, 19, 37, 121, 190–1, 206, 269–70, 277, 278n
"Argentinian Doctrine," 269
Arinos de Melo Franco, Affonso, 277n
Arnstein, Senhor (São Paulo), 251
"Art" (Andrade), 241n, 248n
Arte Tradicional do Brasil, A (Severo), 255n
"Arts in Brazil, The" (Smith), 242n
"Aryan," 120, 121, 177, 191, 224, 227
Ascoli, Max, 162
Asfora, Perminio, 14, 228
"*Aspectos de um seculo de transição*" (Freyre), 120n
Aspectos del Vivir Hispánica (Castro), 43n
Assis, Machado de, 13, 14, 164
Assis Chateaubriand (industrialist), 14
Atkinson, G. Anthony, 33
Atlantic Federation, 183
Atlantic Monthly, The, 3
Aurora, Count d', 110n
Australia, 170
Aventura e Rotina (Freyre), 183n
Ayres, L. Cardozo (painter), 13, 228

i

INDEX

Azevedo, João Lucio de, 50, 53
Azores, 182-3

Bahia, 12, 59, 64, 75, 82, 91, 106, 108, 118, 122, 132, 151, 213, 218
Baker, Joseph E., 94
Baldwin (locomotives), 218
Balkans, 190
Ballou, Maturin M., 164n
Bandeira, Manuel, 13, 212, 229
Barbosa, Ruy, 14
Barreto, Lima, 13, 14
Barros, Ademar de (mayor), 279
Bates, Henry, 25, 117, 142, 175
Bates, Marston, 24, 25, 144
Bavarians, 131
Beals, Carleton, 171
Belém, 235n, 241
Belgian Congo, 27
Belgians, 27, 198
Bell, Audrey F. G., 45, 58
Bello, Julio de Albuquerque, 228
Belo Horizonte, 252
Bemis, Albert F., 248n
Bennett, Frank, 239
Bews, J. W., 95
Bilden, Rüdiger, 175
Bingham, Hiram, 173
Bland, J. O. P., 19, 238n
Blumenau, 29
Boas, Franz, 74, 198
Bolívar, Simón, 172, 185
Bolivia, 74, 158
Bolsheviki, 76; see also Russia
Bonifacio, José, 61, 136, 138
Bonn, Moritz Julius, 95
Bopp, Raul, 165
Bororos, 136
Brasileiro em Terras Portuguesas, Um (Freyre), 183n
Brazil, Dr. Vital, 7, 37, 122
Brazil (Fuss), 30
Brazil (Hill, ed.), 36, 164n, 241n, 248n
Brazil (Scully), 138n
Brazil: A Study of Economic Types (Normano), 73n, 103n, 181

Brazil: An Interpretation (Freyre), 3
Brazil: Its People and Institutions (Smith), 242n
Brazil: Today and Tomorrow (Elliott), 75n, 131n, 133n
Brazil and La Plata: The Personal Record of a Cruise (Stewart), 168n
Brazil and the Brazilians (Fletcher and Kidder), 29, 176n, 247n
Brazil and the River Plate (Hadfield), 148n
Brazil Builds (Goodwin), 250n, 251n, 255n
Brazil under the Monarchy (Creary), 77n
Brazilia, 282
Brazilian Federal Department for the Protection of the Indians, 136
"Brazil's Foreign Policy" (Oliveira Lima), 185n
Brennand, F., 13, 228
Brites, Dona (Pernambuco), 9
British, see English
Bryce, James, 120, 179
Buarque, Sergio, 229
Bureau of Indian Affairs (U.S.), 174
Bureau of Intercultural Education (U.S.), 173
Burle-Marx, Robert, 253
Burma, 156n
Burton, Sir Richard Francis, 119-20, 242n
Butantan Institute (São Paulo), 7

Cabral de Melo Neto, João, 228
Café Filho, João, 17
Callado, Antonio, 14, 229
Calvin, John, 173
Cambridge University, 147
Camões, Luis de, 75, 240
Campista, David, 161
Canaan (Graça Aranha), 219-25
Canada, 18, 72, 74, 206
"Canudos War," 150
Cape Verde Islands, 182-3
Cardozo Ayres, L. (painter), 13, 228

ii

Carneiro, Gomes, 136
Carneiro da Cunha, Vitorino, 217
Carthaginians, 48
Casa-Grande & Senzala (Freyre), 255*n*
Cash, W. J., 193, 194, 195
Castilianism, 99, 102*ff*
Castro, Americo, 43*n*
Catalans, 106
Catholic Church, *see* Christianity
Caxias, 263
Ceará, 107
Celso, Afonso, 225
Celts, 47
Cendrars, Blaise, 230
Ceylon, 126, 284
Chaco, 74
Chagas (scientist), 122
Chamber of Deputies, 160; *see also* Parliament
Chateaubriand, François René, 172
Chile, 19, 37, 121, 206
China, Chinese, 3, 18, 27, 31, 38, 58, 63, 66, 106, 120, 128-30, 142, 148*n*, 170, 177, 230, 231, 233, 237, 243, 257*ff*
China and Europe (Reischwein), 64*n*
Christianity, 4-5, 8, 21, 39-40, 42-6, 52, 53, 56, 60-2, 68-71, 87-9, 111, 117-18, 121, 124, 134, 137, 138, 142, 151-3, 156-69 *passim*, 172, 195-201, 210-11, 214, 223, 225, 284
"Chronicas Lageanas," (Creary), 47*n*
Church, R. J. Harrison, 145
Cid, El, 172
Civilizations, 3
Clark, Hamlet, 77
Clash of Culture and the Contact of Races, The (Pitt-Rivers), 199*n*
Cleveland, Grover, 133
Climate of Portugal, The (Delgado), 47
Clough, Shepard Bancroft, 31*n*
Coelho Pereira, Brites, 49
Coelho Pereira, Duarte, 49
Cole, Charles Woolsey, 64*n*

Colonial Policy and Practice (Furnivall), 156*n*
Colonies (Walker), 155, 157
Color and Culture in South Africa (Patterson), 197
Colquhoun, R. S., 32
Colton, Walter, 175
Columbia University, 78, 199
Comintern, 277
Communism, Communists, 228, 275, 275-6, 279, 281, 283-5
"Comparison of the Effects of Certain Socioeconomic Factors upon Size of Family . . . , A" (Griffing), 88*n*
Comte, Auguste, 124, 220
Concerning Latin American Culture, 42*n*
Conference on Tropical Architecture (London, 1953), 31-2, 33
Conference on Tropical Architecture, 32
Congress of Regionalism in Brazil (Recife, 1926), 32, 93, 228
Conquest of Brazil, The (Nash), 55, 76*n*, 176*n*, 177*n*
Conselheiro, Antonio, 150
Constant, Benjamin, 172
Cooper, James Fenimore, 135
Corbusier, Le, 248*n*, 252
Costa, Lucio, 234, 248*n*, 249, 253, 280
Cotteril, R. S., 84
Council Against Intolerance in America, 173
Council of Immigration and Colonization of Brazil, 138
Council on Intercultural Relations, 173
Coutinho, Afranio, 94*n*
Coutinho, Morais, 228
Couto, Ribeiro, 108
Creary, R., 77
Cruls, Gastão, 14, 165
Crusades, 48, 260
Cruz, Oswaldo, 37, 122; Institute, 7
Cuadernos, 43*n*
Cuba, 126, 195

INDEX

Cult and Culture (Vogt), 253*n*
Culto da Arte em Portugal, O (Ortigao), 64*n*
Cunha, Euclides da, 14, 150, 217, 224, 225, 226
Cunha, Vitorino Carneiro da, 217

Dalgado, D. G., 47
Dampier, Sir William Cecil, 74
Dantas, Julio, 183
Danton, Georges Jacques, 172
Darwin, Charles, 38
Dean, Vera Micheles, 281*n*
Debret, J. B., 255*n*
Deck and Port (Colton), 176*n*
Denmark, 121
Dent, Hastings Charles, 148*n*
Dias, Cicero, 13, 91, 211, 228
Díaz, Porfirio, 175
Dickens, Charles, 77
Diem, Ngo Dinh, 279
Diplomatic Relations Between the United States and Brazil (Hill), 195
Discurso aos Surdos (Lourival Fontes), 278*n*
Dixon, Roland B., 74
Documentary History of American Industrial Society (Phillips), 72*n*
Domestic Architecture of the American Colonies and of the Early Republic (Kimball), 256*n*
Domville-Fife, Charles, 147*n*, 148*n*, 235*n*
Drew, Jane, 248*n*
Dumont, Alberto Santos, 12, 37
Dutch, Dutchmen, 26, 27, 30-1, 76, 83, 99, 121, 134, 156, 159, 197, 198, 223-4, 243, 255*n*, 256*n*

East India, East Indians, 7, 29, 35, 48, 63-4, 65, 98, 233, 236-7
Economic History of Europe (Clough and Cole), 64*n*
Ecuador, 74, 90, 126, 158
Egypt, 77, 126, 198
El Greco, 43*n*

El Greco y Toledo (Marañon), 43*n*
Elliott, L. E., 75, 131*n*, 132-3, 138
Encyclopedia Americana, The, 3
Encyclopedia of the Social Sciences, 126-7, 169*n*, 187*n*
Engenho Novo, 59
England, English, 4, 7, 34, 48, 58, 65-6, 76-9 *passim*, 83, 89, 97, 99, 124, 127, 130, 138, 142, 143, 148*n*, 153, 156, 159, 160, 170-5 *passim*, 184, 190, 198, 205-6, 221, 222, 225, 239, 243, 261, 262, 267, 269
Entralgo, Dr. Laín, 43*n*
Epocas de Portugal Economico (Azevedo), 50*n*
Equatorial America (Ballou), 164*n*
España como Problema (Entralgo), 43*n*
España en su Historia (Castro), 43*n*
Espirito Santo, 132
Estadista da Republica, Um (Franco), 277*n*, 278*n*
Estado Novo, 101-4
Evolving House, The (Bemis), 248*n*
Ewbank, Thomas, 118, 119, 214
Export-Import Bank, 274

Fair Employment Practices Committee (U.S.), 174
Family and Civilization (Zimmerman), 254*n*
Family and the Nation, The (Dampier), 74
Fascism, 103, 171, 188, 190, 192, 262; see also Nazis
Faulkner, William, 217
Federal Council of Churches of Christ in America, 174
Federal Department for the Protection of the Indians, 136
Federal Farm Board (U.S.), 126
Fernandes, Annibal, 228
Fernando, King of Portugal, 51, 52
Ferrero, Guglielmo, 220
Ferrez, Gilberto, 256*n*
Filko, José Mariano, 255*n*
Fischer, Eric, 152

iv

Fischer, Eugen, 40
Flavio Carvalho, 35
Fletcher, J. C., 29, 30, 176, 247
Fonseca, Rabbi Aboab da, 38
Fonseca, Hermes da, 217
Fontes (scientist), 122
Fontes, Amando, 218
Fontes, Senator Lourival, 276, 278n
Foreign Affairs, 3
Forty Years in Brazil (Bennett), 239n
France, French, 7, 12, 38, 48, 76, 83, 89, 99, 102, 125, 134, 153, 160, 170, 171, 172, 179, 186, 190, 198, 205, 222, 225, 230, 243, 252, 261, 262, 267; Revolution, 171
Franco, Affonso Arinos de Melo, 277n
Franco, Francisco, 171
Frank, Waldo, 107, 112
Franklin, Benjamin, 172
Freiburg, University of, 22
Freyre, Gilberto, 3, 13n, 28, 37, 64n, 77n, 86n, 120n, 183n, 255n
Frontin, Paulo, 125
Frontini, Senhor (São Paulo), 251
Fry, Maxwell, 248n
Furnivall, J. S., 156
Fuss, Peter, 30
Future of Underdeveloped Countries, The (Staley), 283

Gaines, Francis Pendleton, 83, 84, 85
Gallop, Rodney, 236
Gamio, Manuel, 74
Ganivet, Angel, 40
Ganzert, Frederic William, 164n
Gaston d'Orléans, Prince, 11
Gauls, 47
Genetic and Endocrine Basis for Differences in Form and Behavior (Stockard), 121n
Geographical Review, 26
Germany, Germans, 10, 29, 35-6, 37, 48, 59, 89, 102, 125, 131, 137, 144, 147-8, 148n, 153, 155, 158-61 passim, 175, 180, 184, 186, 190,

Germany (continued)
191, 213, 221, 222, 224-5, 261, 262, 267, 269
Giddings, Franklin, 99
Giedion, Siegfried, 33, 245
Gillespie, James Edward, 64n
Gladstone, William Ewart, 172
Glicerio, Francisco, 124
Gobineau, Joseph Arthur, Count de, 175
Goetz, Walter, 188
Gomes Carneiro, Major, 136
Gonsalves de Melo, J. A., 256n
"Good Neighbor Policy," 173, 273, 275
Goodwin, Philip L., 248n, 250-1, 252, 255n
Goths, 48
Goulart, Jango, 279
Gourou (scientist), 25
Goyaz, 75
Graça Aranha, José Pereira da, 219-25, 229
Granville, Granville George Leveson-Gower, Earl, 130
Greco, El, 43n
Greco y Toledo, El (Marañon), 43n
Greece, 172, 192
Griffing, John B., 88n
Grivet (Swiss philologist), 38
Guenther, Konrad, 22-3, 24-5, 114-15, 134-5, 175
Guimarães Rosa (novelist), 14, 229
Gunther, John, 120n
Gurvith, Georges, 265

Hadfield, William, 148n
Halecki, Oscar, 154, 155
Hanke, Lewis, 192
Harper's, 171n
Harrison Church, R. J., 145
Hartt, R. L., 38
Harvard University, 73
Hayes, Carlton J. H., 78
Hearn, Lafcadio, 37
Highlands of Brazil, The (Burton), 120n, 242n

INDEX

Hill, Lawrence F., 36, 164n, 195, 241n, 248n
Hindus, see India
Hispanic American Historical Review, The, 77n
History of Brazil (Southey), 78
Holland, see Dutch
Hollanda, Sergio Buarque de, 229
Holsteiners, 131
Hood, Thomas, 77
Hoonholtz (family), 163
Hooton, Earnest A., 73, 74
House, Edward M., 170
House of Representatives, see Parliament
Human Ecology (Bews), 95n

Ihering, Rudolf von, 115
Imperial Academy of Medicine (Brazil), 88
India, 27, 29, 51, 52, 58, 90, 147, 154, 198, 200, 241n, 243, 284; see also East India
Indians, see Amerindians
"Industry, Commerce, and Finance" (Ganzert), 164n
Influence of Overseas Expansion on England, The (Gillespie), 64n
Inquisition, 5, 42, 45, 68
"Integralismo," 192
Inter-American Conference of Philosophy, 93
Inter-American Development Commission, 274
Inter-American Financial and Economic Advisory Committee, 274
Irish, 59, 163
Isabel, Princess, 11, 203, 207
Italy, Italians, 29, 35-6, 89, 126, 131-2, 144, 147-8, 153-4, 158, 159, 160, 162-3, 164n, 170, 180, 181, 186
Itamarati, 10

Jacks, G. V., 145
Jaiyesimi, S. O., 32
Jamaica, 78
Jango Goulart, Vice President, 279

Japan, Japanese, 18, 36, 64, 89, 137, 144, 147, 153-4, 155, 158, 159, 170, 181, 184, 261, 262
Jardim, Luis, 228
Jefferson, Thomas, 171, 172
Jesuits, 44, 45, 60-2, 64, 69-71, 74, 108, 110, 136, 137, 143, 188-9
"Jesuits" (Goetz), 188n
Jews, Judaism, 38, 42-6, 48, 50-3, 58, 59, 153, 161, 163, 190, 211, 227; Sephardic, 45, 46, 48, 52, 58
John (João) VI, King of Brazil, 203, 216, 217
Journal of Heredity, 88n
Journal of World History, 154
Juárez, Benito, 173
Junior, Cyril, 160
Jurema, Aderbal, 256n

Keyserling, Count Hermann, 120n
Kidder, Daniel P., 29, 30, 176, 247
Kimball, Fiske, 236
Kinsey Report, 260
Koenigsberger, O. H., 32
Kohl, Johann Georg, 47
Kohn, Hans, 40n, 168-9
Konder, Marcos, 165
Kontinent, 3
Koster, Henry, 78
Ku Klux Klan, 187
Kubitschek, Juscelino, 17, 280

Lafayette, Marquis de, 172
Lamartine, Alphonse Marie Louis de, 172
Las Casas, Bartolomé de, 61
"Latin American," 259-60
Lattes, Cesar, 37, 164
League of Nations, 170, 263
Le Bon, Gustave, 220
Le Corbusier, 248n, 252
Lee, Douglas H. K., 26
Legendre, Maurice, 240
Lentz, Fritz, 174-5
Letters Home from Spain, Algeria and Brazil (Clark), 77n
Lewinson, Paul, 169n
Library of Congress, 77

Life in Brazil (Ewbank), 118*n*, 119*n*, 214*n*
Ligurians, 47
Lima, Jorge de, 212
Lima, Manoel de Oliveira, 185
Lima Barreto (writer), 13, 14
Lincoln, Abraham, 172
Lindley, Thomas, 254*n*, 255*n*
Lins, Osman, 229
Lins do Rego, José, 14, 91, 212, 217, 218, 228
Listener, The, 3
Livermore, H. V., 242*n*
Livro do Nordeste, 120*n*
Lobato, Monteiro, 226
London, University of, 3
London Labour and the London Poor (Mayhew), 77
Lopes Neto, Simoes, 229
López, Solano, 263
Lorente, Mariano Joaquin, 220*n*
Lott, General Teixeira, 279
Luis, Washington, 217
Lund (Scandinavian geologist), 38
"Luso-tropical civilization," 154*ff*
Luther, Martin, 110, 173

Macao, 147
Machado, Alcantara, 75, 229
Machado, Brazilio, 276
Machado, Pinheiro, 81
Madeira, 182, 280
Magalhães, A., 228
Magalhães, Basilio de, 75
Malaya, 126, 154
Malê Revolt, 151
Mann, Thomas, 91
Maranhão, 59, 67
Marañon, Gregorio, 43*n*
Marinho, Joaquim Saldanha, 104
Martin, Percy F., 240–1
Martius, Karl Friedrich Philipp von, 175
Mary (Virgin), 196–7, 202, 204
Masters and the Slaves, The (Freyre), 13*n*, 255*n*
Matto Grosso, 72, 75

Mattos, Gregorio de, 213–14, 215, 217
Mauá, Viscount de, 14
Maura, Bishop of, 172
Maurice, Count de Nassau, 256*n*
Mauro Motta, 228
Mayhew, Henry, 77
Mayo, Elton, 216
Mead, Margaret, 202
Meade, Richard Kidder, 185
Mello, Silva, 122
Mello family, 201
Melo, J. A. Gonsalves de, 256*n*
Melo Neto, João Cabral de, 228
Memoria sobre a populacao e a agricultura de Portugal . . . (Rebello da Silva), 48*n*
Men, Manners, and Morals in South America (Bland), 238*n*
Mencken, H. L., 66
Mendes, Murilo, 212
Menotti del Pichia, 164
Mexico, 13, 58, 90, 98, 126, 144, 150, 158, 167, 170–1, 175, 263
Meyer, Augusto, 164
Miall, Bernard, 115*n*
Mignone (musician), 164
Milliet, Sergio, 165
Milton, John, 172
Minas Gerais, 13, 17, 75, 88, 97, 102, 108, 109–10, 118, 122, 132, 211, 229, 242*n*
Mind of the South, The (Cash), 193
Mindlin, Henrique E., 33, 164, 249, 253
Misericordia, 168
Modern Architecture in Brazil (Mindlin), 33
Modern Colonization (Church), 145
Mogul, 32
Mohammedanism, Mohammedans, 12, 40, 42–4, 117–18, 151, 153, 198–200; *see also* Moors
Mongoloid, 47, 174, 175
Monroe Doctrine, 269
Monroe Doctrine, The (Bingham), 173*n*

INDEX

Monteiro brothers (painters), 13
Montenegro, Olivio, 228
Moog, Vianna, 164, 218
Moors, 12, 26–30, 40, 42–4, 48, 51,
  53, 54–6, 58, 62, 147, 198–9, 227,
  232–57, 260; *see also* Arabs
Morais, Venicius de, 212
Morais Neto, Prudente de, 229
Moreira, Juliano, 186
Moreira de Barros, 128
Morgan, Edwin, 278
Morrow, Glenn R., 93
Moscow Conference, 171
Motta, Mauro, 228
Mucambos do Nordeste (Freyre),
  255*n*
Müller, Lauro, 124, 161, 191
Müller, Max, 38
Mumford, Lewis, 27–8, 248*n*
Mundo que o Portugues Creou, O
  (Freyre), 37, 64*n*
Murphy, James, 57

Nabuco, Joaquim, 14, 17, 82, 91, 207
Narrative of a Voyage to Brazil
  (Lindley), 254*n*, 255*n*
*Narrative of a Voyage to the South
  Atlantic* (Webster), 77*n*, 80*n*
*Narrative of Travels on the Amazon
  and Rio Negro, A* (Wallace), 77*n*
Nash, Roy, 55, 76, 176–7
Nassau, Count Maurice de, 256*n*
National Assembly, *see* Parliament
National Association for the Ad-
  vancement of Colored People
  (U.S.), 173
National Conference of Christians
  and Jews (U.S.), 174
National Museum of Natural His-
  tory of Brazil, 10
"Native Policy" (Ots y Capdequi),
  188*n*
"Natural Eugenics in Brazil"
  (Griffing), 88*n*
Naturalist in Brazil, A (Guenther),
  22–3, 115*n*, 135*n*
*Nature of the Non-Western
  World, The* (Dean), 281

*Naturalist on the River Amazon,
  The* (Bates), 117*n*, 142*n*
Nazis, Nazism, 158–9, 188, 190, 192,
  262
Negroes, 5–6, 8–12, 14, 26, 48–58
  passim, 71–3, 76*ff*, 90–2, 101, 104,
  108, 111, 116–40, 143–65 *passim*,
  167*ff*, 185, 186, 190–2, 198–200,
  210, 214, 218, 219, 222–34, 242*n*,
  255*n*
Nestor, Odilon, 33, 228
Netherlands India, 156*n*
Neto, João Cabral de Melo, 228
Neto, Prudente de Morais, 229
Neto, Simoes Lopes, 229
"New Christians," 42
"New Lusitania," 53
*New Viewpoints on the Spanish
  Colonization of America*
  (Zavala), 60, 60*n*
New Zealand, 170
Newton, Sir Isaac, 172
Ngo Dinh Diem, 279
Niemeyer, Oscar, 234, 248*n*, 249,
  252, 280
Nigeria, 32, 34
Nordic(s), 54, 76, 97, 192, 260, 264
Norman architecture, 29
Nossa Senhora do O, 59
Notices of Brazil in 1828 and 1829
  (Walsh), 97*n*
Nuñez, Mendieta, 74

Old South, The (Cotteril), 84*n*
Oliver Twist (Dickens), 77
Orient and Occident, 40*n*, 169*n*
Orléans, Prince Gaston d', 11
Orleans-Bragança family, 257
Orozco, José Clemente, 211
Ortigão, Ramalho, 64*n*
Osman Lins, 229
Ots y Capdequi, José, 188
Oumansky, Constantin A., 170–1
Ouro Preto, 109, 118, 253

Pakistan, 198, 284
Palmerio, Mario, 14, 229
Panama, 179

Pancetti (painter), 13
Pará, 59, 64, 72, 108, 115
Pará; or Scenes and Adventures on the Banks of the Amazon (Warren), 86n
Para-Fascists, 103; *see also* Fascism
Paraguay, 18, 71, 188, 190, 195, 263
Paraíba, 218
Paraná, Honorio Hermeto Carneiro Leão, Marquis of, 81
Paraná, 132, 154
Para-Nazis, 158–9; *see also* Fascism; Nazis
Pareto, Vilfredo, 216
Parliament (Brazil), 10, 104, 123, 160, 161, 162, 163, 277n, 284
Passing of the European Age, The (Fischer), 152
Patronato Agricola, 131
Patterson (medical scientist), 38
Patterson, Sheila, 197
Paulding, James K., 85
Peçanha, Nilo, 124, 191
Pedro I, Emperor, 203
Pedro II, Emperor, 10–11, 119, 123, 129, 172, 176, 185, 203, 204, 207, 216, 217, 237, 240
"Pedro the Third," 12
Pena, Carlos, 228
Pendleton, Robert L., 26
Pennsylvania, University of, 93
Pereira de Souza, Washington Luis, *see* Luis, Washington
Pernambuco, 5, 9, 30–1, 59, 82, 103, 106, 118, 132, 134, 163, 213, 218, 239
Perón, Juan, 285
Peru, 75, 158, 195
Pessôa, Epitacio da Silva, 129
Petropolis, 12, 148n, 237
Pfeiffer, Ida, 77
Philip II, King of Spain, 60, 70, 99–100, 113
Phillips, Ulrich B., 71–2, 85, 92
Philosophy and Phenomenological Research, 94n
Phoenicians, 47–8
Pichia, Menotti del, 164

Pierson, Donald, 175
Pilla, Raul, 162
Pinheiro, Machado, 81
Pinotti, Mario, 164
Pinto Roquette, E., 36, 74, 100, 177
"Pita, Tio," 129
Pitt-Rivers, Fox, 199
"Place of Christendom in the History of Mankind, The" (Halecki), 154
"Plantation: The Physical Basis of Traditional Race Relations, The," 84n
Plantation and Frontier (Phillips), 72n
Poland, Polish, 77, 144, 147, 153–4, 155, 158, 159
Polynesian, 119
Pombal, Sebastião José de Carvalho e Mello, Marquis of, 21, 44, 240
Porque me ufano do meu paiz (Celso), 225
Portinari, Candido, 13, 33, 164, 211, 280
Porto Seguro, Baron of, 269
Portrait de l'Espagne (Legendre), 40n
Portugal: A Book of Folk-Ways (Gallop), 236
Portugal and Brazil: An Introduction (Livermore, ed.), 242
Portugal of the Portuguese (Bell), 45n, 58n
Portuguese Africa, 18, 147, 182–3
Portuguese Asia, 182; *see also* India
Portuguese East India, 147; *see also* East India
Portuguese India, 183; *see also* India
Portuguese Pioneers, The (Prestage), 64n
Potter, Pitman B., 96n
Prado, Paulo, 75
Prestage, Edgar, 64n
Progress, 3
Protestants, 4, 14, 38, 40, 46, 168, 223; *see also* Christianity
Prussia, 102, 205
Putnam, Samuel, 150

INDEX

Quadras, Janio, 279
Queiroz, Raquel de, 10, 14, 212, 218

Race, Class and Party (Lewinson), 169n
"Race Conflict" (Kohn), 169n
Race Relations and the Race Problem (Thompson), 84n
Radosavlevich, F. R., 174
Ramalho, João, 61
Ramos, Arthur, 36
Ramos, Graciliano, 14
Rape of Earth, The (Jacks and Whyte), 145
Rebellion in the Backlands (Cunha), 150
Rebello da Silva, L. S., 48n
Rebouças, André, 11, 104
Recife, 26, 28, 30, 32, 33, 38, 118, 228, 255n, 256n, 282; Congress of Regionalism, 33, 34, 93; law school, 88
"Regionalism: Pro and Con . . ." (Baker), 95n
Regionalist Manifesto of Recife (1926), 33, 34, 93, 228
Rego, José Lins do, 14, 91, 212, 217, 218, 228
Reischwein, Adolphe, 64n
Revista do Serviço do Patrimonio Historico e Artistico Nacional, 256n
Ribeiro, João, 95, 222
Ribeiro Conto, 108
Ricardo, Cassiano, 75–6
"Rio Camapuão," 148n
Rio de Janeiro, 6–7, 10, 12, 28, 29, 38, 59, 82, 103, 105, 107, 108, 112, 118, 122, 128, 132, 165, 168, 185, 195, 203, 219, 226, 227, 229, 231, 235, 237, 248n, 250, 251, 252, 256n, 278, 282
Rio de Janeiro, University of, 256n; School of Architecture, 33
Rio Grande do Sul, 13n, 59, 72, 102, 106, 107, 108, 110, 111, 153–4, 160, 188, 189, 229, 239
Rio Pardo, 59

Ríos, Fernando de los, 42
Rivera, Diego, 211
Roberto brothers (architects), 249, 252, 253
Rodriguez, Pedro Sainz, 43n
Roman(s), Rome, 27–8, 29, 48, 54, 172, 192, 211, 232–57
Rome, University of, 162
Romero, Sylvio, 91, 139, 224, 225
Rondon, Candido Mariano da Silva, 136, 179
Roosevelt, Franklin D., 273, 275
Roosevelt, Theodore, 66, 101, 178
Root, Elihu, 15
Rosa, Guimarães, 14, 229
Rosas, Juan Manuel de, 190
Rosen, Laura, 248n
Rosen, S. McKee, 248n
Rothschild family, 221
Russia, 3, 15, 18, 40–1, 58, 77, 113, 120, 142, 167, 168–72, 173, 174–5, 237, 261, 276–7, 279, 283, 285

Sainz Rodríguez, Pedro, 43n
Salas, Herberto, 218
Salvador da Bahia, 15, 28, 118, 231, 254n
Sampaio, Theodoro, 75
Sancho II, King of Portugal, 53
Sanderson, Dwight, 62
Santa Barbara, 132
Santa Catharina, 35, 132, 153, 155, 161, 191
Santo Aleixo, 29, 31
Santo Amaro, 75
Santos, Constantino José dos, 51n
Santos, Paulo, 33, 256n
Santos (city), 6, 133
Santos Dumont, Alberto, 12, 37
São Paulo, 7, 12, 35, 82, 102, 106–7, 108, 112, 122, 131–2, 145, 148n, 154, 160, 225, 226, 227, 229, 231, 244, 251, 265, 276
São Paulo, University of, 143n; law school, 88
São Paulo Congress, 105–6
São Vicente, 67
Sarton, George, 260

Saturday Review of Literature, 95n
Savelle, Max, 31
Schmidt, Augusto Frederico, 164
Schulten, Adolf, 40
Scottish, 24, 34
Scully, William, 138n, 148n
Seeds of Liberty (Savelle), 31
Select Committee on Coffee and
 Sugar Planting, 78
Sephardic Jews, 45, 46, 48, 52, 58;
 see also Jews
Sergio, Antonio, 49, 51n
Sergipe, 122
Sertão, 115
Sertoës, Os (Cunha), 150, 217, 225,
 226
Severo, Ricardo, 255n
Shakespeare, William, 66
Shaw, Paul, 143
Sigaud, J. F. X., 38
Silva Rebello, L. S. da, 48n
Silva Rondon, Candido Mariano da,
 136, 179
Sinimbú, 59
Siquiera, Jacintha de, 119
*Sketch of the History of Portugal,
 A* (Sergio), 51n
Slavs, 36
Smith, Lynn, 242n
Smith, Robert C., 242n
Smith, Robert S., 33
Sobieski (Polish traveler, *c.* 1611),
 45
Sobrado na Paisagem Recifense, O
 (Jurema), 256n
Sobrados e Mucambos (Freyre),
 28, 255n
"Social Life in the Middle of the
 19th Century" (Freyre), 77n, 86n
"Social Pioneering" (Ramos), 36
Society for the Defense of Re-
 gionalism, 32-3
Society of Jesus, *see* Jesuits
Sombart, W., 52, 143
"Some Considerations on the Prob-
 lem of Philosophy in Brazil"
 (Coutinho), 94n

South Africa, South Africans, 152,
 197-8, 268
*South America: Observations and
 Impressions* (Bryce), 120n, 179n
South American Journey (Frank),
 112
Southern Plantation, The (Gaines),
 83
Southey, Robert, 78
Soviet Union, *see* Russia
"Soviet Wooing of Latin America,
 The" (Beals), 171n
"Spain in the Epoch of American
 Civilization" (Rios), 42n
Spencer, Herbert, 220
Staley, Eugene, 282
Stalin, Joseph, 171
Stephens, H. Morse, 147
Stewart, C. S., 168, 175
Sticks and Stones (Mumford), 27
Stockard, Charles R., 121
Stratford, Wingfield, 143
Study of War, A (Wright), 96n
Suassuna, A., 228
Suevi, 48
Sumner, William Graham, 108
Swiss, Switzerland, 29, 38, 269
Syrians, 147, 154

Taunay, Affonso de E., 75
Tavares, Odorico, 212
Taylor (naval officer), 269
Taylor, Robert Love, 83
Technics and Civilization (Mum-
 ford), 248n
Technology and Society (Rosen
 and Rosen), 248n
Teixeira de Freitas, Augusto, 37,
 254
Teixeira Lott, General, 279
Tempo dos Flamengos (Gonsalves
 de Melo), 256n
Thompson, Edgar T., 84, 85
"Thoughts on Housing for the
 Humid Tropics" (Lee), 26
*Through Five Republics of South
 America* (Martin), 240n, 241n

INDEX

Through the Brazilian Wilderness (Roosevelt), 66*n*, 178*n*
Time, 171*n*
Torquemada, 43*n*
Torres, Alberto, 225
Torres, Antonio, 10
Toynbee, Arnold, 154, 155
Travels in Brazil (Koster), 78*n*
Travels in Portugal (Murphy), 57*n*
Treaty Ports (Abend), 170*n*
Tropical Architecture (Fry and Drew), 248*n*
"Tropical Architecture and Building Standards," 33
"Tropical Planning Problems" (Koenigsberger), 32
Tropics: World of Tomorrow, The (Wilson), 276
Turks, 51
Turner, Frederick Jackson, 73, 94, 103

Ubirajara, 172
Ugarte, Manuel, 191
Unamuno, Miguel de, 40
UNESCO (United Nations Educational, Scientific, and Cultural Organization), 263
United States of America, 15, 18, 19, 27–30, 71–2, 79, 82–92 *passim*, 97–104, 120, 124, 126, 132–3, 144, 149, 150, 162–3, 170–208 *passim*, 228, 236, 237, 248*n*, 251, 258*ff*
United States of Brazil, The (Domville-Fife), 148*n*, 235*n*
"Universalism versus Regionalism in International Reorganization" (Potter), 96*n*
Uruguay, 19, 190, 206, 269
Urupés (Lobato), 225–6

"Valorization" (Whittlesey), 126–7
Vargas, Getulio, 103, 110–11, 113, 159, 204, 207–8, 276, 278, 279, 282–3
Varnhagen, Adolpho de, 269
Vauthier, 255*n*, 256*n*
Veblen, Thorstein, 87

Velloso de Oliveira, Henrique, 188
Venezuela, 18, 265
Verissimo, Erico, 14, 218
Verissimo, José, 225
Vespucci, Amerigo, 9
Vieira, Antonio, 14, 223–4
Villa-Lobos, Heitor, 12, 212
Visigoths, 54
Vitoria, Francisco de, 43*n*
Vogt, V. Ogden, 253
Voltaire, 172
Voyage autour du Monde (Pfeiffer), 77*n*
Voyage Pittoresque et Historique au Brésil (Debret), 255*n*

Wagley, Charles, 242*n*
Walker, Eric, 155, 157
Wallace, Alfred Russel, 25, 37, 77, 175
Walsh, R., 97*n*
Warren, John Esaias, 86
Washington, George, 171, 172
Weber, Max, 278
Webster, W. H. B., 78, 80
West Indies, 78
Westward Ho! (Paulding), 85
Where Winter Never Comes (Bates), 144
Whethams, *see* Dampier
Whittlesey, Charles R., 126
Whyte, R. O., 145
Willems, Emilio, 36
Wilson, Charles Morrow, 276–7
Wilson, Woodrow, 170, 171, 173, 205, 208
Wint, Guy, 20
Wright, Quincy, 96*n*
Wright brothers, 37

Xavier, St. Francis, 64

Yale University, 93, 173
Year Book of Education, 3
Year in Brazil, A (Dent), 148*n*

Zavala, Silvio, 60
Zimmerman, Carle C., 254
Zola, Emile, 111

xii

A NOTE ABOUT GILBERTO FREYRE

GILBERTO DE MELLO FREYRE was born at Recife (Pernambuco), Brazil, on March 15, 1900. After study in Brazil, he did graduate work at Columbia University, New York, under Frans Boas, Franklin Henry Giddings, Carlton J. H. Hayes, and Charles G. Seligman, and continued his studies at anthropological and ethnological museums in England, Germany, France, and Portugal. While serving as secretary to a governor of Pernambuco, he helped to establish at Recife the first chair of modern sociology in Brazil; he was active later in establishing in Rio de Janeiro both the first chair of social anthropology in South America and a pioneering chair in social research. He has been visiting professor at many universities in the United States, England, Portugal, France, and India. Freyre's numerous books have been translated into most Western languages. Among the most important of them are *Casa-Grande & Senzala* (1933; second English-language edition, as *The Masters and the Slaves*, 1956), *Sobrados e Mucambos* (1936), *Nordeste* (1937), *Região e Tradicão* (1941), *Sociologia* (1945), and—a labor of many years—*Ordem e Progresso*. The Patten Foundation Lectures that Freyre delivered at Indiana University in 1944 were reprinted as *Brazil: An Interpretation* (1945). When not traveling, Senhor Freyre lives and writes at his ancestral home in Recife.

This book was set on the Linotype in Janson, a recut-
ting made direct from the type cast from matrices
made by Anton Janson some time between 1660 and
1687. Janson's original matrices were, at last report,
in the possession of the Stempel foundry, Frankfurt
am Main.

Of Janson's origin nothing is known. He may have
been a relative of Justus Janson, a printer of Danish
birth who practiced in Leipzig from 1614 to 1635.
Some time between 1657 and 1668 Anton Janson, a
punch-cutter and type-founder, bought from the Leipzig printer Johann Erich Hahn the type-foundry which
had formerly been a part of the printing house of
M. Friedrich Lankisch. Janson's types were first shown
in a specimen sheet issued at Leipzig about 1675.
Janson's successor, and perhaps his son-in-law, Johann
Karl Edling, issued a specimen sheet of Janson types
in 1689. His heirs sold the Janson matrices in Holland
to Wolffgang Dietrich Erhardt, of Leipzig.

Composed, printed, and bound by KINGSPORT PRESS,
INC., Kingsport, Tenn. Paper manufactured by P. H.
GLATFELTER CO., Spring Grove, Pa. Designed by GUY
FLEMING.